I've Got
JOHN

I've Got JOHN

My Tutorials from the Other Side of the Looking Glass

S H E R R Y   A N N   W H I T E

BALBOA
PRESS

A DIVISION OF HAY HOUSE

Balboa Press books may be ordered through booksellers or by contacting:

Balboa Press
A Division of Hay House
1663 Liberty Drive
Bloomington, IN 47403
www.balboapress.com
1-(877) 407-4847

Because of the dynamic nature of the Internet, any web addresses or links contained in this book may have changed since publication and may no longer be valid. The views expressed in this work are solely those of the author and do not necessarily reflect the views of the publisher, and the publisher hereby disclaims any responsibility for them.

The author of this book does not dispense medical advice or prescribe the use of any technique as a form of treatment for physical, emotional, or medical problems without the advice of a physician, either directly or indirectly. The intent of the author is only to offer information of a general nature to help you in your quest for emotional and spiritual well-being. In the event you use any of the information in this book for yourself, which is your constitutional right, the author and the publisher assume no responsibility for your actions.

Any people depicted in stock imagery provided by Thinkstock are models, and such images are being used for illustrative purposes only.
Certain stock imagery © Thinkstock.

Printed in the United States of America.

ISBN: 978-1-4525-7114-0 (sc)
ISBN: 978-1-4525-7113-3 (e)

Balboa Press rev. date: 06/06/2013

"On the other side of the looking glass"
Artwork by : Olivia Banfield
Age 10 August 23rd, 2009

PREFACE
A PROMISE KEPT

On Christmas morning of 2008 I made a promise to my seven year old niece, Shannon, that one day I would take her on her first horse ride. Her father, who was gravely ill, over heard me make this promise to his daughter. Our eyes met at which time he gave me a wink and a smile. Less than a month later, on January 20th, he was in Paradise.

On July 26th, of 2010, I was able to fulfill this horse back promise. On that sunny southern California morning, Shannon's mother Bobbi, her brothers Dale and Shane, my grandchildren Kyle and Olivia along with myself, saddled up for an hour and half horseback adventure.

Before the children could mount their steeds, they were given the dos and don'ts of horsemanship from their cowgirl teacher. I watched as Shannon intently listened to every word of advice given to her. Bravely she climbed up onto the saddle and held the reins. She looked back at me and flashed me a very nervous smile, all the while holding the saddle horn with a death grip.

Off we went. In a single line. First our cowboy leader then the rest of us. I was at the rear of the line where I could keep an eye on all the buck-a-roos.

After riding along the dusty trail for about fifteen minutes, we all noticed a beautiful ancient elm tree where perched high on top was a magnificent Peregrine falcon. The falcon watched our every stride. He felt to me like an old friend. It was a few minutes after this that I felt a cool breeze flow by. I even felt a slight chill come on which caught me by surprise as this was a very hot day with temperatures in the 90's. I gathered my reins of my horse, whose name was Rope, and ran my hands along his mane.

The chill soon disappeared to be replaced by a very relaxed calmness. I looked ahead at our group of riders to see Shannon's pony tail bouncing along with the gait of her horse. Then once again that strange cool breeze came upon me.

Then I heard a whisper in my ear say "Thank You". I knew instantly that it was Doug, Shannon's father. "You're welcome", I whispered.

We rode along in silence. Each of us in our own world. We soon came upon a sign which was an advertisement for glider rides at the nearby community airport.

I asked Bobbi, my sister in law, if she was ready for our next adventure? "How about a glider ride". Bobbi then told me about a birthday gift she had given her husband, Doug, many years past. This birthday gift was a glider ride. She told me that Doug had told her that this was by far the best gift he had ever been given. That this glider ride was a life time memory for him.

I then knew that Doug was informing me that this horse ride would be a life time memory for his children.

It was after reflecting on this message that I came to realize that Doug's spirit was now watching the seven of us ride by through the eyes of the Peregrine falcon we saw sitting high upon that elm tree. Seconds after this, the falcon soared by our group on wings of magic. Gliding silently as he did when Doug was flying in the glider many years past. Only this time he was flying in the company of Angels.

Three days later I was back home getting ready for another day of work. I had the Golf Channel on as I did my book work. It was then that a commercial aired which was to confirm to me Doug's message to perfection.

This commercial featured a young child. A message ran across the bottom of the screen which read:

> "The smallest moments in life can make the
> biggest impacts on a child's life".

> "Take Time to Be a Father".

Then incredibly, at the far right of the screen appeared a small image of an eagle, or it may just have been a Peregrine falcon, in flight.

07/26/2010

Dedicated to our mother "Dixie"

My mother knew and understood my love for music and especially my love for the Beatles. Allowing me to cover my room from floor to ceiling with pictures of the Beatles taped to every inch. I pleaded for a Beatle record player, Beatle dolls, jewelry and of course tons of Beatle magazines. She also took it in stride when her eldest daughter started to wear a Beatle wig.

Mom supported most my crazy ideas when it came to the Fab Four. One of those ideas' was to have an English tea party on my thirteenth birthday with my Beatle loving bird (girl) friends.

Mom helped me set up for this gala event. She made English bread pudding and served us hot tea. A grand time was had by all. We sipped hot tea and ate pudding while we listened to the latest Beatle songs. We were so British on that glorious day.

Mom had a little joke she would play with me. She would call all the Beatles "Ringo". Telling me "well, they all look the same to me and Ringo is the only name I can remember." I do remember her asking me one time "who's this one?" as she gazed at a picture of John Lennon. "He is very handsome". I told her his name is John Lennon. "Well, mom said, "I'll still call him Ringo."

All her life mom loved to sing. At Christmas time if you came to her home during the holidays, you would be asked to sing along with Dixie. Mom was not always in tune when she sang, but we did not mind. Mom's favorite carol was "Silent Night." Every holiday season when I now hear this song, I think of mom.

Mom was diagnosed with ovarian cancer on October 2nd, 1980. She lost her battle on December 13th, 1981. She was only 47 years of age.

The night before mom passed my husband and I were with her, as were all her children, husband, sister and many others who loved Dixie. She would go in and out of consciousness and thankfully did not seem to have much pain.

The last night of her life, we turned on the TV. To watch the Jim Nabors Christmas special. We all sang Silent Night together one last time with mom singing the lead as she always did.

Randy (my husband) and I were with mom in the very early hours of the morning when she awoke from her slumber to ask me "Why is he here?" I looked at the doorway she was pointing to and saw no one. "Who Mom? Who do you see?" I asked. "He's standing right there. What does he want? Why is he all dressed in white?" She pleaded an answer. I looked again expecting to see a doctor or nurse. Again the doorway was empty. Now mom was actually getting aggressive. "Well, Sherry Ann (mom always added my second name when it was important that I listen) you know his name. I cannot remember it. Ask him what he wants". I did not know what to reply. She fell back to sleep.

The next morning, Sunday the thirteenth of December, at 7:00 a.m. I was at her side when she sighed first then took her last breath. It is now over thirty years. I think of her and miss her every day. I've also wondered who the gentleman was who was standing at her hospital door? Mom just could not remember his name.

09/04/2008

Our mother "Dixie" and myself. 1970. We love
you and miss you every day in every way.

John Lennon and the Number 9.

Most people are very familiar with the number 9 and John Winston Ono Lennon. For those of you who are not familiar, here are just a few of the well documented 'coincidences'.

John Winston Lennon was born on October 9th, 1940.

Beatles first Cavern club date was February 9th, 1962.

John met Yoko Ono on November 9th, 1966.

The Beatles first appearance on the Ed Sullivan television.

Variety show was on February 9th, 1964.

Number 9 dream was recorded on John Lennon's L.P.

Walls and Bridges. This album was his 9th solo album.

Sean Lennon was born on October 9th, 1975. This was also John Lennon's 35th birthday.

John recorded three songs which included the number nine-

One After 909

Revolution # 9

Number 9 Dream.

John Lennon was shot on December 8th, 1980. Due to time differences, it was December 9th, in Liverpool England.

There were many other number 9's in John Lennon's life.

This Photo was taken in Palm Springs California at the Lennon art exhibit. Right before this photo was taken I was asked by a news reporter if he could interview me for his report later that evening. He asked me for my thoughts on John Lennon. My answer was that I love John Lennon for many reasons. For his music, his poetry, art, and of course for his efforts for world peace and the women's movement. That most of all I love him because, right or wrong, he always spoke his truths as he saw them. I think John liked my answers. I refer to this photograph as a "Wink from John". PS…can you find the image of a Kitty?

Contents

Chapter 1

LIFE BEGINS IN NEW ORLEANS

TWO DAYS FAST GALLOP, NORTH east from the city of New Orleans, in the city of Franklin, lived a young African American slave girl who was known by the name of Daisy. She was a sweet girl who loved to dance and sing. She was also as lovely to the eye as the flower she was name for.

As was the custom, her last name was the same as her masters which was Wells. Daisy did not know her birth parents as she was sold at auction to Gemstone plantation when she was two years of age. Her birth mother had died at the age of seventeen. Some say she died because she fell on a piece of farming equipment, a pitch fork, most whispered it was no accident. Her husband, Daisy's father, mysteriously disappeared after his young wife had died.

Daisy's life was simple and although she lived in slavery she felt herself blessed to call one of the most beautiful of plantations in Washington Parish, her home.

For all of her life, Daisy attended to her master and his wife's daily needs in the mansion. She felt only honor that she was a "house maid," as she did receive certain privileges. She was not required to toil in the hot sun like the field slaves did, with back breaking work, the skin on their fingers cut to the bone, knees that gave way to the crippling effects at a very young age. The lives of the field slaves were lives cut short by the demands of a cruel and unjust society. Daisy wore clean clothing and bathed daily. Her Mistress demanded such.

Daisy did not know any other life then the life she had been given by her master. Her daily chores included housekeeping, cooking, and fetching water each day from one of the many wells on the plantation.

As she walked along the pathway to one of the wells with her pail in hand, she would sing. Her voice was carried along with the wind.

Daisy loved to sing into the sides of the well. As she sang she thought her voice was that of a nightingale. However, most would say she had more of the tones of a goose.

One day as she sang for all her might into one of the many wells on this plantation, an older slave could not bear the singing any longer and pleaded to her "child stop that awful wailing into the well." Daisy thought he said "child you sing well." So she sang all the louder. The man shook his head and quickened his step to get away. Daisy also had a hearing disability.

When she was allowed, Daisy would walk down to the small shanties that were grouped together to form what was known as the "long house." This was where the field slaves lived. Daisy would then gather with her slave family to sing songs and to celebrate life. Daisy always was first to start a sing along. No one could tell her not to. So they sang and danced along with her, bringing out the pots and pans to basically drown out Daisy's singing. Daisy would just sing louder.

Daisy lived in the mansion in a small room off the pantry. In this room she dreamed of meeting a man and having children of her own someday. She could not see this man's face, but knew someday he would walk into her life. He would be of African heritage. He would sing songs of their homeland and life would then be complete after they jumped over the broom.

Sometimes dreams do not come true. The master's wife was unable to conceive children. She had great pain when her husband would come to her for intimacy. It was for this reason the master began to visit Daisy in the late hours of the night in her little room off the pantry.

Nothing was said about this affair. Although everyone seemed to know, even the master's wife. No one dared to say anything about it. Instead they would look the other way and avoid eye contact. Daisy continued to attend her master's every need.

As time went by Daisy discovered she was with child. She continued to attend to her chores with a song as a new life grew within her. Even though everyone knew who the father was, not a word was whispered. The master was known as a kind man; however he could and would punish those with the whip if they did not obey him. Fortunately for Daisy, he was kind to her. So she kept the secret. Only one person cared about the birth of her baby and that person was the master's wife.

On the night of August 22nd Daisy began to feel the pains of birth. The Master's wife was the only person who was there to help Daisy give birth. The labor continued through the night and into the morning of the 23rd.

As the morning sun brought forth beams of light through the shaded window the woman known to Daisy as "mam" realized that Daisy would not survive the birth of her baby. Finally God kissed Daisy and she was no longer in pain. Her last breath had been drawn. The Master's wife knew what she must do. The baby was cut from her womb.

The master's wife put the tiny baby on Daisy's breast. "You have a daughter", she whispered into her ear. Daisy had told her the name she had chosen which was Sarah Anne. From the other side of the looking glass Daisy smiled.

The date was August 23rd in the year of 1819. I was born into this reality once again.

Everyone on the plantation grieved when Daisy died. She was a sweet and lovely girl who brought joy and laughter to everyone she met. Her life was as brief as a cool breeze in summer. She was greatly missed.

The master was not the same man after Daisy's death. He became bitter and took out his anger on everyone.

He was most angry towards God. After Daisy passed away he never again attended a church service.

He could not understand why God would take a woman who had so little. She never once complained or gave any indication that she was anything other than overjoyed with becoming a new mother. He felt ashamed that he never told her he welcomed the life within her womb. He would only look the other way, always avoiding eye contact.

Sarah was a chubby and happy baby. She proved to be a child of sweet nature and very little trouble which proved to be a blessing as no one felt comfortable showing any sort of affection towards Sarah. This left Sarah alone for most of the time. Thankfully, her Guardian Angel looked after her when no one else would.

When Sarah was ill, which was seldom, everyone looked the other way and tried not to get involved. Especially the house slaves who were in fear of being reprimanded if they responded to Sarah's crying.

Sarah's skin was light olive; her hair was light brown with wispy curls that formed around her round face. Her eyes were the color of coal and it seemed like the baby came into this world with a smile. Her features, hair and skin color gave little doubt that her father was Caucasian.

The master was tolerant of baby Sarah but would grow very angry when she would cry. At such times the master would blame

Sarah for the death of his Daisy. He could feel the anger within and tried to not punish the baby. It was difficult for him.

The master's wife (Sarah's Mam) insisted the baby live in the mansion with her. She had not been able to conceive and because of this, she became a step mother to Sarah.

As time went by, Sarah learned the ways of her adopted mother. She learned about the importance of cleanliness. How to keep your body healthy and strong. She learned of proper nutrition and the importance of daily hair, skin and dental care which were the utmost of concern because of disease. Her step mother proved to be an excellent teacher in many ways. Problem was, never once did she tell the little girl that she loved her.

Sarah was asked to call her adopted mother "mam". However when the masters wife could not hear her, Sarah called her "mammy".

Through all her difficulties Sarah grew to be a healthy and happy little girl. Because of her heritage and the knowledge that she was the master's 'love' child, the slaves were indifferent toward her. They did not accept her into their family of Africans, being not unkind to Sarah, just not accepting of her.

When Sarah attended church services with the master's wife, she was treated again with indifference. Not that Sarah was treated unkindly by the white folks it was just that no one was sure how to treat her. So she was basically ignored by most.

So it was that Sarah realized that she was different from others and never really had a family in the true sense of the word. She was neither white nor Negro.

As the years went by and Sarah grew from a little girl to a young lady, she began to favor her mother more each day. For the master, this resemblance rekindled his grief for Daisy. He missed her more than anyone ever realized.

By this time, Mam had grown to resent Sarah. She began to abuse her verbally at first then she began to slap her when she would not perform with complete compliance her every request.

She also had great distain towards her husband and no longer had any desire for him. She complained of great pain and refused any intimacy with him.

The master found kindness and physical love from a lady who owned a successful brothel in New Orleans. Her name was Rose.

In his lifetime there were only two women who loved the master. One was Rose the other was Sarah. Sarah desperately needed love and constantly tried to get the masters approval. She did not know that the master was her father. She thought that her father was the Lord Jesus.

Not only was the master having marriage problems at this time, he was also having financial difficulties with the plantation. The slaves were in rebellion and the master had to rule with great discipline to keep them from trying to escape. Because of all of these difficulties the master began to find comfort in a bottle of whiskey. This was at first an occasional habit. Then it became a daily need.

On Sarah's ninth birthday, the master called her into his private room at the mansion. He studied the young girl when she walked into his room. Shy and innocent, she was beautiful. The master told Sarah that her mother's name was Daisy. He told her that her last name was Wells. Incredibly no one had told her this until this day.

The master then gave Sarah a birthday gift. The gift he gave Sarah was a large black laced fan that had blue butterflies on it. The master told Sarah that he had given it to her mother the night she was born. The same night that Daisy went to be with Jesus in Heaven. Sarah started to cry as she felt it was her fault her mother died. The master, for the first time, took Sarah into his arms and caressed her. This was to be the first of many secret nights.

Nine year old Sarah began to learn from her master, the ways in which she could please men. In the late hours of the night, the master would awaken Sarah and take her to their secret school room. Sarah, in her innocence and her need to be touched and loved, proved to be a willing and able student. She learned quickly the skills she would need the rest of her life.

In the winter of 1830, the master died suddenly. He was known all over the area for his equestrian skills, but one day while on his way to New Orleans, to visit Rose, he was thrown off his horse. He broke his neck and died immediately. The master's name was Joseph Francis Adams.

When the master, Joseph died, the plantation was near bankrupt. His wife was not able to manage not only the plantation but also the slaves who were in hysteria over the idea that they would soon be sold in auction.

Joseph's wife could no longer care for Sarah, let alone comfort her. Sarah missed her master and her friend Joseph terribly. She was all alone. When the master's wife looked at Sarah she could only see her husband's mistress, Daisy. Her resemblance to her mother was now uncanny. Her dark eyes held the same soul and the master's wife held great contempt for her because of this.

In April of 1831, Sarah along with forty members of this plantations slave family, which included men, women and children, were taken to New Orleans to be sold at auction.

At the age of eleven plus, Sarah was about to get the education of a lifetime. Her life was about to be changed forever.

The slave auction was held at one of New Orleans finest hotels that stood right next to the shores of the Mississippi river. The slaves were first taken to a large room to be examined closely by the interested bidders and the auctioneers.

The men were forced to show their muscles and lift weights to show their strength. If asked, the men removed their clothing. Whip scars on their backs meant that this Negro was disrespect full and disobedient, so the price would go down.

When Sarah was examined, a crude and unclean finger was forced down her throat. She gagged but refused to cry. The perpetrator gleaned an evil smile and exclaimed that "this one has all her teeth!" Sarah felt like a horse and thought to herself if she were a horse; she would kick the man hard in the head.

The women were treated no better than the men were. The bidders would snicker and leer as the women took off their clothing to reveal the size of her breast. The larger the breast the more milk she would produce. Which in turn would provide the needed nourishment for future investments (children.) The children would be asked to dance for the entertainment portion of this horror show. While all of this was being done, the cries of desperation could be heard as the mothers and fathers of the children realized that they were very likely going to be sold to different locations. This meant that many families would never see each other again. The children would try to reach their mother's arms only to be kicked and slapped by the bidders who by now were either intoxicated by alcohol or by pure evil.

The slaves were then taken to a large stage that stood in front of the hotel. More refreshments, mostly whiskey, were served.

When it came Sarah's turn to walk onto stage, she knew what she must do. She glanced at the men in the audience. She remembered the dance her master Joseph loved to watch her perform for his pleasure.

As she stepped onto the stage she heard her mother Daisy's sweet tones in her inner ear. She also heard the drum rhythm of her ancestors.

The auctioneer made the announcement loud and clear "We next have a beautiful mulatto girl who is approximately eleven plus years old. For your pleasure gentlemen, start the bidding." The auctioneer motioned for Sarah to move forward with a toothless grin.

Sarah stepped onto the stage, alone with only her butterfly fan, she began her dance. Taking a deep breath and then saying a silent prayer asking for help from Jesus and her mother. Sarah stood alone on that large and cold stage. She was terrified however she knew what she had to do.

Slowly Sarah put her hand on her hips. Moving her hands slowly to her breasts then up to the nape of her neck to her hairline and the small ribbon that held her hair in a bun. She untied the ribbon and then shook her head to release her hair which then fell to her tiny waistline. She held her butterfly fan in front of her and let it spread its wings of lace. Next she untied the single strap that held her dress in place, letting it fall to the floor. All the while, she slowly rotated her hips to reveal her agility and gracefulness. The rowdy noisy men grew silent as Sarah danced her dance of seduction to perfection. She had to this point had her back to the audience. She finally turned to face the men. Smiling sweetly at them. Her fan and her hair covered her breast and intimate parts. She was innocent but dangerous. A tasty combination.

The bids began high. Sarah's eyes scanned the bidders. Amongst the sea of men dressed in black was one spot of red. It was Madam Rose from the bordello that Master Joseph had once introduced Sarah to when she had traveled with him to New Orleans.

Rose was the only person that Joseph had told that he was Sarah's father.

Rose was the high bidder and became not only Sarah's new master but also her step mother.

She vowed she would do what she could for Sarah. However she was a business woman first and foremost. She recognized Sarah's beauty and potential. Times were hard, Sarah would be an asset. Her youth and her beauty would bring welcome income.

Thus began Sarah's new life living at one of New Orleans finest brothels. A new life and a new name.

As was the custom of many brothels, the first names the women were known by were not their birth names. At this house the ladies were known by names given them by Rose. Rose was very fond of flowers. Thus she gave 'her girls' flower names. Sarah felt this was a good omen and a special blessing, as she knew her mother's name was Daisy.

Rose would name her girls after a flower that started with the first letter of their birth name. Thus Sarah was to be known as "Sunflower" for the rest of her life.

Sunflower was now approaching twelve years of age. Her duties around the house included cooking, cleaning and helping the working girls with their daily needs in any way Rose asked.

The women soon grew to appreciate Sunflowers knowledge about health and cleanliness. Sunflower was well liked by all the women.

Life was hard but good for Sunflower. Like her mother, she would sing songs from her homeland as she performed her chores. She loved singing gospel songs.

Being much too young to perform the work she was purchased for, Sunflower was asked to watch the ladies as they entertained the gentlemen callers in the parlor. She soon learned many skills that she would need throughout her life. Seductive skills that worked on the mind as well as the body. Rose taught her well. How to look beautiful inside and out. Her father, Joseph taught her well how to tease and titillate any man.

Most of the women who worked at this establishment were Caucasian. Sunflower was the only girl of mixed race, a 'mulatto.' There were times she would resemble her mother. Other times her father. She was a Chameleon, changing her look as desired even at this early age. She grew more beautiful with each sunrise.

Iris was a diminutive woman who proudly told everyone about her homeland, India. She would sit for hours in a very uncomfortable position and pray to her God while chanting "Shiva, Shiva, Shiva," over and over again. Iris was very beautiful. She had long black hair that hung to her knees. Many faithful men friends cared very much for her. The men loved to watch her stretch and hear her chant and sing.

One man, Sir George, fell in love with Iris. He asked her to marry him. Sir George was a very wealthy man who owned several very successful tobacco farms.

Another lady who worked at the brothel in New Orleans was a woman of Mexican ancestry who was known as Rosemary.

Rosemary loved to cook and often prepared great meals from

her culture. She also loved Christmas and every holiday season she would be in charge of decorations. The house never looked so lovely then at Christmas time when Rosemary took charge and the house became a palace of green and red.

There was one Asian lady at the house who went by the name of Orchid. She was as beautiful and delicate as the flower she was name for.

One day, Sunflower was asked by Orchid to come to her room. Orchid loved Sunflower and wished to talk with her about their chosen profession in which Sunflower would soon begin.

She told Sunflower how sometimes women can honor men and have the ability to make him very content without using her body.

Orchid talked about the Geisha's of her homeland. How beautiful and delicate women can make a man feel as though he were an Emperor. In turn he will treat you as a princess.

After Orchid concluded her lesson, just as Sunflower was about to leave, a large Japanese beetle flew into the room and landed on her shoulder to rest. Orchid smiled and told Sunflower "This is a good omen. You will have good fortune for seven years." At that the beetle flew away.

Sunflower never had a biological sister. Alice, who was known as Angel Trumpet, (although everyone called her Angel), was as close to a natural born big sister Sunflower would ever realize.

Angel was an American Indian born on the bayou. Her black hair framed her natural beauty to perfection. Angel was the house spiritual leader. She was a great comfort for all when times were at their worst. She was truly the Angel of the house. "Trumpet call for Angel," was the cry when one of the ladies got the blues.

Then there were the African ladies of the house. The prices for services rendered were different for each lady. Some were paid more than others. The African ladies sadly were paid the least. Thus it seemed they also had to serve the toughest and the cruelest of clients. It was just the way it was.

One Negro girl whom Sunflower felt close to was a lovely lady by the name of Lily. Lily came from a land that was referred to as the "land down under", Australia. Lily often talked about her Aboriginal brothers and sisters and her magical and mysterious homeland that was so far away. Sunflower would listen to Lily explain her spiritual beliefs long after all the ladies of the house had satisfied their gentlemen friends and retired for the evening.

Many times, Sunflower, Lily and Angel Alice would dance in the moonlight together. The three ladies would gather on the shores of the Mississippi to ask God to bless them and also to bless Mother Earth. Angel Trumpet Alice would bring her drum, rattles and a small golden bell. Angel would then sing her song to Father/Mother in her native language. Lily would sing her song in her Aboriginal tongue. The symphony would ebb and flow with the river. The dance was always in a secret place. It was a secret life that was shared with only the three sisters. All inhibitions disappeared. Their dance was performed in the nude. Although Sunflower felt her Spiritual beliefs were those of the Christian faith, she honored the beliefs of her sisters, Alice and Lily. Sometimes Sunflower would giggle in delight during these dances. Her beliefs, though somewhat different, blended. Her song was contained within her spirit. When it was put to voice, she would hear herself sing in a language she did not understand. The language was that of her ancestors in Africa.

These ceremonial dances continued for fifteen years when the moon was full. Starting when Sunflower, who was the youngest, was fourteen. The dances ceased in the summer of 1848.

In that summer, on a humid summer evening, Lily disappeared mysteriously never to be seen again. That was the night that a cruel and evil man who would torment Lily took her for a horse driven carriage ride.

When this man came to call at the house his visits were kept secret. He was a very respected and wealthy citizen of New Orleans. He was also a man of the cloth.

Lily's body was never found.

These women of pleasure became Sunflowers family. Together the women laughed, cried, shared their religious beliefs and of course how to make the most money possible and get the most requests for company.

Sunflower's day began at six in the morning. She would rise, stretch and then go to her mirror to wash and clean. She would brush her hair one hundred strokes in the morning. After she had put on a fresh dress of cotton, she would go to the kitchen to help prepare breakfast. A typical breakfast of potatoes, eggs, fruit and corn bread. The women of the house would arise at eight in the morning. Breakfast was served at nine.

After breakfast the chores began. Sunflower would help clean up the kitchen then if asked would go into town to help purchase food for lunch and dinner and the next day's breakfast.

Lunch was served at one in the afternoon. Soup would always be on the menu along with fresh fruit and vegetables.

After lunch Sunflower was given two hours of schooling from Rose, who was an excellent teacher. She learned to read from the Bible, poetry, the works of Shakespeare, and from other literary masters of the time. Sunflower was also taught geography, and some math skills.

After her lessons were over, more chores and kitchen duty. Dinner was at six. Dinner was always a feast. Each lady of the house would once a week suggest a meal. Thus the dinner menu always changed.

After dinner the women would get ready for the men to arrive, which always started at eight in the evening. This was the best time of the day. This is when the ladies would laugh, play card games and chat about life.

There was always a table full of sweets for the men and the ladies to enjoy before or after their appointment. Most men were quite hungry after. Rose discouraged alcohol. However behind closed doors it was permitted. A minimum of two very intimidating men were always on staff for security if needed. This was seldom.

The last client would be asked to leave only when he was satisfied. If it required an all night stay, then the lady he chose would accommodate him. However, Rose made sure that this privilege was not abused.

Sunflower was allowed, if asked, to escort the men to the proper room and give them a sponge bath before the requested lady arrived. She learned quickly to be comfortable around nudity.

Her bedtime was ten. One hundred brush strokes before bed. Clean her teeth and then retire.

When Sunflower was seventeen years of age, Rose could no longer avoid the requests from her many clients. Rose had one rule of her gentlemen callers and that was that Sunflower remain a virgin. This request was not unusual and could be accomplished by the right woman.

Sunflower loved most all of her gentlemen callers. She enjoyed what she did for a living having little regret. She loved her friends, the ladies of this establishment as sisters. She remained a virgin until at the age of thirty, when she met a man by the name of August.

My Tutorials

"Sarah Anne Wells 8/23/1819 Franklin, Louisiana"

I really did not have any reason to think that my first name was Sarah when I wrote of her birth.

It was a couple of days after I finished typing my thoughts about the birth of Daisy's baby girl that I was to receive a message that confirmed to me that Sarah was the right name.

Right after I finished writing of Sarah's birth a customer came into our bicycle shop to purchase some items and greeted me with "hello Sarah." How are you today?" I replied that I was fine, but that my name is Sherry. The customer corrected himself, "I'm sorry," he said "for some reason I really thought your name is Sarah." "No .problem," I told him that maybe my name was Sarah in a past lifetime". "Maybe so," he said apologizing once more.

Many years later, right before I was to submit this manuscript, I began to wonder just how many miles a horse could gallop in one day. Having grown up on a horse ranch I feel 35-40 miles in one day would be reasonable. I found a map of Louisiana. I rested my finger on New Orleans. Tracing north then slightly east, 70 some miles my finger came to rest on Franklinton. In 1819 (Sarah's year of birth) the city of Franklin was founded. In 1826 the name was changed to Franklinton.

In my life I've been surrounded by many "Franks". My birth name is Sherry Ann Franks. My son's name is Frank as is his father, his grandfather and his great grandfather. A gentleman whose first name is Franklin introduced Randy (my husband to be) to me in the year of 1975 at a golf course he owned where Randy and I worked at.

I have not been able to document that Gemstone Plantation existed. I do know that in Franklinton there is a golf course by the name of "Gemstone Plantation Golf Course." In later chapters Gemstone will be explained.

XOXOXOXOX

"Seventeen"

Seventeen seems to be a pivotal year for John Lennon and myself.

John lost his mother Julia when he was just seventeen.

My mother was just seventeen when she gave birth to me.

I had my first near death experience when I was just seventeen.

XOXOXOXOX

"My first near death experience at the age of seventeen"

I've heard it has been said that we are given five outs during our lifetimes. Five times is the maximum we have before we step to the other side. I've had two times where I can say I've used these outs.

It was the year of 1967 and the summer of love. I cannot say that I was a hippy. I cannot say that I was a preppie. I did not participate in many school activities. I do know that I was seventeen and I loved to party!

As we all know some of the most incredible music happened during this time in history. Some say this musical magic happened because of drugs, mostly LSD.

I have received messages from John Lennon (during readings) that yes he admits that some of his genius was induced. Not all though. Some of the drug use helped and some of it hurt in his musical ventures.

As for myself, my drug use almost cost me my life. Oh, how I loved to party at the age of seventeen. At these parties I had many chances to try drugs of all kinds. I had somehow managed to keep my drugs to pot, booze, bennies (speed) and reds (downers). Don't get me wrong, I'm not proud of this at all, but at this time in my life it was an accomplishment of sorts. I never tried LSD.

One very memorable party was held in a garage that had been converted into a party room. This party room featured strobe lights, and black light posters. We were so cool!

We danced to "Incense and Peppermints." We smoked joints and guzzled Coors beer. At some point someone put on the new Beatles album "Sgt. Pepper's Lonely Hearts Club band". Life was good.

Then our host brought out a new party favor for our pleasure. He had brought a canister of Freon and a large balloon.

The idea was to fill the balloon with the Freon gas and then inhale it. Our host telling us that his was harmless fun! It was just like inhaling helium. Except instead of a high squeaky voice, the party animal would have a low baritone voice.

The balloon was passed around and everyone was laughing to the point of tears and falling over. I was the only girl at the party and all the guys were excited to hear my voice. The balloon was passed to me. I remembered the guys telling me to take a really big hit of the balloon as I would sound really funny. So, of course I did, like a girl with no brain, as I was asked to do. I inhaled with all my might.

When I did this, at first, nothing weird happened. However, when I did speak my voice was very deep. "Ho! Ho! HO!" I said and the boys began to fall over laughing. I did sound like the jolly green giant and I laughed too. Then I stopped laughing. Then it happened.

As I looked around the room, it started to have a frame around it. It was like looking at life through a picture frame. I could see all the boys were starting to get smaller and farther away from me in this frame. Then they stopped laughing. Their smiles faded. I tried to reach for them, but they were much too small and far away for me to reach.

Reality and the picture started to disappear, which most would assume would be really frightening, but it was not. It was interesting.

Then I could no longer see any of my friends. I could hear their voices. I heard them asking "What happened?" "Sherry are you o.k.?" I heard my boyfriend (who was later to become my first husband Frank) ask if we should call someone? I could hear panic in his words. Suddenly the music and the voices faded away. Then just blackness.

It was then that I started to see in my "mind's eye" a small blinking light. It was very bright. It seemed to me that it was a star in a very black blanket of space. The light began to get brighter and brighter. Then I could hear "ping, ping, ping", as the light got closer and brighter. Every time the light would blink, it would ping. The ping became unbearably loud. Then out of this blackness came a voice. Loud and clear this voice said to me "THIS IS IT! THIS IS ALL THERE IS AND ALL THERE EVER WILL BE". It was absolutely terrifying. It was no longer interesting. I wanted to come back so desperately. However I could not voice my desire. I was helplessly staring at the light. The ping was now ear shattering I was utterly helpless.

Then the light began to fade. The ping grew silent. Slowly the music came back and I could hear my friends and their concerns for me. I was surprised to find myself on the floor. I did not remember falling. Then I came back fully to this reality.

It was only a matter of a minute or two, but it felt like an eternity that I was face to face with this light, the ping, and the voice.

The next day, a newspaper article appeared that reported the abuse of Freon. How there had been a couple of deaths as a result of this abuse. Neither I nor my friends ever did it again.

I believe the voice I heard was that of my Guardian Angel and that I was being given a warning. This experience kept me from using any "hard drugs" for the rest of my life. I did continue to smoke pot, and I drank way to much alcohol, but that was it.

That night, John Lennon's music was with me. I could hear him singing to me as I returned from that awful place. I could hear "A Day in the Life", as I returned to this reality.

I was so happy to be alive and yes, John's voice was a welcome back for me.

As for my beliefs on life after this life now that I am nearing the age of sixty: I do not believe that all there is on the other side is a blinking light, a loud ping and a voice telling me over and over again "THIS IS ALL THERE IS".

I believe this message was a harsh warning for a very foolish girl, who wanted to please at any cost. Also a girl who really liked getting high. I needed this and it was perfect.

This near death experience was actually a blessing as it helped to lead me in the right direction and toward a light that is beautiful beyond belief.

XOXOXOXOX

"Reverend Arlene Raedel"

Before I begin to reveal all the amazing coincidences and Synchronicities that I have learned about the date of August 23rd and the number 23, I need to introduce my Guide and my friend Reverend Arlene Raedel.

As the years went by, I could no longer ignore all the coincidences that were occurring in my life. I began to feel the need to find someone who might be able to confirm my suspicions and answer my question "Why".

I began to wonder if a psychic Medium could help. I started my search at a "new age" retail store in our city. I went with great anticipation and excitement.

I'd been to gypsy fortune tellers in the past and enjoyed the novelty. This time it was different. I was very curious about the possibility of connecting with one of my loved ones. Or perhaps connecting with the entity responsible for all these coincidences that had been happening for many years.

I walked into the store and was greeted by a man of about my age. He was sitting behind the counter strumming his guitar. I took a deep breath and informed the man that I would like to sign up for a reading. To my surprise, he did not give me "the look", and asked for my name. Then he collected the twenty dollars for the reading. I waited a few minutes before my reading with a psychic by the name of Joey. My first reading with her was with tarot cards. It was interesting, but no connection.

I continued looking for "the one", who I would know was the right spiritual advisor. The one who my invisible friend would be able to speak through. I was about to give up and then decided to give it one more try. I finally found her after about three months and five readings.

Once again I walked into the little shop (Shine on Moon), (not real name) and was greeted by the guitar man. He looked up and smiled. By now he knew my name and signed me up. "Who is working today?" I inquired "Arlene," he answered "You'll like her." He went back to his strumming. I went to the comfy couch to wait. The fragrance of many types of incense filled the air and was intoxicating in a wonderful way.

This time the reading was different. I walked into the cubical to see a lady sitting at the little desk. There were no Tarot cards. Arlene wore a lovely print dress and had golden hair to her shoulders. Most of all she had a very sincere smile as she greeted me. I thought she might be about the same age as me, maybe a few years older, but it was hard to tell. She was not loaded down with a lot of jewelry, she had just enough on that told me that each piece was special to her. The little room was lit with soft lighting and had a faint smell of incense. Arlene asked me my name as I took my seat across from her. She clicked on her tape recorder which was the only item on the small round table. 'I always start my readings asking for guidance from our Creator and for protection,' she informed me. "I also give all credit to God". Then we began our first of what was to become what we both call "conversations with our friends".

I knew right away that I had finally found "the one". Reverend Arlene was comfortable to talk with and very reverent. Nothing earth shattering happened at this first session other than just about everything we talked about seemed to connect with me on some level. Maybe it did not exactly ring true, but it felt right. I liked her references to Father and Mother God.

This was a very spiritually uplifting experience for me. I did not feel it was wrong at all. Just a nice talk with someone whom I felt was honest and secure in her own beliefs.

What I liked most of all is that Reverend Arlene did not mention the Devil or Hell one time during the session. We only talked of positive things in life. We talked mostly about life and how much God love's each of us. I was very impressed with Arlene's Biblical knowledge. I left store with a smile along with a smile and a great feeling of "one" ness".

Arlene finished our reading by telling me to look for a bird to connect with me in the next few days. He will find you and you'll know immediately you have connected. He is one of your animal tokens.

I had no idea what she meant, but sure enough a couple of days later a beautiful blue bird met me outside in my back yard as I went to feed our turtle "Grumpy". I had forgotten about the bird message until this moment. This bird was very curious about me. He would chirp several times and seemed very unafraid. This little fellow stood his ground even when I was only a few feet from him. He would cock his head, ruffle his feathers then chirp at me once more. After a few minutes he flew away.

This proved to be the last day I would see this bird. His mission was done.

So began, and continues to be, my journey with Reverend Arlene. We've had over thirty readings as of this date.

Some of these readings are funny some sad, some tell of future events and some feel very spiritual.

Here is a funny example as recorded on tape at a session:

Arlene: "Sherry, why is John showing me the back side of a jackass?"

Sherry: "Ha! Ha! Ha! I have no idea."

Arlene: "Well he is and it's not pretty! Is he trying to tell me something?"

Sherry: "Ha! Ha! I hope not!"

A few minutes later we started discussing music. I asked her who her favorite entertainers were and what kind of music she likes. She told me that she loves the music from the late 50's early 60's. She told me that she loved the music of Frankie Lane. I asked her if she could remember her favorite song by this artist. She replied "I always liked—Mule Train". We both got the connection and we had a good laugh.

After several readings I informed her that I had my suspicions that one of my Guides was John Lennon. I had not told her this until we had met several times. It was only after I had been given several confirmations that I began to believe that she was indeed connecting with him.

Reverend Arlene is able to hear John's voice in her mind and then see images, and respond with incredible insight. Don't get me wrong, she's not always right, but she never gets it all wrong, and sometimes it is quite remarkable the way she connects. I asked her once if she actually is able to see John. How does he look? She told me he looks like a little blue light most of the time. This little light floats about the cubical. Most the time she cannot see him at all. She just feels his presence and hears his voice in her inner ear.

Since you are reading this book I'm guessing you are a bit interested in these phenomena and hopefully you have an open mind. Not that

I want anyone to just except all of anything anyone tells you about spiritual matters. In fact when I'm sitting across from Arlene I'm always asking for some kind of verification. Sometimes I'll actually ask myself "what am I doing here?" Then something wonderful will happen and I am just amazed and happy to be connected with so much love.

I've never gotten a scary or evil message. Nor have I ever received a message I am ashamed of. The messages always feel like a tutorial. In fact they are indeed just that.

It's always a message of hope, love, happiness, and tutorials about life.

All the messages convey a feeling that everybody, all that is, is connected and go on forever.

I feel very blessed to have been given this gift and hope that by sharing I can somehow give back this wonderful knowing that "we are ONE'.

XOXOXOXOX

"John and Cynthia Lennon"

John Winston Lennon married his sweetheart, Cynthia Powell on August 23rd, 1961.

XOXOXOXOX

"Hollywood Bowl—August 23rd, 1964"

August 23rd, 1964 is one of the most memorable days of my life. In fact I can say that this day set in motion all the days to come for me. On this day I attended a Beatles concert at the Hollywood Bowl.

My best girlfriend was a skinny gal with long brown hair. Her name was Bonnie. At the tender age of twelve, Bonnie and I were hopeless Beatle-maniacs. We had wall to wall Beatle pictures taped to the wall of our rooms. We dressed like The Beatles, tried to talk with an English accent and were never without our copies of Sixteen Magazine.

As the school year ended and summer began our favorite radio station KRLA announced that there was going to be a Beatles concert on August 23rd at the Hollywood Bowl. Bonnie and I did not know how we were going to get to the concert, but we knew we were going to attend it. Nothing could stop us! We did not tell our parents of our grand plan.

Bonnie and I saved our allowance (which was about $1.50 per week) and some of our lunch monies, to get enough for our tickets. The price of the tickets was $5.50 each! When we finally saved enough money we made the journey to the local AAA (yes, the American Auto Association sold the tickets). When the big day arrived, Bonnie and I marched into the AAA with our money in hand.

I think I must have looked at that ticket a hundred times. I kept it hid in my jewelry box with the dancing ballerina on top. Only problem was, we did not have a ride to the show. Hollywood was about 60 miles away. It might as well have been China! However just holding and having the ticket was magical. So about three days before the concert, Bonnie and I could not keep the secret any longer. It was time to ask our parents if we could get a ride to Hollywood to see the Beatles. The times were different back in the sixty's then today. This was a really big thing in our lives. We were innocent little girls and these tickets were not something our parents would normally approve of. Especially the way we obtained them. I clung to my ticket and held my breath as I gazed upon my mother and fathers expressions when I told them about the ticket. They knew of my puppy love for the Beatles. My room looked like a Beatles museum! They were tolerant and kind. However, this was too much! This may be out of the question, I feared.

Dad gave me "the look, "and asked me to give him the ticket. Gulp! Which I did. "Now go to your room young lady" my father said "Your mother and I need to talk" Not a good sign.

Finally I heard mom approach my room and say to me "Your dad and I want to talk to you." Holding back my tears and hoping beyond hope that this would work out I bravely marched back to the living room where dad was sitting in his easy chair. I told my parents, I was very sorry for not asking them first. That was all it took! Dad's face (although still not exactly smiling) softened. He asked me "Now young lady, just how did you figure on getting to Hollywood to see these bugs?" "Beatles, Dad," I corrected him (I knew he knew they were called the Beatles, but this was dad's way of trying to cope with my, well obsession). "Well" I said, "I hope that Bonnie's parents can take us". "Alright, if they can take you then it's alright with your mother and I," dad said with almost a smile while he picked up his can of Spanish peanuts. "I love you Mom and Dad," I cried.

I ran to the telephone to call Bonnie. She informed me that her parent would indeed provide the ride. Bonnie was an only child, and her parents did tend to overindulge her, so we felt we had a good chance on getting a ride from them. Well, we hoped anyway!

Off to Hollywood we go, but first, what am I going to wear to a Beatles concert? I had only one choice. The one "Mod" thing I had in my closet. It is a bit hard to describe but here goes! It was a newspaper dress. It was styled like a man's button down dress shirt that came to my knees. The fabric was cotton, but it actually looked like a newspaper. I looked like I was a walking newspaper add! I thought it was very grown up and very mod. I finished my outfit with my beloved Beatle boots. Only problem was my curly hair. No problem. Out came the iron and I ironed my hair to straighten out the curls.

Bonnie looked beautiful with her long (and straight) hair that hung to her shoulders. Cut in the style that was so popular in the mid sixty's. Bangs that hung straight across her eyebrows. She wore her favorite "I love the Beatles", white tee shirt and short black skirt. Her Beatle boots finished her assemble also. We made quite a fashion statement, well as best we could, after all we were only twelve years old.

Into the ole Buick land yacht and off we went to Holly- Wood, two little girls with some mighty big dreams. I had never been to Hollywood before so every car we passed had a movie star driving it, or so I imagined. It seemed to take forever but finally we arrived. There in the distance was the Hollywood sign I had seen on the "I love Lucy" TV. Show. Was that Lucy in the car we just passed?

When we arrived at the Bowl, Bonnie's parents parked the car and thankfully let us walk alone the short distance to the entrance of the Hollywood Bowl. As we walked, holding hands, we spied a huge billboard which was advertising "London Fog" fashion wear. We both froze in our Beatle boots and did what came naturally. We screamed! We were joined in our song by several other girls.

I felt cool, except my curly hair was starting to frizz! Plus there were so many pretty older teenage girls. Very mod girls and very mod boys. I soon forgot about my frizz, because it just really didn't matter. This was magic.

Finally we got thru the gate and into the Hollywood Bowl. Beautiful as the Bowl is, the only thing that my eyes saw was Ringo's drums on stage with "The Beatles", printed on the front of them. Plus the three guitars we knew so well. We found our row "G" for George Harrison, who was my favorite Beatle. Bonnie's fave was Paul. Everyone had a Fave Fab.

Then like a wave of sound it happened. It started way back in the farthest row from the stage, and then made its way to the front of the Bowl.

WE LOVE YOU BEATLES

OH, YES WE DO

WE LOVE YOU BEATLES

AND WE'LL BE TRUE'

WHEN YOU'RE NOT NEAR TO US

WE'RE BLUE

OH BEATLES WE LOVE YOU

YEAH, YEAH, YEAH, YEAH

Once finished it would start over again. Finally the lights dimmed.

Our favorite D.J. Bob Eubanks from radio station KRLA, appeared on stage to make the announcement. You could hardly hear what he was saying until he said the words we had been waiting for, "HERE THEY ARE. The Beatles!"

How can I explain what happened next? Christmas, birthdays, trips to Disneyland, hugs from your family, a Puppy's warm tongue against your cheek, a kitten softly purring next to you as you take her to the land of dreams, all of these wonderful things mixed into one and then some. That was the feeling. There they were, in real life! John, Paul, George and Ringo. The scream that was let loose as they walked onto stage was and is beyond description.

From our seats the Beatles were about one inch tall. Thousands of girls were in front of Bonnie and me. However, during "She Love's You." Bonnie screams to the top of her lungs that Paul just waved to her! I remember thinking "Really?" Oh well, maybe he did. So I hugged my friend and screamed a little louder.

When the show ended we all sort of went into a mass depression. It was over. Now the long walk back to the Buick.

However, just as we got to one of the driveways leaving the Bowl, a big black Cadillac Limousine appeared. We were asked to stop by one of the policemen to let it pass by. Bonnie and I once again froze to attention. In the Limo was a head with a very unmistakable hair style. Then out of the window came a hand that waved to me. Was it? Well, in reality, probably not. However, maybe, just maybe, on August 23rd, 1964 I really was given a wave and a "hello' from John Lennon. I like to imagine I did.

XOXOXOXOX

My Beatle friends 1965

"Trinity is born on August 23rd, 2003"

On August 23rd, 2003 our granddaughter Trinity was born. Trinity is a beautiful little girl with light blonde hair and big blue eyes that can melt your heart. She has a zest for life that makes everything seem so wonderful. She loves animals and hopes to someday become a veterinarian. I for one believe she will accomplish this goal. She is an Angel in human form.

XOXOXOXOX

"August 23rd. 2006. A Miracle in Duluth"

On August 23rd 2006, I was witness to a miracle in Duluth Minnesota.

On August 17, 2006 my father and his wife, Lori, were involved in an automobile accident in the city of Duluth, Minnesota.

Dad and Lori's car was hit on the driver's side door by an elderly woman. Dad and Lori were on their way home from a month's vacation. Two innocent people who happened to be in the wrong place at the wrong time.

Dad broke three ribs. Lori broke her collar-bone and had to be hospitalized. I guess there is not much anyone can do for broken ribs so dad was not hospitalized. He sat and slept next to Lori for two days while in extreme pain himself.

The staff fell in love with the two "Youngsters" and they soon earned the nick names of Mr. and Mrs. Smith.

Mr. Smith, dad, would joke around with the staff and try to make the best of it as he sat with his wife. Unfortunately he had a secret. He was in the early stage of developing pneumonia. When a young intern came in to check on Lori's vitals he noticed dad sitting in silence in the corner of the room. He did not look good. He was immediately taken to urgent care, and then later admitted to the intensive care unit at Saint Mary's hospital in Duluth Minnesota with pneumonia.

On August 19th my two sisters, Kathy and Vicky, along with our younger brother Mark and myself flew from California to Minnesota to be near our father who by now was on life support.

Before I left for Minnesota I went to the Shine on Moon to visit with Reverend Arlene for support and prayer. I was given a prayer from Arlene that I printed out to take with me for comfort. In this prayer was this statement that read:

"After the third day, we the children of John (our father) should expect to see a miracle. We will not accept anything less than full recovery. That we will know that our father will return to health and will not be asked to give his life in this matter".

"We, the four children of John, will simply not let this happen".

It was a bold statement and the kind of prayer I was not accustomed to. It proved to be very hard to hold on to these thoughts when it became very evident that dad may not re- cover.

Before we were about to board for the long flight to Minnesota, we received a call from Lori. Dad was slipping away. Lori was weeping hysterically and asked if there were any way we could get a faster flight? There was no way.

It was heart wrenching. The only hope I could hold onto at that moment was the printed prayer I held in my pocket.

It was not the right moment to reveal it to my brother and sisters. I did however feel a great sense of "it's going to be all right." As I boarded the plane I told Kathy that dad will be fine. Don't give into negative thoughts!

I think I was actually trying to convince myself as much as anyone. I told Kathy that I believe in Miracles and that my Guardian Angel, John, would soon send me a message. I felt it and I knew he would with all my being.

The message came on the last leg of the flight. When we boarded our last connection before we arrived in Duluth, I noticed as I stepped into the cabin of the jet, that Edgar Winter was on board. He smiled as I walked by. A surreal moment.

As fate would have it, my assigned seat had me sitting next to one of Edgar Winter's band members. Before too long I found myself telling him all about dad and the reason we were on this very late flight.

During the course of our conversation, I learned that the Edgar Winter band was on their way to Minnesota to star with several other bands in an all oldies show. One of the other bands that were to perform at this show was Iron Butterfly. The lead singer of this band is Martin Gerschwitz. I have known him many years and we have shared many special moments together. I asked my new friend to pass along a note to Martin, which he did do. The next night I received a phone call from Martin which was of great comfort to me.

I knew John was using Edgar Winter and Iron Butterfly to let me know he was with me at this time. Here is how I know:

In 1970 John Lennon wrote a song entitled "Rock n Roll People." Edgar Winter recorded this song on his album "John Dawson Winter III" in 1974. John is sending Mr. Winter his love and would like to congratulate him for his "FAB"ulous rendition of "Rock n Roll People."

Edgar Winter had a hit song by the name of "Frankenstein!" Another Frank!

The butterfly is my insect token for Aquarius. I was aboard butterfly wings of Iron on the way to see our father.

We arrived at the hospital around 1:00 a.m. We were escorted into dad's room where we saw him for the first time. I cannot speak for Kathy, Vicky or Mark, but I can say this for myself, I almost fainted when I saw him. I don't know what I expected but I surely was not prepared. Dad was in an induced coma. I stood staring at the monitor that blinked his vitals. I had no idea what I was looking at. I had never seen anyone hooked up to so many life support lines.

The nurse who escorted the four of us into dad's room said little to us. We all stood in shock over dad. We stayed for an hour then left for our hotel room.

Dr. "O" greeted us at 8:00 a.m. the next morning. He gave us very little hope for our father. This was August 20, which was the first day and it was a very grim and hopeless one.

Dad had developed a third type of pneumonia and was now in an induced paralyzed state. I'll never forget Dr. O telling us, "I don't think you kids' realize how serious your father's health is right now. Dr. O never smiled once that day.

I clung to the Prayer I had in my pocket. The second day, August

21st all seemed hopeless. Dr. O showed us dad's x-rays that had just been taken. Not one of us really knew what we were looking at until Dr. O explained the shadows to us. Dr. O first asked us if dad were a tobacco smoker. "Yes, he is", I answered. Dr. O only said he thought so. He shook his head and left the room. It was a long sad day. All of us took turns trying to find something to be positive about. We sat for hours at a time staring at the blinking lights and graphs of the life support lines while holding dad's hand.

We had another conference with Dr. O. the next day. August 22nd was the third day and I could tell by his eyes, that Dr. O was not going to give us much hope. Dad's condition was now grave.

At that point, I needed some time to myself. I left dad's room to use the lavatory. Instead I just started walking, not sure where to go. Then I found the hospital chapel.

The hospital chapel at Saint Mary's hospital was about to begin service. I took my seat and held onto Reverend Arlene's prayer. I cried as I've never cried before. I also prayed as I've never prayed before. I'm afraid the services were interrupted by my sobs. It did not seem to matter to me. The only one who mattered to me at that moment was God and my dad.

After the service was over the Chaplain asked me if he could help. I looked up. He was very young and of mid- Eastern ancestry. I could hardly believe my reply to him "Thank you Father, but I do not subscribe to your religion," I told him through my sobs and nose blowing. When I heard myself say this to the kindly Father, I was taken by surprise and to be honest shocked! I had just repeated the line that is used in the Beatles movie "Help". Ringo says this line to the Priest who is about to sacrifice him. Ringo's line in the movie is—"Here's your bloody ring! I don't subscribe to your religion anyway." Again it was a surreal moment. John Lennon sure has a way of interjecting humor at the most odd times. I could hardly believe I had said that and just tried to ignore my statement. Fortunately the young priest just put his hand on my shoulder. He did calm my sobs a bit. However, I did feel a slight giggle inside. Even through all the sadness. I told the young Chaplain that I was not a Catholic. I told him that his service was very lovely but that I believe that everyone goes to Heaven no matter what religion. I also told him I believe there is no such thing as Hell

The Chaplain answered me by telling me that he has many friends and family in India who are not Catholics either. His kindly eye's told me that it was alright that I was not of his religion. I was surprised by this, and he offered me some comfort.

I left the Chapel and started to walk back to the intensive care unit. I was so afraid of what I might find out since I had been away from dad for over two hours. I stopped at the elevator then turned and walked the opposite direction. I was very afraid.

I cried out to John that I could use some "Help" actually saying this out loud as I stumbled my way through the hospital corridors. I thought to myself that if anyone knew who I was praying and talking to, would think I was mad. Maybe I was. However I really did not care anyway.

I walked out the doors of Saint Mary's. I just had to get away and walk. For an instant I thought about going to the small bar that is across the street from the hospital. Just get lost in a bottle. I knew that this was not the answer.

I did not know where to go. Just walk I told myself. I walked a few blocks and stopped in front of a used book store. In front of this store was a little black kitty laying at the threshold of the store. This little kitty reminded me of our shop cat Dyno who keeps me company every day at work. When I saw this kitty I knew I must enter the book store. So I did.

The lady behind the counter had probably seen many people like me over the years being so close to St. Mary's Hospital. By now my face was swollen and red from crying. I was a mess!

She smiled and said "Hello". I gave her a nod and made my way to a corner of the store.

Every step of my way, the little black kitty followed me. He nuzzled me and somehow took some of my sadness away. A little white dove in the corner of the store cooed at me from his cage. I could tell his wing had been broken. Just as I felt my spirit had at this moment in time.

I found myself in front of the "L" section of used books. "O.k. John where are you?" I thought to myself. I knew there must be a book for me. This had to be the reason I was led to this store. The little black kitty's eye's followed my every move. Then I found the book. The only book on the shelf about John Lennon. It was May Pang's book which is entitled "Loving John" (1983).

For those who do not know, May Pang worked as a personal assistant and production Coordinator for John and Yoko. In 1973 John and Yoko separated. This led to a relationship between John and May. This lasted 18 months. John later referred to this as his "Lost Weekend".

I had wanted a copy of this book for many years. Now I found it, at a book store in Duluth, Minnesota. So far from home. Seeing John's pictures inside the covers made me feel better. "Thank You John for helping me discover this book. I know there will be a message from you to me within these pages", I said to myself as the little black kitty blinked at me once again.

I took the book to the counter and asked the lady if she had other books about John Lennon in the store. "No" she answered, while looking at her computerized inventory. "No, this is the only one." I noted that she was about a woman of my age who had long gray hair that reminded me of our shared youth in the sixty's. I then found out that she was from California too, and that she had moved to Duluth to open her book store a few years ago. I found out that her little black kitty's name was Crow. "Black Crows" I thought to myself, remembering their hit song "She Talks to Angels". Once again, appropriate as this was exactly what I'd been doing the last few days.

So I purchased the book and walked back to the hospital. I gave Crow a kiss before I left the store. Crow gave me another nuzzle and our eyes connected and I knew some- how everything was going to be fine. I could return to be at dad's side, no matter what.

When I entered the hospital and the intensive care unit, I held the novel "Loving John" and the printed prayer from Reverend Arlene tightly. I walked into dad's room to see him still in the induced coma state with all the machines that were keeping him alive. I thought to myself about the night before when dad's heart had stopped twice. As I kissed dad goodnight, thoughts of losing him were starting to overcome my confidence that we his children and all who love this incredible man would not allow this to happen. We may just not be able to overcome this, I thought. We may just loose him this night. I wanted to believe, as Arlene's prayer stated, that by the end of the third day we would see a miracle, but it was so hard to stay in that frame of mind.

Kathy and I went back to our shared hotel room that night with heavy hearts. Kathy is my younger sister who is three years my junior. As most sisters do, we've shared many special moments. Kathy is a truly wonderful person. She loves her family, her pets, her friends and just about any stranger she meets with a heart of gold that is so special. She was married to her sweetheart "Ja" at the age of sixteen. They are still happily together. When her time comes and she faces her life's decisions, I believe our Creator will simply say to her "Kathy, you did well."

That night in our room, before we fell asleep, Kathy and I shared some very special and private memories with each other. I told her about my experiences that day. About the Chapel, the book store, and the little black cat by the name of Crow. I also told her about finding the book "Loving John." I shared Reverend Arlene's prayer with her. When I did, I felt an amazing lightness come over me. I felt happy and content.

Before I fell asleep I thought about my two other siblings who were by now asleep in the room next to us. Through all the sadness, this experience had brought me closer to both Vicky and Mark who are quite a bit younger than I.

Sweet Vicky is one of the most honest and brave women I have ever known. Brave because she is true to her heart. At this time Vicky's lover was fighting a battle with breast cancer. She had recently been diagnosed and was being treated with very aggressive chemotherapy. Vicky was torn between her love of her father and her friend. Two life changing events at once. Her courage and her smiles helped everyone. Very seldom did I see fear in her eye's just hope. My little sister Vicky was a rock.

Then there was Mark. My brother is thirteen years my junior. Mark was only sixteen when we lost our mother. Sometimes I think his grief was the deepest. Mark handled dad's accident as only a man is able. Trying his best to guide his older sisters and our dad's wife, Lori, with as much brotherly advice and guidance he could. Sometimes he would offer up some comic relief at the most unusual of times. He helped us all cope. Just as he did when he was sixteen and we lost mom.

I slept well that night. It was now the end of the third day.

The next morning, August 23rd, I awoke to a beautiful summer day. Blue skies and big fluffy white clouds. This was my granddaughters third birthday. I told Kathy, let's get to the hospital. Dad is going to be fine. Kathy smiled back at me and said "Let's go then". Off we went.

So, bright and early we made our way to the intensive care ward. We were asked to meet with Dr. O at 8:00 a.m. We had not checked on Dad and had not had a phone call during the night so we really did not know what to expect. Kathy and I met Lori, Mark and Vicky at the nurse's station to wait for Dr. O. Within a minute or two he walked in with a big grin. This was a first! He told us that dad had a good night! That he felt dad will recover! This was the first time Dr. O had given us any hope! Hallelujah! We hugged and kissed each other. Little sister Vicky gave Dr. O a big kiss on the lips! We were dancing for dad! Dr. O then told us he would bring dad out of the induced coma state he was still in sometime in the afternoon.

Then he smiled and said "you kids will have your dad home soon. You have your Miracle".

Miracle is sometimes a word that is too lightly used in my opinion. However I'm going to use it! That it happened on August 23rd makes it even more special.

Just as Reverend Arlene's prayer stated "By the end of the third day our dad would recover".

Even that was to pass. It was at the end of the day that dad was to wake up and be able to look us in the eye and hold our hands. He was not able to talk as he was still on the ventilator and had a tracheotomy tube. Many other machines too. However, we knew, for the first time, that our father knew that his wife and his "kids" were at his side.

Just as the prayer stated, by the end of the third day, we knew our dad was going to survive this unfair event. August 23rd, 2006.

Two days later Kathy and I flew back home. Although dad was still in intensive care, Dr. O felt confident it would not be long until dad would be re-evaluated and admitted to a step down room in the hospital. Well, sometimes things just don't go as well as we wish.

Dad was not recovering as we hoped. Things were again turning the other way and dad was extremely depressed. His battle was not over, not by a long run.

Kathy and I decided to return to dad's bedside six weeks after our return home. Things were just not going all that well for dad. This time, Kathy and I made a vow to each other that we would not return home until dad was out of Saint Mary's hospital and into a rehab facility.

Before we left for Duluth, once again I went to visit Reverend Arlene for prayer and guidance.

Reverend Arlene told me this time I should be firm and not give in to any doubt that dad would be coming home. She told me to bring courage with me. Then she said "Get this man to laugh and smile again! Your dad needs a good laugh!" Then she did what I have seen her do many times. She is silent for a couple of seconds, and then turns her head and smiles. She then asks me "Sherry is your dad a cowboy?" Reverend Arlene could not have known this. "Yes, dad is and always will be a cowboy at heart!" "Sherry, when you walk into your dad's hospital room this time, no matter how sick he looks or how worried you are, I want you to smile and greet him with—Hello cowboy!"

Then Rev. Arlene asked me, "What is your dad's fascination with the Lone Ranger?" I thought for a few minutes but I could not think of any time dad had ever mentioned the masked lawman. "Maybe in his youth, but Reverend Arlene I don't think he ever mentioned the Lone Ranger to me," I replied in earnest to her. "O.k.", Rev. Arlene said "I still think that there is a connection, look for it."

When we landed in Duluth, Kathy and I immediately took a taxi ride and headed to Saint Mary's hospital.

We were greeted in the nurse's station by some of the nurses who we had met the last time we were there. "Thank God, you've come", said one of dad's favorite nurses (her name was Julia) "Your dad is not doing so well. He needs hope, love and encouragement. Lori needs this also."

Well that did it for me, Kathy too. We looked at each other and said "let's get it done".

As I walked into dad's room for the first time, seeing him once again hooked up to every kind of machine, my wind was taken out of my sails. However, Kathy and I were very determined. I looked at dad and greeted him as Rev. Arlene had said I should except I said "Hello John Wayne! I love you, now let's get to work and let's get you out of here!" Dad smiled with tears in his eyes back at me. Tuff cowboy.

So began the hard part, Dad's slow recovery.

I had been reading May Pangs book "Loving John", on and off since I purchased it six weeks past. I was only about half way through the novel. I mention this, because John was about to send me another message of love and hope. May's book was going to be, once again, the catalyst for this message.

It was on the fifth day of our return to Duluth that I noted that a concert was being held at a casino that Kathy and I walked by every day after our day at the hospital to our hotel room. The concert that night was with the "Little River Band".

I love live music. However with all that was going on I was not sure if I should attend. I asked Kathy and she said "go." She would wait for me inside the casino playing our favorite slot machine "Nurse Betty." It felt right, so I told her I was going to attend the concert.

I had a blast. The Little River Band was fantastic. The October night was cool but not cold. The air was fresh and it felt so good to happily sing along. Great music along with the healing presence of the Great Lake "Mother", Superior just a short walk away from the venue. It doesn't get much better than this!

I joined a group of fellow music lovers and we held hands and sang along to "Reminiscing." This was not one of my favorite songs, until this night. It was beautifully performed and touched my heart.

After the concert Kathy and I walked the two remaining blocks to our hotel. That night, I picked up May Pang's book, "Loving John", and finished it to its conclusion. At the end, May wrote about how she and John Lennon listened to "Reminiscing", by the Little River Band over and over again one night. How this had been a favorite song of John's. I was blown over. Once again John had come through with a powerful message of love and hope for me. I kissed the book and told John thank you before I fell asleep. I smiled when I realized I would have never known that this song was one of John's favorites had I not walked into the little book store on August 22nd. Then it hit me. Reminiscing. Kathy was asleep by now, so I had to keep all of this to myself, for now. However when Kathy woke up, I told her about John's message the best I could. "We've got to get dad back to loving life again! I'm going to reminisce like I've never reminisced before in my life" I told my little sis who agreed. "Now let's get back to the hospital and love -our John-, our dad".

So out the front door of our hotel room Kathy and I marched. Determined to do our best this day to get dad out of his depression. As we were about to press the down button on the hotel elevator, I heard "Hold, Please." Into the elevator cab stepped a familiar face. In walked Glenn Shorrock, the lead singer for the Little River Band. To say I was surprised to see him is a huge understatement. I had no idea that he was registered at the same hotel as Kathy and I were.

I thanked Glenn for the wonderful evening of entertainment and told him I especially loved hearing "Reminiscing." I wanted to ask him if he realized that Reminiscing was one of John Lennon's favorite songs, but I could tell he was in a hurry to get where he needed to be. Somehow I think he knows.

Then it hit me as I watched him hurry away to the parking lot and then disappear from sight. What an amazing synchronistic-moment it was. That Mr. Shorrock would be hailing the elevator at that exact moment in time! Had Kathy and I not left our room when we did, I would have never had the opportunity to thank Glenn for his song. Wow! Amazing another message from John that I need to get started reminiscing with dad. On Kathy and I marched with renewed determination at our side.

You may think it easy to just start blabbing away to a loved one who is sick and depressed. It is not. In the last few days I had read many articles from the National Geographic magazine (dad's favorite) to try to get him to smile. I think I just bored him. We would watch TV. But then he would just fall asleep. We tried everything with not much success. It was so sad to see him sitting in a chair with his head down. No smiles. About all he was concerned with was, well not much.

Today was different. Today we shall reminisce. Now what to reminisce about? My mind went blank. Geese, not now I told myself! Then I remembered Rev. Arlene's question about dad being a cowboy. "Dad, do you remember the pinto horse you had many years ago?" Dad just sort of shrugged his shoulders and went back into his lonely place. "Kathy", I asked her "do you remember dad's brown and white Pinto?" "Yes", I do she chimed in. No one but dad could ride him." I asked her if she could remember the horse's name as I could not. "No I can't remember it either", she replied. "What was his name?" I asked the walls. I honestly tried to remember, but could not recall the Pinto's name. Then I felt a hand on my shoulder and looked down to see dad mouth something (he could not talk because of the tracheotomy tube still in place). Then I saw that dad was telling me the name of his beloved Pinto horse "TONTO". I looked at dad and asked him to repeat.

'T.O.N.T.O". This time I could read his lips and could hardly believe it. My mind went into overdrive as I realized Rev. Arlene's message had come true. The Lone Ranger's Indian friend. His name was Tonto.

I got so excited that I started giggling like a silly school girl. I guess it was contagious because Kathy and Lori giggled too. Then it happened, Dad smiled, and although he could not audibly giggle, he giggled. "Tonto", he mouthed it again. I told him how marvelous his memory is.

There was no way I could tell him exactly why I was so excited about Tonto, but Tonto's spirit opened the door just a bit more to help dad recover. The Lone Ranger to our rescue.

After this, dad was still very guarded, but nobody ever talked about anything other than getting out of the Intensive care room he was still in.

The day after Tonto, I tried another approach with dad with music. I had brought my cd player with me to listen to before I fell asleep. I had only one C.D. with me for dad to listen to. It was a c.d. my father in law, Ralph, had recorded. Ralph is a very gifted singer. "Have a listen Dad," I said, as I put the ear phones on him. "This is Ralph." Dad smiled ear to ear. Then he gave me thumbs up. I was so glad I thought of this. I have thanked Ralph many times for his beautiful voice and how he brought joy to dad that day. After that I purchased every country CD that they had in the gift shop. Johnny Cash, Willie and Hank Williams Jr. You gentlemen do not know it, but you also helped to bring our cowboy dad into this reality and I thank you for your beautiful music.

The next couple of day's dad continued to take little steps at first, and then huge giant leaps towards recovery. First he was off the ventilator. Next the tracheotomy tube came out. At which time dad spoke his first words in over two months, "I have the most beautiful wife and daughters in the world." We were very proud of dad. Kathy and I were also very proud of ourselves, calling our journey with dad "our finest moment."

It had now been over three weeks that Kathy and I had been basically living at the hospital at the intensive care unit at Saint Mary's. Dad and Lori, well over two months. A word here about dad's wife, and our step mother, Lori. She is an amazing woman. She stood toe to toe with the nurses, the doctors, anybody anytime and absolutely made sure "her John," got only the best of care. No if ands or butts. If "her John" needed something, Lori made it happen. I have never seen a woman's love for her man more evident than Lori's for her John. Lori had to rely on the kindness of strangers while dad was in the hospital. She lived in the homes of some of the hospital staff and friends that she did not know before the accident. My heart was filled with new hope for the human race because of the good people of Duluth, Minnesota.

Life in the intensive care ward was far removed from my daily routines. My admiration for the doctors, nurses, cleaning staff, ministers, counselors, and of course the people I met whose loved ones were hospitalize with dad at the time, will never leave me. What the staff lives with on a day to day basis is incredible. They live with the highest of hopes, and the lowest of low. How they are able to do this year after year leaves me with a feeling of awe.

There are too many nurses who helped dad for me to mention only one name. Please just know, for what you did for our dad will live forever in our memories. Bless you. Dr. "O," as we called him is from South Africa. Just as I believe Sunflowers ancestors were born. Perfect.

When the time finally came for dads release into the rehab center, most all the tubes were gone. Except for his stomach feeding tube. I marveled at the thought that dad had not eaten a mouth of food or a drink of water in over two months. He had lost about forty pounds since the accident. He could barely walk more than three or four steps at a time when he was released, but those were mighty big steps as far as we were concerned.

With pomp and circumstance we rolled dad, in his wheel chair, across the indoor walkway over the main street of Duluth, to his new home at the rehab facility. We were mighty proud and very happy. One of the nurses from Saint Mary's saw dad and Lori and said to them "Well Hello, Mr. and Mrs. Smith. So good to see you!"

Dad got to his new room and one of the first things we needed to do was to initial his socks, skivvies, and jogging pants and tee shirts. So I got out my sharpie and put his initials on his personals. "J.L."

Well it was only a few days later that Kathy and I booked our flight home. Dad and Lori booked their flight also.

Update:

It is now over five years since dad and Lori's accident. Dad is now home and quite happy. He is currently the Commander of his chapter of the VFW in his home town in Arizona. He is playing golf again, and going to the casino and playing the slot machine "Nurse Betty", with Lori.

Dad and Lori did make a return trip to Saint Mary's hospital a couple of years after the accident, thanking the hospital staff and most especially Dr. "O."

Our prayers were answered, Dad was not meant to sacrifice his life and step to the other side of reality. It was simply not his time to do so.

I thank our Creator for the miracle that happened on August 23rd, 2006.

XOXOXOXOX

Our cowboy dad Mr. John M. Lovell

"Donnie our Bmx Angel # 223"

Donnie came into our lives in 1984. He was an extremely active six year old. We met him at our local bmx (bicycle moto-cross) track. Donnie loved to race and was by far the highest ranked amateur in our district.

Donnie also had one of those charismatic personalities that drew young and old to him like a rock star. He had a smile that any movie star would desire. He walked like a peacock, a wonder to behold.

Our children, Frank age 13 and Crystal age 10, were also racing bmx at this time. We had a lot of fun and the memories will never fade away. Our bicycle shop was only a couple of years old and this family sport became pivotal in its growth.

We started our bicycle team with our children and a couple of their friends. After a month or two our team had grown to a team of about ten racers. One of those racers was Donnie.

What a time we had! We raced all over California, Nevada and Arizona. Our team was not the number one team, but in our minds we were!

Donnie quickly moved up the ranks and soon was racing in the expert class against the very best seven year olds in the nation.

As time went by the racers on our team came and went. When Donnie was nine he decided to race motor-cycle moto-cross.

Now we go forward into time. It is now April of 2005.

It was a beautiful spring morning. I had decided to visit Rev. Arlene at Shine on Moon. I felt a real 'push' to do so.

As was our custom we started with a prayer of thanks to our Creator.

Arlene: Did your husband ever race moto-cross?

Sherry: No, he did not. However we own a bicycle shop and many years ago we did have a bicycle moto-cross racing team.

Arlene: Did your racing team happen to wear jerseys with your shops name on them as I am see a vision of this jersey.

Sherry: Yes, our team did wear jerseys with our shops name on the front. However this was many years ago.

Arlene: Time does not matter. I also see the number 23 quite clearly. Did these racing bikes have a number plate on them?

Sherry: Yes, they did have a number plate on them in order
for the spectators and the announcer to identify the
racer.

We then went on to discuss any other personal or spiritual questions I had for that day. Just as our visit was about to end she asked me a couple more questions:

Arlene: Does the date of May 17th have any relevance for you?

Sherry: Nothing comes to mind at least at this moment
anyway.

Arlene: May 17th is important.

Then as if she were talking to someone other them myself, someone only she could see and hear, in a very low voice she say's to this person "Yes, I know. May 17th is the beginning by May 20th it is finished."

I went home thinking about this conversation all night. Over and over I put the cassette tape into the recorder to listen to and make sure of the dates. I went to bed, then right before I was to fall asleep, I remembered the importance of May 17th. On that terrible day in 1987 Donnie lost his life. It was a beautiful Sunday in southern California. Donnie was his usual competitive self. Sometime in the morning he and his friend fired up their engines on their motor bikes and began to race each other. Donnie was told to never ride his motor bike on this very busy street. Sometimes little boys don't always obey their parents. Donnie was hit by a car and died instantly. He was ten years old.

His reality in this world ended on May 17th. His memorial service was held on May 20th.

I know with 100% certainty that Rev. Arlene did not know about Donnie. At this time she did not even know I owned a bicycle store, thinking instead that I owned a motor cycle shop. Eighteen years had passed since Donnie's death. With all my heart and soul I know this was a divine message.

I thought about Donnie all night after I remembered the importance of May 17th. I felt sad when I realized I never told him how proud I was that he raced for our shop. The next morning I opened a folder of memories I keep at the shop. I looked into this folder and discovered a photograph of Donnie. I had forgotten I had this photograph until this very moment. It was from a newspaper clipping that featured a picture of him riding his b.m.x. racing bicycle. He was wearing our bicycle shops racing jersey. His bike had a number plate on it with number '223.'

The number '22' is from a special lady whose name is Louise. She is my sister Kathy's mother in law. From her slice of Heaven she has sent Kathy many wonderful messages of hope and love. Usually these messages are proceeded or ended with the number '22.' This being the date she was born, Feb. 22nd, and the date she stepped to the other side of the mirror, Feb. 22nd.

The number '23'was given me from Donnie. I believe he was thanking us for all his wonderful BMX memories. I also believe he was helping me discover ONE more connection in order to help me in my search for Sunflower Sarah. Most important of all I knew he was asking me to pass this message along to his family. I did not know how I would do this, because after his death his mother, father, and sisters moved away and simply disappeared.

Thank you "Donnie" I love you and will try my best to get this message to your mother and all your loved ones who miss you so very much.

Update: April 10th, 2013. ----Of all the messages I've put to word for this novel, this message BMX Angel 223 was by far the most challenging. These next two confirmations from Louise and Donnie.

Message from Louise:

I had been trying to locate Donnie's family for over ten years. I finally was able to locate his mother and my friend, Patti. . I worried that I might offend her if her spiritual beliefs were not open to this message. I finally sent her an email with this message I received from her son so many years ago. She wrote me back and thanked me. I am over-joyed.

As a way of letting me know that I did 'good' Louise sent a message the same day I received Patti's email while I was at work. As stated, BMX racers use number plates on their racing bicycles. Unfortunately BMX racing has slowed way down and most bikes shops do not even stock number plates. Well, we still do keep number plates in our inventory even though we sale maybe one every six months. Right after I received the letter from Patti, a man walked into our store and asked to purchase a number plate! Then he asked if he could purchase a couple of numbers (stickers) to put on it. I asked him what number he wanted and he told me #22. I was lucky not to have a bug fly into my open mouth! I could only asked the gentleman why his son wanted the number 22. Is it his birthday? "Nope, the man replied. He just picked number 22 as his favorite number. No reason really". No coincidence. Thank you Louise. Hugs to all in Heaven.

Update: May 17th, 2013---- A confirmation and message from Donnie to his mother----I opened my Facebook page today to see a message that Patti had written. In this message she wrote:

--------Today is an ugly day. Miss you Donnie and love you. The hurt never goes away.

I wrote back to Patti and told her I was thinking of her and praying that she will find peace. I also told her to hold her kitty "Bailey." As our wonderful animal pets have such a wonderful way of taking pain away. Only minutes after I sent this email to Patti, a young couple walked into the shop and purchased a beautiful sky blue bmx bicycle. Their last name is Bailey.

XOXOXOXOX

"New York City August 23rd, 1966"

The Beatles last concert in New York City –8/23/66

XOXOXOXOX

"Flash! UFO sighting in NYC 8/23/1974"

I have never seen a UFO. Believe me, I've wanted to. I've been searching the heavens all my life in hope of a close encounter, I could call my own.

When I discovered this next message, I went from being just open minded and not sure, to being a believer.

On August 23rd, 1974 John Lennon and May Pang, from their apartment building in New York City, saw a UFO from their balcony!

Many years ago I had read about John's sighting but quite honestly never gave it much thought. Until I read the date it happened, August 23rd! I discovered the date when I read "Loving John" by May Pang, which as stated in a previous message, I acquired while in Duluth, Minnesota.

In May Pang's novel, she describes the event. May was in the shower when she heard John shouting for her to come to the balcony right away. May was still drying off and shouted back to him 'in a minute.' John became even more insistent and called once again for her to come to the balcony right now!

When May stood next to John and asked him what the matter was, he pointed out to an object that was surrounded by blinking white lights. May goes on to say that she too was convinced that a UFO was hovering very close to the two naked people standing on their balcony who were in complete shock. John started to laugh and made the comment to May that the extraterrestrials probably thought that everyone stood naked like Adam and Eve on the East Side.

May wrote that John was afraid no one would believe him and what he saw. Thinking everyone would accuse him of being on something!

After that May and John called a few friends to ask if they too had seen the UFO. One of these friends was photographer Bob Gruen, who told John and May that there had been other sightings and that the newspapers and Police had been alerted.

More from May: WWW.ufoevidence.org

"It was shaped like a flattened cone and on top of it was a brilliant red light, pulsating as on any aircraft we'd see heading for a landing at Newark airport.

We could make out a row of lights that ran around the entire craft."

"I would estimate it to be the size of a Learjet. It was so close if we had something to throw at it, we probably could have hit it quite easily."

This sighting was eventually recorded in the official UFO journals.

Now I know that some of you, including myself, when I read of this account, thought "Yeah right." Why would an alien decide to cruise around John Lennon's apartment? Well, actually when I thought about it some more "why not?" If these entities are smart enough to travel "Across the Universe" then it only figures that they would select an interesting human subject to study and visit. It seems to me they would have the ability to figure out where John Lennon lived and probably would have no problem knowing his habits. I think John Lennon is a perfect choice to study!

While I was researching John and May's UFO sighting I came across another sighting that is very interesting. On August 25th, 1974, less than 48 hours after John and May saw the UFO in New York City, another incident occurred in Coyame, Chihuahua, Mexico.

In Coyame, Mexico a crash and recovery of an unknown object was tracked over Mexico as it soared toward the United State airspace—it then disappeared at the same time a small civilian plane was lost on radar and apparently the disappearance of both the UFO and small aircraft. Both crashed in Mexico.

This sighting and cover up was so intriguing the History Channel produced a documentary about this. If you are interested in reading further about this subject, then check out www.mexicoroswell.com. If you do indeed go to this site you will see an artist rendering of the space craft that to me looks remarkably like John and May's UFO as they described it. It is fascinating and if you open your mind, then perhaps this was the same UFO that John and May saw a couple of nights before, on August 23rd, 1974.

John wrote this message on the liner notes of his album, 'Walls and Bridges'

On August 23rd, 1974 at 9: O'clock I saw a UFO—J. L.—There's UFO's in New York and I ain't too surprised—As John sings so brilliantly—"Strange days indeed. Most peculiar Mama!"

XOXOXOXOX

"August 23rd, 1968. Ringo says I quit"

On August 23rd, 1968 Ringo Starr made an announcement that he was going to quit the Beatles. Telling the lads that he felt they no longer needed or even liked him. John being his usual witty self-told Ringo "Oh, I feel the same way!"

Anyway Ringo did not quit the band.

Well, after discovering yet another August 23rd, link, I felt confident that I had finally discovered the connection between John and Ringo that I had been searching for.

Little voice in my head would just not let it be. I had just purchased a copy of Ringo's new novel "Post Cards from the Boy's." This has to be the reason for all of my Ringo thoughts!

After all, I too have a post card collection. No, there has to be more!

Then for some reason James Bond popped into my head. Then I remembered once again that Mr. Bond would always bet on red 23rd on the roulette wheel of fortune. Yes, of course the number 23 once again! Then I recalled that Ringo's wife Barbra Bach was a "Bond Girl". That's it! That's the connection. Nope not yet!

Most all of us of a certain age remember the incredible Sean Connery as James Bond. However there was one more "Mr. Bond" that I recall with a smile. Peter Sellers starred as the secret Agent in "Casino Royal." I then began my search to find the connection with an actor I have always loved and who is indeed one of my favorite comedians. I think the man was and is a genius!

As I started my research the first thing I discovered was what a goon John Lennon was! In England in the late fifty's there was a TV. Show called "The Goon Show". This show was very popular and a young John Lennon was glued to the TV set every week to watch it. Peter Sellers was one of the stars of this show. He was John's favorite goon!

Of this show John wrote a review for the NY Times in 1972—

"I was twelve when the Goon show first hit me. Sixteen when they were finished with me. Their humor was the only proof that the world was insane".

Another interesting Peter Sellers/John Lennon discovery I found was this: "Ze King and I" by John Lennon

"There was really only one person in the United States that we really wanted to meet—not that I'm sure he wanted to meet us—and that was Elvis Presley. We just idolized the guy so much.

It was a real thrill to meet Elvis, though—especially to play with him. And because we were both Peter Sellers fans, I remember saying to him, "Zis is Ze way it should be. Ze small homey gathering wiz a few friends and a leetle music!"

This of course in reference to the brilliant acting of Peter Sellers as Dr. Strangelove. Both Elvis and John were huge fans of the movie and Peter Sellers.

So this is all very cool I thought to myself, but why do I still get the impression that there is still more Ringo connection!

In 1970 Ringo starred with Peter Sellers in a movie called "The Magic Christian." I did not realize this until just recently but John Lennon appeared in this movie too! In the movie a look alike pair to John and Yoko with long hair and glasses appeared on screen. These two actors serve to distract from the real John Lennon who wore a short wig, false nose and no glasses.

At this point I thought all of these discoveries about John's love and admiration for Peter Sellers was meant to be a nice tribute to him. John must have had many happy memories of "Tele Goon" during troubling times of his youth. I think John just wants everyone to know how much he thanks Peter Sellers for his talents and for just "being there".

That's it! After I typed this last paragraph I remembered another movie in which Peter Sellers starred. "Being There." This was the last movie Peter Seller made in 1979. I'm sure John loves this movie as much as I do! I'm hard to please when it comes to comedies. This movie is awesome! It makes me laugh no matter how many times I watch it!

I searched the internet for information about this movie and found the movie poster that was used to promote it.

In this poster is a picture of Peter Sellers who starred as "Chance the Gardner" walking away from the camera. Chance is walking in thin air. In the background is a gothic building and big fluffy white clouds and blue sky. It reminds me so much of the first time I saw the Dakota! Just perfect!

Then I remembered who co-starred with Peter Sellers in 'Being There'. One of the funniest ladies ever—Miss Shirley Maclaine. Of course I thought to myself. I was taken back to where I started this entire Ringo Starr and August 23 message.

Shirley Maclaine starred in a movie called "Postcards from The Edge." Back to Ringo's book "Post cards from the Boy's". Perfect!

Shirley Maclaine is also known for her beliefs in reincarnation. Perfect.

My final thoughts on all of this is summarized by Chance the Gardner

—Peter Sellers—

At the very end of the movie 'Being There" is this final thought which closes out the movie—

"LIFE IS A STATE OF MIND" I really think John Lennon likes this statement. I know I do.

In this message we met Chance the Gardner. In the next message we will meet Samuel the Gardner.

XOXOXOXOX

"Soul of a Man"

In 2006 Eric Burdon (lead singer—-The Animals & Eric Burdon and War) released a new C.D. called "Soul of a Man." It is a compilation of blue's classics. Each song as interpreted by Eric is performed to perfection. When I listen to Soul of a Man, I can only compare it to reading a fabulous novel. Each page is a masterpiece and tells a complete story.

On August 23rd, 1868 American poet and author Edgar Lee Masters was born in Garnett, Kansas. Edgar Lee Masters is perhaps best known for his "Spoon River Anthology", he published in New York City in 1916. Spoon River is a collection of his poetry. Incredibly there are 244 poems that are a collection of post-mortem autobiographical "Epitaphs," Two Hundred and forty four citizens of the fictional city of Spoon River, Illinois tell us the truth about their lives-before and after their deaths. Whew! What an imagination Edgar Lee Masters had! The poems are quite fascinating.

One of the poetic Epitaphs is number 217- which happens to be my husband and my favorite number to wager. In this Epitaph we meet Samuel the Gardner.

I who keep the Greenhouse,
Lover of trees and flowers,
Oft in life lay under this umbrageous elm.
Measuring its generous branches with my eye,
And listened to its rejoicing leaves

Lovingly patting each other

With sweet Aeolian whispers

And well they might:

For the roots had grown so wide and deep

Aught of its virtue, enriched by rain,

And warmed by the sun,

But yielded it all to the thrifty roots,

And how shall the SOUL OF A MAN

Be larger than the life he has lived?

Poem by Edgar Lee Masters.

The first time I heard Eric Burdon sing "Soul of a Man", I was mesmerized and put into a sort of hypnotic spell. In the song Eric asks over and over again: "Can anybody tell me, what the Soul of a Man is?" He asks this question over and over.

I believe that Edgar Lee Masters, through the memories of Samuel the Gardner answers this question. Perhaps this is the greatest of all the August 23rd messages I've been given.

The tree of life goes on forever. The tree represents the soul of a man or woman. We can never be larger than the life we live one life at a time. We just keep growing. The roots of the tree representing beginning of life, the top most branches representing our current life and times. Each of us trying to reach the sky. We never give up. Carry on Sky Pilot.

I cannot complete this message without a mention of Blind Willie Johnson. It was he who wrote "Soul of a Man". Thank you for your prayer and your song Blind Willie.

XOXOXOXOX

"Kobe Bryant. August 23rd. 1978"

Our son Frank, as you will discover in future chapters, was a devoted and very talented cyclist. He competed for placement in the 1996

Olympic Games in Atlanta. He came closer to being one of our American Olympiads than anyone I know. We are very proud of his accomplishments. I asked Frank, just a few days ago, who is his current sports hero? He told me his hero is Kobe Bryant of the Los Angeles Lakers. As Frank explained to me, he admires Kobe because when Kobe was faced with diversity and scandal, he faced the error of his ways with dignity and honesty. Kobe Bryant was born on August 23, 1978.

Today is October 9th, 2010. This would have been John Lennon's 70th birthday. All over the world celebrations are being held in his honor. Yoko is in Iceland to light the Peace Tower once again which will remain lit until December 8th, 2010. John's day of transition.

Fans are gathering in Liverpool, at Strawberry Fields Park in NYC, and indeed all over the world. There have been several specials on the news letting fans know of this special day.

Last night I watched Larry Kings special from 2007 where he interviewed Paul McCartney, Ringo Starr, Olivia Harrison, and Yoko Ono in Las Vegas before they attended another presentation of the spectacular Circ De Solie "Love" show. Many really great memories of John were shared on this telecast.

At John's star in front of the Capitol Records building at noon today, is a 70th birthday party with many fans and celebrities in attendance.

So, when I woke up this morning, October 9th, I felt a bit "guilty" about not having planned anything to honor John. It was just another work day for me.

Then this thought occurred to me and I heard a little voice in my head say "You don't need to do anything at all other than to have a great day and let me give you a present."

So I said to this voice in my head "O.K.!" "I will expect a message!"

I got to work and did my usual routine of getting our bike shop ready for a busy Saturday.

It did not take John long at all to give his present to me on his birthday. The first lady who walked into our bike shop was wearing a Kobe Bryant of the Los Angeles Lakers jersey.

XOXOXOXOX

"Johnny Cat. August 23rd, 2008"

On August 23rd, 2008 we added a new addition to our family. His name is Johnny and he is a cat.

We have a wonderful friend who has worked for us for over ten years. His name is Mike and he is one of the kindest men I have ever met. He truly is a gentle soul who loves animals of all kinds and gives so much. He has limited time and funds but does what he can to help all of God's creations, be it fur, feathers, scales or even insects, Mike does what he can to make their lives a little better. He is also very kind and I have witnessed patience beyond measure through the years as he tries to help people with their bicycle needs or just about anything else for that matter.

On August 23rd, 2008, Mike was on a bicycle test ride, when he thought he heard a little noise come from under a bush. The little noise became a meow. Mike scooped up the little kitten and brought him back to the shop. The little guy was in need of a home.

"We'll take him" we announced to Mike. We named the beautiful grey striped tabby kitty "Johnny." He lives with us at home. We love him very much.

XOXOXOXOX

"Your Mother Should Know"

On August 23rd, 1967, the Beatles were in London at Chappell recording studio's working on Take #9 of "Your Mother should know."

Today is May 8th, 2011. It is Sunday. It is also Mother's Day.

I got up this morning, had my cup of coffee. Then Randy gave me a beautiful card and roses.

I next read my emails, watched a bit of the Sunday Morning TV show I like. Then I turned off the TV. To listen to Breakfast with the Beatles with Chris Carter.

The first song I heard this morning was "Your mother should Know". Perfect timing. Of all the Beatles songs recorded, this could not have been more perfect for me. Recorded August 23rd, 1967.

XOXOXOXOX

"August 23ʳᵈ, 2009 and our Table for Two"

Before I begin this next message I feel I need to explain to those of you who do not know this, John Lennon had many connections with the number nine. If interested I recommend surfing the net and find out how many wonderful times the number nine touched his life.

Just about every message I have received from Spirit has come from left field as they say. There is no way I can plan or make up these messages. I'm just not that clever! However there have been a few times that I've requested a message. Or should I say I've challenged John Lennon in advance to communicate with me. Whenever I do this I am quite apprehensive about doing so. I just don't want to be disappointed so I keep my requests to a minimum. There was a special weekend coming and I was really hoping I would get an answer to my request. Wow! Did I ever get my wish!

On August 22nd and 23rd I made special plans for my ten year old granddaughter, Olivia, and I to attend a Beatles Fest at the Queen Mary in Long Beach. The festival was in celebration of the Beatles Hollywood Bowl appearance on August 23rd, 1964. Forty five years ago and I was there.

Olivia is a beautiful girl who has grown up around the music of the Beatles. Her grandmother on her mother's side loves the Beatles too and lived in England when the whole British music scene exploded in America in the sixties. Olivia's Uncle Otis is an accomplished guitarist and together she and her uncle sing Beatles songs. Then there is me, or as I'm known, Mau Mau, need I say more?

So off Olivia and I went on August 22nd to Long Beach. We were staying two nights aboard the spectacular Queen Mary ship. We had a beautiful state room which was luxuriously decorated in dark stained oak. It was actually a very large room with a king sized bed and a large free standing bath tub. We felt like Queens on the Queen!

That evening we attended a concert by the Beatles Tribute band called "American English". The band performed the music of the Beatles to a very difficult to please hard core Beatles fan audience. The band, although not the real thing, did an admirable job and I think all the Beatlemanics had a grand time of it.

On the morning of the 23rd, I awoke early and watched from my porthole, the people set up their booths to sell their merchandise. It was an absolutely perfect sunny day in southern California at the beach.

It was so hard to believe that it had been 45 years (4+5=9) since that morning that Bonnie and I had went to Hollywood. I soaked in the memories of that day as I sat looking out the porthole. Once again the world was magic. Just like it was, August 23rd, 1964. Except today is August 23rd, 200+#9. "O.K. John I'm ready to receive!"

Olivia woke up around 9:00 a.m. "Good morning, Mau Mau" she said as she swished her long brown hair away from her eyes. "Good morning beautiful, I said to my little angel." I hugged her then we got ready for our Beatle adventure.

I felt like a kid again. All giggly and ready to have some fun. I did feel John's presence and I knew something magical was going to happen. Just as it did when I was twelve and going to see the Beatles in Hollywood.

Olivia and I decided to have Sunday Brunch aboard the Queen Mary. It was a bit pricey, but this was a special day and I wanted

Olivia to share this with me in style. So off we went, skipping along the way to the Grand Ballroom.

Before we entered the Ballroom we stopped and had a couple of photos taken by the ships photographer. He had set up a special Beatles photo-op. After our photos were done we chatted with the photographer. He told us he was from Liverpool. For a second, maybe a bit longer, I felt like I was 12 again and frozen in my Beatle Boots. This time I did not scream in delight, but believe me, it was still somewhere in there.

When we walked into the entry of the Grand Ballroom, a Maître Dee in dressed in a black tuxedo greeted us. He presented us to our waiter. "Please follow me ladies". I smiled and took Olivia's hand in mine. Olivia whispered in my ear as we walked into the Grand Ballroom "I feel like Rose did when she walked down the stairway to meet Jack on the Titanic." I kissed her and gave her hand a squeeze.

Inside the Grand Ballroom were many formal tables with dressed in white linen. I found out later that the Grand Ballroom aboard the Queen Mary will seat up to 1400 guests. It is a very large room.

We followed our waiter who took us to our little table for two. "Your table ladies" our waiter bowed to us. Sitting in the middle of this huge room amongst many other tables that were occupied was our little table. We had not made any reservations so this was a random seating. OUR TABLE WAS NUMBER 9!!! When I saw that the table was number 9, I giggled in delight. Olivia looked at me with eyes the size of saucers and said "Mau, Mau, John's favorite number is Number "9". John made sure we got this table!". "Yes" "he did" I said; as I gave her a big ole Beatle hug. "Indeed he did!" I was beyond happy and knew for certain my message had come.

Of all the messages I've received over the years, this message was perhaps the sweetest and so special. Sweet because my granddaughter was witness and special because I had asked for it.

Forty five years to the day. 4+5=9. So many nines. We dined with John Lennon by our side.

I received one other message on August 23rd, 2009. I must first explain that I have told Olivia that I have a special connection with John Lennon but I do not go into great detail with her. I try to keep my connection simple with her. She is much too young, and I do not want to influence her spiritual beliefs. I tell her that John is one of my Guardian Angels. I tell her that he is my Angel on my shoulder. I have a little pin I wear when I am far from home, or at times when I feel like I need a friend. It is a pin of John from the Beatles cartoon series. So when I tell Olivia about my Angel, I point to the little John pin.

After our Grand Breakfast, Olivia and I went to the Beatles Festival where we saw lots of Beatle souvenirs and watched the people play the new Beatles Guitar Hero on stage. We took some funny pictures of ourselves and then went back to our stateroom. We wanted to explore the Queen Mary.

We spotted a sign on board that was an ad for the Queen Mary ghost tours. "Mau Mau I want to go on the ghost tour" Olivia informed me. I was a bit apprehensive at first, but after talking to other passengers who had taken the tour, I was assured that it was very kid friendly. Just some special effects. Kind of like the haunted mansion at Disneyland. So I said yes and off we went for our spooky tour.

Our guide for our tour was Ron. He reminded me of Lurch from the ole Munsters TV. Show. He had a very spooky face that was made really spooky with the black light effects. He would hide, as we took the tour, then jump out and say 'BOO!". Very funny and fun. The tourists would scream and jump. All in good fun.

The tour took us to the very bottom deck of the Queen. Spooky lighting, some special sound effects, along with some specially placed webbing made it almost real. As we went along the darkened deck, Ron told us a bit of history about the magnificence Queen Mary. He told us about the many mysterious unseen guests who are still aboard the Queen. We did see the famous 'haunted swimming pool' which was unnerving. But once again, even though the swimming pool was dark and spooky, it was done in the adventure of fun. Olivia had a great time, as did I.

At the end of the tour, we took an elevator to reach the Main deck. It was a large elevator and was able to hold about twenty people I would say. I believe this was the count on our ride. Olivia was standing next to me with her hands wrapped around my arm. Ron was at the elevator controls making funny faces in the darkened cab. Doing his best to keep up the spooky atmosphere. It was then that something happened that has never happened to me before or since.

I felt two taps on the back of my shoulder. Two pokes! Not real hard, but enough to know someone had poked me. I was 100% sure someone had done so. Right after these two pokes, Ron announced "Oh, by the way that poke you just felt was not from me!" I had not said anything at that point. It was perfect timing on Ron's part. I looked at everyone's face for some kind of confirmation or tell -tell sign that someone was joking around. I started asking everyone "did you poke me?" Everyone looked dumbfounded. Olivia had her hands around my arm, so I know she didn't. Ron was too far away to have been the poker. I actually looked for some kind of mechanical hand that came down and poked me! There was no mention before we entered the elevator that it had any special spirits who poked, or appeared.

I asked Ron after we got off the elevator if this had happened before, and he told me that 'yes' it has. He gave me no further explanation, he just shuffled away.

We were approached by a young couple who asked me if I had an 'experience?' I told them about being poked. They told me that they too have had experiences of their own on the Queen Mary. "Well", I said to the young couple "Why did this spirit poke me, in an elevator?" Future chapters will explain why. Olivia gave me the best answer to my poking question when she looked up sweetly and said, "Mau Mau, you forgot you have you an Angel on your shoulder. It was John who poked you." I knew then that she was right.

Taken aboard the beautiful Queen Mary on August 23rd, 2009.
My granddaughter Olivia Banfield and me, her Mau Mau

"His Name was Joseph"

On February 12th, 2010 I went to see Dr. Sally Cernie who is a certified Dr. of Hypnotism. I wanted to experience a past life regression while under hypnosis.

I had been hypnotized once before at one of those funny Las Vegas shows. I enjoyed being under and had a blast doing silly things on stage. So I knew what to expect and understood that I was not going to become a zombie.

With great expectation, I went to see Dr. Sally Cernie. She had reserved three hours for me. The first hour we spent talking about my feelings toward hypnosis along with some of my spiritual beliefs.

After getting to know each other a bit we started my hypnotic past life regression session.

I had just begun writing Sunflowers life story and was fully aware of her existence at this time.

A word about what it feels like to be hypnotized. The best I can explain my experience with hypnosis is that it is fun! It is also very relaxing.

Dr. Sally began my session with soothing talk of relaxation, telling me to relax my head, neck, back, stomach, legs, hips, and feet—basically starting at the head and moving down. Her voice was soothing and I started to feel like I was going to fall asleep.

She asked me to go back in time to when I was a young girl. Then we went further back into another existence.

It was easy to remember my existence as Sarah. As I was remembering what life was like in the 1800's, my logical mind was telling me that I was just relaying my novel to Dr. Sally. However as I spoke and remembered it felt so natural.

When Dr. Sally asked me to remember how it was I died I became somewhat confused. I thought that my master, whom at this session I called Adam, pushed me down the stairs and I broke my neck and died.

While I was telling Dr. Sally this memory, I felt that what I was telling her about my death was wrong. It felt familiar but not correct. I also told her that my master's name was Adam. This was not his first name, however I do believe his last name was indeed Adams. I felt a very strong feeling of falling down.

Which brings me to how I came to the realization that my master's name in my former life was Joseph?

Many years before I began this novel, as stated in a previous message, I began to search for a psychic Medium to help me discover why it was I get so many messages from those on the other side.

Before I met Reverend Arlene, I met Joey. I had two readings with her. Joey was a small lady who was born in the Philippines. Joey's specialty was reading Tarot cards.

She would spread the cards out on the little round table and then ask me to pick out the number of tarot cards that matched the number of letters in my first and last name which was eleven. Then she asked me to cut the cards and to pick six, the number of letters in my first name.

The actual tarot card reading was interesting but in all honesty, pretty generic. We had some laughs about the possibility about my hitting it big in Las Vegas (I was going for a short vacation in a couple of weeks). Other than that, nothing especially relevant.

Then just as I was about to leave, after she had turned off the tape recorder, she asked me if I would like to know how I died in my last lifetime. She sort of caught me off guard when she asked me this and I really was not sure if I wanted to know. I must add that the whole atmosphere had changed and Joey, who was until then quite upbeat, was now quite serious in her tone of voice.

"O.K, Joey "how did I die?" "You were a woman who was quite well known for your horsemanship. One day, while on a journey of some distance, your horse threw you. You died of a broken neck. You did not suffer". After Joey told me this, we both just sort of stood there not knowing what to say. I told her thank you and added "I think."

I never gave this horse accident broken neck theory much thought after that. Until I started writing Sarah's life story. Many times I thought about the name of her "master'. Thinking as I told Dr. Sally, it was Adam.

Then when I began to write the chapter about where and how he met his death, the horse accident came back to memory. I realize now that Joey had not envisioned Sarah, but had indeed envisioned her master (her father) in that accident. I also knew, without a doubt, that his name was Joseph. I believe his last name was Adams.

It was years later, after writing about my believe that the master's name was Joseph Adams, I was able to find some proof that Joseph Adams did indeed live in or around the Franklin , Louisiana area in the early 1800's. I did a search on Louisiana history, with the history of Washington Parish as a focal point. I was able to find a short article in which I believe I found Joseph Adams. In this article were a list of names of those who were granted "Headrights." Property was granted to settlers in Washington Parish by an act of Congress in 1820. Most settlers had taken up land prior to 1810, and not later than 1815. As I scrolled down the list of names I found Joseph Adams listed as a resident of the Varnado Vicinity (about five miles east of Franklin.)

I read next about 'Headrights' and slavery. I learned that settlers were given land if they owned slaves. Approximately four acres for each slave or indentured servant owned.

Authors note: The time period is perfect. Even the Varnado Vicinity is perfect. This is exactly where I believe Sarah lived until the age of thirty. On a personal note, isn't it amazing that only one hundred and ninety three years have passed since this 'incentive' by the government? Thankfully things do change for the better.

"Buddy""

Thru an amazing set of circumstances, I found a John Lennon three set C.D. that features almost three hours of taped interview with him. I would have never discovered this gem, entitled "Lennon in my Life" if Buddy our tabby kitty had not led me to it.

Buddy was a beautiful orange tabby cat whom our daughter found when the tiny kitty was only about five weeks old. She found him trying to cross a very busy street. So it was that Buddy shared our lives with us for over twelve years.

When we lost Buddy on, April 26th of 2004, we were devastated. Buddy was fine one day, and then he stopped eating and started to lose weight at an alarming rate... We took him to our veterinarian who tried everything she could to help him. We never did find out why, but Buddy left us three days after taking him to the hospital.

The day we lost Buddy was very sad. My husband and I have owned and operated a retail bicycle store since the early 1980's and really try not to miss many days, however on this day, neither of us could work. Randy, my husband, had received a call from a customer who had purchased a bicycle from our shop a month previously. This customer needed some repair but was unable to drive the thirty miles to our shop at this time. Randy and I decided to drive the distance to this customer's home and perform the repair. This is something we rarely if ever do.

I asked Randy to take me to the mall near the customer's home as I was not up to a visit. Our plan was for Randy to get the repair done, and then pick me up at the mall. We would then go for a hike at nearby MT. San Jacinto.

I walked around the open air mall in a stupor. Hiding my eyes behind darkened glasses. Waves of sadness would come and go. Buddy was such a huge part of our lives.

I sat for a while on one of the benches and watched the people walk by. Then I would get up and wander some more. Mindlessly window shopping. After about forty five minutes I spotted a music store.

I had never been to this store before. It was well stocked with thousands of C.D.s and DVD's. Of course, as I always do at a store such as this, I searched for the Lennon/Beatles/and Animals section.

At this point I feel I need to explain that along with John Lennon I have one other major influence on not only my musical tastes, but also a man who has influenced many of my spiritual beliefs. His name is Eric Burdon and he was a member of the British group called "The Animals." He continues to this day to not only amaze me but also confound me! Anyway, I love Eric Burdon as I love John Lennon. Both men when it comes to music are geniuses as far as I'm concerned.

I found all the usual music choices with one exception. A three set C.D. I quickly took it to the counter to purchase. A bargain at only $9.99!

On this amazing three disk set, John talks about many subjects which include, education, music influences, love, religion, spiritualism, and his thoughts about women's rights. John also reflects on his thoughts about positive projection.

What were particularly interesting to me were John's thoughts about education. John mentions a test that is taken in the United Kingdom called "the Eleven plus Exam". This exam is given in the U.K. to help determine which area of education would best suit each student. After John talks about the eleven-plus exam, he mentions how many students during this time were more interested in listening to early American rock then in their studies. He mentions Mick Jagger and Eric Burdon by name. I was extremely happy to hear him mention Eric. I felt contentment.

Because of this message I began to think of Sarah and what year it would have been when she was eleven plus years old. It would be the year of 1831. I knew then that this would be the year of a life changing moment for her. Buddy's death in April was a clear message to me that this moment in her life happened in April of 1831.

I miss Buddy to this day and will never forget him and thank him for leading me to this discovery.

𝒳𝒪𝒳𝒪𝒳𝒪𝒳𝒪𝒳

"The Red Rose"

In one of my first readings with Reverend Arlene, she asked me if I had recently been given a red rose.

I thought for a second and then remembered that a month ago I had indeed been given a red rose from my brother in - law for a Mother's Day gift. Reverend Arlene was silent for a few seconds after I told her. "The rose you received was also from your son" she informed me. I did not want to correct her, as this made no sense to me at all, so I just let it go.

I did not realize the meaning of this message until many years later.

I received the red rose "symbolically", from my son John, in a former life. The Rose was also being used as a way of reminding me of my former madam. It was Rose, who was dressed in red taffeta on the day of the slave auction. It was Rose who became Sarah's mother or at least a motherly influence for many years.

XOXOXOXOX

"The Sunflower with a Heart"

My first realization that sunflowers had great meaning for me came to me when I first visited Strawberry Fields Park in New York City.

This park sits across the street from the Dakota Apartment building on Central Park West and 72nd Avenue. John and Yoko's home.

The date was August 11, 2001.

This was my first visit to New York City. Of course one of the first places I wanted to visit was the Dakota and the Imagine mosaic at Strawberry Fields Park.

There was only one flower on the Imagine Mosaic that beautiful warm August morning. It was a sunflower.

I did not know the meaning of the sunflower at this time. I just thought it beautiful that it was left.

I have since that time learned much about this magnificent flower. One of the most meaningful is that to many the sunflower is the flower of peace and Spirituality.

I took a picture of the sunflower that was left on the mosaic.

When I took the picture out of the packet of photos that we had taken while in NYC, I was amazed to see that the pod of this sunflower held a secret. The pod is in the shape of a heart.

"The Sunflowers"

A few years ago I was involved with a group of online friends who were all John Lennon fans. We called ourselves the Sunflowers.

Just a week or two later, after we had picked the name of our group "the Sunflowers," the Travel Channel aired a show about tours in Liverpool, England. One of the most popular destinations is Strawberry Fields Park. Standing at entrance is a gate where fans from all over the sign their names. On the right hand corner of this wall someone had scribbled "The Sunflowers were here".

XOXOXOXOX

"The Sunflower Glove"

On a crisp morning in early January of 2005, I went to see Reverend Arlene when I probably should have just stayed home instead. I was in a blue mood.

Reverend Arlene started out our reading as she always does with thanks to our Creator. I don't think she got much further than "How are you today?", when my dam burst and the tears started to flow. I was very distraught over a lot of things that morning. Not important now, just know that I was at the end of my rope. Rev. Arlene handled the situation with love and caring words.

It was a few weeks after this reading that I wanted to return to Arlene and thank her for being there for me that sad morning. I was much better, the sun was shining again and all was right with the world. I also wanted to bring her a gift as a way to thank her.

On the way to the Shine on Moon, I stopped at our local .99 cent store. I walked into the store asking John to help me find something for Rev. Arlene.

As I walked around the store it was almost like I knew where to go before I thought about it. Like I had a guiding hand taking me along. I walked up to a really strange wall ornament when I saw it I laughed and said to myself "Really John? You want me to give Arlene this?"

I felt the invisible hand again push me towards the checkout counter. I thought to myself as I paid for it, this has got to be the strangest gift I've ever given anyone. I drove the five minutes' drive to Shine on Moon, and was happy to see that Arlene was indeed there. I made an appointment and waited on the big comfy couch. I breathed in the wonderful smells left from the many candles and incense that filled the air. I felt wonderful.

Arlene smiled and gave me a hug as I entered her little room. We talked a bit about love, hope and joy. It was all very positive. Then she told me that John is showing her a glove. Arlene asked me if John Lennon wore gloves a lot. I told her that I did not know. "Well," she said as she cleared her throat "John is defiantly showing me a glove." I was not connecting and told her that hopefully I will find a picture or something showing me a glove and then I'll understand why he is showing you a glove". I must add here that I had completely forgotten about my gift which was sitting on my lap in a bag!

We changed the subject and that was when I thanked her for all her understanding and kind words for me at our last tearful reading. She told me that she was much honored that she was able to help me that sad day, that I had completely opened up and by doing this, our connection will become stronger. I too, felt this was true.

I thanked her again and then I told her that I had brought a gift for her. I took out the wall thing that was concealed in the bag, thinking to myself, how cheap it was! "Reverend Arlene, I asked John to pick out a gift for you and this is what he wanted me to give to you", I said thinking to myself that I had just blamed John for this cheap gift!

"Sherry, this is perfect! This is the glove John was showing me! This is it, "she said all the while grinning from ear to ear. It was then that I realized the glove she asked me about was this weird looking glove thing I was handing her. I was speechless! All I could say was "Amazing, just amazing!"

Reverend Arlene held the gift in her hands then started to explain the meaning. "The glove is our Creator who holds us all in his hands. It also represents John's presence in your life as directed by our Creator. The Butterflies are you and I. We are Aquarian women and the butterfly is our sign's insect Totem". I told her that Yoko is an Aquarian also. Perfect!

Arlene then gazed across the table and took my hand in hers. Then in a very sincere and heartfelt tone she told me "The Sunflower is you. You were known by the name of Sunflower in your past lifetime."

I will never forget these words. Until this day I thought Sunflower was a nice, albeit corny, name for our Lennon online group. Now I knew differently. John believes that I am Sunflower.

I left the room after giving Arlene a big hug. I felt so awesome. "I love my gift," Arlene told me once again. "I do too," I told her as I had purchased the same wacky gloved Sunflower/butterfly hand wall ornament for myself. We both laughed and both said at the same time "Thanks John!"

It was after this that I started to wonder if I was a woman who was known as Sunflower in a lifetime before this one. If this is true then is she (Sunflower) the reason John has been such a guiding light for me? And who was he in relation to Sunflower?

Because of a sunflower wall ornament, things started to make more sense to me.

XOXOXOXOX

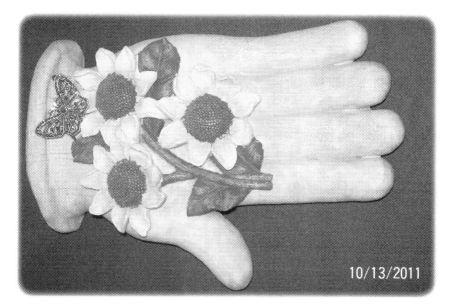

10/13/2011

"Metamorphosis"

I believe the butterfly that was on the glove wall ornament had a dual purpose. First it was meant to trigger a memory in my former life as Sarah. To help me remember the butterfly fan. This until the age of nine, was her only gift.

The other reason was another life message. Life is always changing. The metamorphosis. How each of us will come out of our cocoons and change.

A couple of years ago I watched for the first time the "U.S. verses John Lennon." As I watched the docu-movie I once again marveled at all the life changes John went through. How he was like a butterfly coming out of its cocoon and spreading his wings of peace.

It was a few days after watching this movie that I once again went to visit Rev. Arlene. It was during this reading that I received one of the only messages I've been given from John about world peace. Which I suppose would surprise most people as John was so involved with world issues before his passing. I guess we just have a different relationship him and me.

As a footnote, I do care passionately about our world. Especially the world I believe my children and my grand- children are inheriting from us.

It was at this reading when once again Arlene was able to connect with John that she was a bit surprised to find out that John had been promoted! After she learned this, she explained that, there are promotions on the other side. That John had been working very hard, as he did in this reality, towards world peace.

Arlene bowed her head in deep thought, and then said to me "It will happen, you know, if you want it". I thought to myself that she did indeed sound like John for just a moment. She went silent again, then after listening to her inner ear said "John has told me that it will take three generations of no prejudice against race or religion. Then true peace will become a reality.

After we were told this, Rev. Arlene and I just sat in silence trying to understand what we had just been told.

Arlene broke the silence and asked John, with a slight giggle in her voice, if this promotion is going to make it more difficult for us to communicate? "You're not going to get all hoity toitey on us are you?" Then she told me John told her "Never!"

After this reading was over I thought about the hoity toiety comment. I had just finished reading Cynthia Lennon's new novel "John". How in their youth, John had called her "Miss Hoity Toiety." I believe John wants Cyn to read this butterfly message also. I hope she does.

This brings me back to my butterfly analogy. We all change. Like the butterfly.

As I usually do when I write this book I listen to music. The song that is playing as I finish this is "That's the way God planned it", as performed by Billy Preston at the concert for Bangladesh with George Harrison.

Very appropriate and great timing.

XOXOXOXOX

"Sunflower Lane"

On my 55th birthday, Randy and I went to visit a Spiritualist church in Escondido, California. Reverend Arlene was to be guest pastor for this Sunday morning.

It was a spectacular crisp Sunday morning the 21st of January. We drove fifty miles to the church which is called "Harmony Grove Spiritualist Association." This church is over 114 years old. It sits amongst huge elm, poplar and eucalyptus trees. The setting is absolutely beautiful. As you enter the property you drive under a sign which reads "love is the light, truth is the way."

We entered the small white church and signed the register. There were approximately thirty people at this service. Reverend Arlene did not know I was coming, so when she began her sermon for the day, it came as a bit of a surprise to her to see me sitting before her.

The service was not like any other I had ever attended. We did sing hymns, however the songs were popular songs. Easy rock. After singing about three songs, Rev. Arlene asked the congregation if there were anyone who wanted to share a message of hope and love today with the other people in attendance.

Several people stood up and told of receiving messages from loved ones who have crossed over. One lady told the congregation that she saw an elderly person seated amongst the living in the church. She informed us that this elderly man wants to tell us all that life on the other side is lovely, just like this beautiful, peaceful place. She went on to describe the man, what he was wearing and the color of his hair, beard and hat.

One by one several other people stood up and told of receiving message of love and hope from loved ones who have passed who were seated amongst us. Can they all be hallucinating? Each of these people seems so sincere in their beliefs.

Reverend Arlene then asked us all to gather at the back of the church and to hold hands. She then introduced me. She also told everyone that it was my birthday. Everyone sang Happy Birthday to me! Then she told the group of people, which included Randy, that I have a special Guardian Angel whose first name is John (she did not mention his last name) and that my Angel is now a big influence on her life also.

She continued telling all that John is an amazing and very gifted entity. She then told the congregation that John was my son in my former incarnation. I had never told anyone before this moment that I believed this! This was in fact my 'coming out' moment! Arlene then told everyone that my name was Sunflower in my past lifetime.

When this happened I was very fearful that Randy would now think I have lost my mind! He knows who my special Angel John is. However, we had never discussed any of this. I had never told him about Sunflower. I must say he took it well. We did not talk about it, but, as of this day I'm still married to him!

After the sermon, Randy took a couple of photos of Arlene and me. Then we left for our drive to Hollywood. We were to see the Director David Lynch and Donovan who performed at the Kodak theatre.

As we drove out the driveway of the church we noticed a street by the name of "Sunflower Avenue." So of course I wanted to check it out! It was a very short street with perhaps ten houses on it. In one of the driveways a van was parked in front. On the side of this van in huge letters was the name of a photography studio.

The name of this studio was "IMAGINE." I did not know that

there was a Sunflower Avenue near the church and I certainly did not know that there was a van parked on this street with Imagine printed in huge letters. I like to think that this was a special birthday greeting from a friend on the other side of the looking glass.

XOXOXOXOX

Harmony Grove Spiritualist Association in Escondido, California.

"Shiva, Shiva, Shiva"

As a young Beatlemaniac, George Harrison was my favorite Beatle. George with the lovely brown eyes and cute ears. He broke my heart when I was fourteen when he married Pattie Boyd on my birthday January 21st, 1966.

Today is November 29th, 2008 and it is seven years since George Harrison passed on to the other side to make music once again with his mate John Lennon.

Being in the bicycle business I must comment on George Harrison's song called "Pieces Fish." In this song George sings about riding his bicycle next to a river where rowers are gracefully gliding on the river. Flying along with him as he rides his bike are Canadian geese. Who, of course, do what geese do, crap next to the river bank. What a peaceful scene George presents! Then his bike next does what bikes do. His chain falls off and wraps around his crank.

Oh George how I love you and I can tell that you did ride your bicycle a mile or two. A perfect day, a perfect ride and then your bike messes up! You need a good mechanic! As far as the Canadian Geese, well try to avoid the crap next time!

When I think of the music of George Harrison I think of how in his search for his truths, he found grace and tried to teach each of us. I only have to put on my head set and listen to George Harrison's music and my head is in Heaven.

Today a lovely woman came into our bicycle shop along with her two teenaged children. I had not seen this lady for a couple of years and was delighted to see her once again.

She is from India and she is a teaching missionary. Her beliefs are of the Hindu faith. We exchanged our thoughts about the recent terrorist attacks that had taken place at the Taj Hotel in Dubai. She told me she is very familiar with the area.

I had recently listened to George Harrison's song called "Brainwashed." I was very curious about something he chanted over and over in this song. I asked my friend from India what was the meaning of——

"Shiva, Shiva, Shankara Mahadeva".

My friend told me what the mantra meant. Now I know. I believe George Harrison wanted very much to ask each of us to never stop searching for our truths.

God Bless the people of Dubai.

XOXOXOXOX

"Rosemary and George Clooney"

On February 22nd, 2009 I had a most vivid dream. In this dream I met a lady who was very vivacious and very happy. In this dream she walked up to me and introduced herself—"Hello—I'm Rosemary Clooney." Then she stepped back from me and I awoke right after her introduction. Although it was a very short dream, it felt very real.

I chuckled to myself and thought "Rosemary Clooney!" In a million years I would not thought I would dream of her.

The next morning I went to my computer and googled her name. I found out that she was George Clooney's aunt. Although I admire many of George Clooney's movies, I really could not figure out why I would have a dream about George's aunt Rosemary. It took me almost three years to understand the "George connection." Rosemary's message took only a quick reading of her biography to understand. I learned that she had died of lung cancer on my husband's birthday June 29th. That was the connection. I felt she was lovingly reminding me to get him to stop smoking.

The 'George Clooney' connection came to me in 2011 on my Sister Vicky's fiftieth birthday, October 2nd.

Vicky currently lives with her love of her life, Robin and her mother Dorothy. At this time they lived in a city about forty five miles north east of New Orleans in Mississippi.

We were sitting at the breakfast table in Dorothy's home having a wonderful conversation, when Dorothy shared with us a written account of a dream she had many years ago. She had this dream a few weeks after her beloved brother, Paul had passed.

She felt she wanted to share this beautiful written tribute with me after I told her about my novel I was writing.

She explained that this dream was very vivid and felt very real. She also explained that she had not had many 'paranormal' experiences in the course of her lifetime, but that what happened the day after this dream, which occurred about ten years ago, has always amazed her. I will not go into detail about the paranormal experiences she had, as that is up to her if she so desires. What I will share is how I was used by her brother to let his sister know how much he loves her and is never far away.

"I wrote this a few weeks after my brother passed." Dorothy then asked me to read it aloud to my sisters. I was much honored to do so.

The title of this documented dream is

"Oh Brother where Art thou?"

—Last night I had a dream. At the end of this dream George Clooney appeared. He was very real. I had no idea why I would dream about George Clooney, but I did.—

The next day she had a very real paranormal experience where she felt her brother's presence.

When I read about her dream and her visit from George Clooney, I knew instantly that the reason his aunt visited me in my dream was to confirm Dorothy's dream and experience.

I need to share one more amazing spiritual connection in my dream. I had it on the night of February 22nd. On this date my sister Kathy's mother in law, Louise, was not only born but also passed away. This is another confirmation within my dream that those on the other side of the mirror are always near us. Bless you and thank you Louise.

Kathy has received many messages from Louise in which the

number 22 is shown her. These "little hellos" are a great comfort to Kathy.

When dad was finally released from the intensive care unit at Saint Mary's hospital to rehab his room number was #22.

XOXOXOXOX

"The Japanese Beetle"

For our annual summer vacation this year (2011) the kids chose Knott's Soak City water park for our excursion. We spent the night at a hotel near the water park so that we would be able to get an early start for the day's soggy events.

My granddaughter Olivia woke early so we had a couple of hours before we were to go to the water park. We decided to watch a movie on my laptop. Olivia and I have a special love we share for the Beatles and in particular John Lennon. When I asked her what movie she wanted to watch she chose "A Hard Day's Night".

Olivia is now twelve years old and it is uncanny how much she reminds me of myself when I was her age and in love with The Beatles. We laughed together as we watched the movie like two teeny-boppers.

In one scene of A Hard Day's Night, the Beatles are seen rehearsing for their upcoming telecast. In the background behind the stage were several large pictures of beetles (bugs) I commented to Olivia "Look at all the Beetles". Olivia said "Yeah, Mau Mau, I see a Japanese beetle. That's cool." Although I have watched this movie far too many times then I care to admit, I've never really taken notice of these beetle posters.

We finished watching the movie to get ready for our walk to the water park with my sister in law and her children Dale, Shane and Shannon.

As we were walking into the entrance of the water park, something wonderful happened. As I was about to walk over a small bridge, a very large Japanese beetle came flying straight at me. Now, usually when a large insect that looks a lot like a bumble bee flies towards me I would begin to jump about and run. This time I actually felt no fear. I looked the insect in the eye and in my mind said, "Good morning Mr. Beetle how are you?" I was not frightened at all when the insect landed on my shoulder. Olivia saw the beetle and laughed in delight telling me "Mau Mau, if a Japanese beetle lands on you, you will have seven years of good luck." I had never heard of this and thanked Olivia for telling me this. I chuckled to myself and winked at the BeAtle as it flew away—thinking to myself—is it possible??—well anyway I love you John.

After our day of splashing good fun, it was time to take the walk back to the hotel. When we got there, Olivia and I went to the patio to relax before dinner. It was then that we noticed another Japanese beetle. Only this time it was dead. "How sad Mau Mau" Olivia exclaimed. I agreed. Olivia asked me if we should bury it. I told her that we should leave it where we found it, as perhaps a bird would find it and eat it. "God's plan," I reassured Olivia, who was deep in thought as what to do next.

It was about a half an hour later that Olivia squealed in delight "Look Mau Mau. The beetle is moving! He was only pretending to be dead!" I looked at the beetle and she was right! The beetle was moving its legs. It looked to me like it was stretching. Almost like YOGA!

"How about that, Olivia! I really thought it was dead too." "Good thing we didn't bury him", Olivia said. "Yeah good thing" I agreed.

This is another great example of how John teaches and guides. Sometimes with great humor and satire.

So what is the lesson?—Well—

"The beAtle lives!"

Olivia and I love you very much John Lennon.

XOXOXOXOX

"Lily from OZ"

In the year of 1999, I met a woman from Australia. I will refer to her as Lily, which is not her real name.

Lily is perhaps one of the most knowledgeable, devoted, sensitive and protective fans of John Lennon I have ever met.

We met each other on Eric Burdon's web site where she and I would post messages on his discussion board. I learned that Lily lived in Australia (OZ) and that we had a common love and interest in John Lennon.

My dear friend Lily was also always in search of love. In the summer of 2002 she met a man on the internet she thought she might have a love connection with.

Lily decided to travel across the ocean too far away Alaska to meet this man whom I shall call Buck. Not his real name.

After her visit ended with Buck, Lily had a six hour lay- over in Los Angeles before she was to continue her flight home to OZ. Randy and I arranged to meet her and have some fun in L.A. before she was to continue her flight home.

We went with her to John Lennon's star next to the Capitol records building in Hollywood first. Then we cruised Hollywood Blvd. Next we went to an Irish pub for some lunch.

I wanted to hear all about Buck... Lily sipped her drink, and then looked at me with her lovely brown eyes that were usually dancing with mischief, but now were starting to cloud with tears. I also saw fear.

"Sherry," she told me "Alaska was beautiful. I sent you some pictures, did you receive them? "Yes, I answered. I did, thank you." Then Lily, my friend from far away OZ, told me something I shall never forget. "I met Buck at the airport. At first it was wonderful. I felt I had found someone very special. We sat up all night talking. Then a few days before I was scheduled to leave, he started to change." Lily then began to tell me a horrific story of abandonment and terror. How she sat for hours all alone in a little tent, at a lonely lake many miles from the city. Buck had went into the city to be with his buddies leaving Lily alone and unable to go anywhere. He left her alone for hours at a time.

In the late hours of the night it was very cold and very dark. There was no one around except for the bears and scary stuff. Lily was not sure if what she was hearing was real or her imagination. When Buck finally came to get her, he would apologize passionately for leaving her alone. Lily had a cell phone, but it did not work at this location.

Lily forgave Buck. The day before Lily was to leave, Buck told her he had a surprise. He had arranged for them to spend the night at a friend's cabin next to a beautiful lake in the woods. Just like the tent, this cabin was many miles from the closest city. It was very isolated.

It was during the night that Lily came face to face with what she truly believed would be her last night of her life. Many horrific things happened that night. Lily could not tell me everything.

After several hours of mental and physical torture, Lily became so scared that she grabbed a knife from the kitchen and was seriously thinking of stabbing Buck.

She told me she lay on the bed, clutching the knife, shaking and crying uncontrollably, that she could see Buck sitting at the kitchen table. He was drinking from a bottle of whiskey. She felt that the next time Buck came into the bedroom where she laid, she would kill him, or he would kill her. She lay in bed paralyzed with fear.

She also realized she had put herself in a horrible position. Lily had gone all alone to Alaska and really did not tell anyone who she was meeting. This was not her first time she had traveled a great distance to meet someone. This time she wanted to keep her journey a secret from family and friends. She was right, I thought to myself as she told me about this. I did not know anything about Buck. She kept her secret well.

My friend Lily and I had talked about many things over the years.

However one subject we would seldom discussed was spirituality. We each held different views on faith. So we avoided this subject. I was surprised to hear her tell me that she not only prayed to God to save her, but that she also prayed for help from John Lennon that night. I never thought I would hear this from her.

She told me that as she laid on the bed with the knife in her hand, scared as she had never been in her life, she began to hear John sing to her. She told me it was as clear as if he were on the radio. Except there was no radio in the cabin. She knew it was John's Spirit. He was singing "All you need is love." She could see John's face clearly in front of her. Then she felt a very calming presence and knew that she would somehow survive.

Buck had fallen asleep, or perhaps passed out, during this time.

When the sun came up, Lily got herself out of the cabin and found her way to the highway. She had grabbed her over- night bag before leaving which had her passport and her credit cards. She left her large bag with all her clothes with Buck at the cabin.

Lily was able to hitch a ride and get herself to the airport in time to catch her flight home. She told me that the sunrise that morning had never been more beautiful.

After Lily had told me all of this I thought to myself, "Is my friend making this all up? This is crazy!" I could not say this to her as I could see that she was very sincere. I asked her if she called the police. By now Lily was sobbing, "No" she replied "what proof did I have? No one would believe me. Buck had many friends in town which included law enforcement. I just wanted to forget and get out."

I told her how sorry I was and we hugged each other. I never told her about my doubts. I kept them to myself.

We drove her back to the airport later that night. It was true, she had only one little overnight bag to check in for the long flight home. Certainly not enough for someone who had planned to stay three weeks in Alaska.

I kissed her good-bye and wished her well. Thinking to myself, that she is either the bravest woman I have ever known, or the biggest liar.

We walked back to our car to begin the drive home. We turned on the radio to hear the song "Here Comes the Sun." I thought to myself what perfect timing as I thought about Lily's statement about the sun coming up and how beautiful it was to be alive. I have heard this song by the Beatles countless times. This time was like the first time I ever heard it. It was so beautiful and so timely.

When the song finished Jim Ladd (the D.J. and host) came on the air. Mr. Ladd is a fantastic D.J. who has a wonderful way of telling stories and sharing life's experiences with his audience. His voice has a very soothing and calming effect.

"Tonight," Jim Ladd said "I want to share with you the meaning of love. The love we are all searching for. The love of a lifetime. I am dedicating this next song to all women. How in this search for love, some women will leave their homes and travel far away, alone, and trust somehow, someway, they will find happiness. I now dedicate this next song to all women and I hope you will find this love someday."

The song Jim Ladd had chosen for this dedication was "She Talks to Angels" by the Black Crows.

It was an amazing coincidence. Almost like Lily had talked to Jim Ladd. I know she had not.

I felt John's presence and knew then that Lily had spoken only truths. She had indeed talked to an Angel.

XOXOXOXOX

Chapter 2

JAMES AND JOHN ARE BORN

AUGUST WAS A SLAVE BORN of Jamaican heritage. Madam Rose would trade services with his master and then August would perform odd jobs around the brothel.

August was 23 when Sunflower met him. She and the other ladies enjoyed watching him as he worked in the courtyard. As he worked he would sing island songs, which were mostly gospels. Sunflower and the other women would hide behind the curtains and giggle as they watched in secret. At least they thought they were not suspected. As he worked his ebony skin glistened in the hot summer days. When August discovered that the ladies were watching him, he would turn and wink at them. Like school girls these ladies of pleasure, would giggle in delight.

Soon Sunflower was looking for work for August to do, reminding Rose that this or that needed repair.

One hot afternoon in July, Sunflower spotted August working in the garden. Gathering her courage she decided to have a chat with him. She approached August with a glass of sweet tea. He looked up

from his work to see Sunflower approaching him. Sunflower froze
in her tracks. August was the most beautiful man she had ever seen.
Sunflower stood there with her mouth agape. He smiled and asked
"Is that for me, Miss?" Sunflower looked down at the glass of tea
she had forgotten she held and said in a voice that was very shaky
"Would you like a glass of cool sweet tea?" After she asked that, she
thought to herself, "Dumb, of course he would it's hot as hell out
here!" August smiled and took the glass from her thanking her first.
When he finished the sweet tea, he handed Sunflower the glass back
telling her in his island accent "I do believe that this is the finest
glass of sweet tea I've ever had. Given to me from the most beautiful
woman in New Orleans, Miss Sunflower". Sunflower felt her face
flush. Her knees week, she took the glass and sort of shuffled away.
She had never felt this way about any man.

From that day on Sunflower talked about August all the time.
Telling her friend Angel that it must be a good omen because of his
name being the month I was born and that he is 23 years old. Angel
agreed with her love sick friend.

Soon the summer turned to fall and Sunflower could think of
no other desire than August. Sunflower told Angel that she wanted
to give herself to this man. So, in the month of November on a cool
afternoon, Sunflower asked August to her room to help her with
some furniture to rearrange. Sunflower closed her door and August
came very willingly into her arms. Not much was said, just beautiful
moments in ecstasy. At the age of 30, Sunflower was to know what
it was like to make love to a man of her desire for the first time in
her life.

It was soon after this that Sunflower realized that she was with
child. What should be a wonderful miracle was actually a very
difficult situation for Sunflower. When Rose found out she would
be asked to leave. This would leave her and her baby with no place
to live and very little money. She could not turn to August and let
him know of her pregnancy. If she did his life would be in danger.
Many of Sunflower's clients were in love with her and respected her

wishes as far as having no sex with her. If it were found out that a slave man had this pleasure then he very likely would be murdered. Sunflower's allure would be gone to these men, her clients. She had no one she could turn to for help.

August was sold to another plantation. He was sent to Arkansas, unfortunately to a very violent city of Shame. He was never to make love to Sunflower or see her again in this lifetime. He never knew of his child.

As time went by Sunflower's situation was becoming desperate. She had no one to turn to.

Reverend Elmore James had confessed to Sunflower that he had taken the life of Lily. She was the only one he had confessed his crime to. He took great pleasure in her sorrow. He was now her client.

Sunflower knew what she must do.

She detested Reverend Elmore James not only because he had taken the life of her friend Lily, but also because of his unrelenting desire to humiliate and demean women. His idea of making love to a woman always involved pain and humiliation.

Rose was unable to turn down Rev. James patronage. He was well known. He also had many connections within the law enforcement community and persons of political positions thru out the city of New Orleans. His church had many loyal parishioners who loved him dearly. Plus he paid Rose handsomely for his "pleasure and pain".

Reverend James picked Sunflower as his choice because of her reputation. He desperately wanted to rape her. Not that he would enjoy the sex, far from it. He just wanted to break her spirit. Sunflower by now was very skilled. She knew how to play the game and Reverend James, well she could handle him.

Reverend James would prove to be invaluable to her in getting her out of her difficult situation. She confided her plan to only one person. Her dear friend Angel Alice. So it was that Sunflower began to plan and stage her own rape.

Pastor James was never late for an appointment with anyone. He was always on time. On the appointed day of this fateful decision of Sunflowers she told Angel Alice to make sure that she was near her room. She also asked Angel to have one of her most trusted clients with her. There were always two men who worked at the residence as security, so that would make least three witnesses. Sunflower knew Rose would be near, but this was a little harder to arrange. Three witnesses would be enough.

As usual Pastor James was on time. He always brought with him his secret toys. These toys included a whip, a belt with a huge brass buckle, shackles, gloves and a mask. An evil looking mask of a demon he would always wear.

Sunflower knew what she must do. She played the teasing game. Taunting him. Calling him names. Telling him she would tell of his secrets and then his congregation would rip him apart. His wife would divorce him. "I will expose all your evil ways. I know them all" Sunflower grinned. "I know everything about you." Pastor James was enraged. He trusted this woman. He felt, in his own way, betrayed. Sunflower continued to taunt him. In rage he hit her hard across her face with his fist clenched. Sunflower did not whimper, just smiled. He next pushed her hard and she fell on the hard wood floor with such a force that she felt her arm bend in a strange fashion. She got herself up from the floor and looked at her arm. It was bent and twisted in an odd way. For a moment it did not look like her arm. It was strangely bent and very pale in color. She did not make a sound. She next removed her clothing and teased him in a way she knew he would detest. With this he once again hit her on her jaw. For a moment she felt he had broken it. She tasted her own blood in her mouth. Over and over again she pulled his strings of rage. Once again he hit her in her eyebrow. Her eye immediately swelled shut. He next grabbed the shackles and proceeded to rape her, telling her she is the devils virgin and his seed will make her pure. He will save her. Sunflower was in extreme pain because of her jaw and her arm. However she kept quiet, telling herself "not yet."

Finally the moment was right. She felt him enter her. She then whispered into his ear, "This is for Lily." Next she bit off half of his left ear and spit it into his face. Then she screamed for all she was worth for help.

The door burst open to find a bloody shackled Sunflower. Leaving no doubt as to what had happened.

Angel Alice had done what she was asked and brought a very credible witness with her. Security was right behind them. As if to seal his fate and smile upon Sunflower, Rose was not far behind. Reverend Elmore James was holding a bloody rag on his half an ear. In rage he screamed at Rose to look at what her bitch had done! Rose took one look at Sunflower who looked as though she had been beaten to near death. Rose calmly told Reverend James to "Tell your congregation that your horse bit you! Now get out of my house!"

Sunflower now had her father for her baby.

Reverend James paid handsomely for her silence. His marriage would be in jeopardy along with his status in the city if this got out. His parishioners would not understand. So he paid the blackmail.

Rose sent Sunflower and Angel Alice to her brother's farm away from the city. She felt horrible about what had happened and in some ways blamed herself for not being strong enough to deny this evil man his pleasures. She knew them well. Lily had pleaded with her to not ask her to service this man. Rose also remembered her vow to Joseph that she would do what she could to help his only daughter. Once again she would try to keep that vow.

Sunflower's wounds healed quickly. At her new home she and Angel Alice began to make plans for the arrival of her baby. Both ladies helped as house slaves. Angel and Sunflower missed their 'sisters' and their clients very much. Hoping that someday they might be able to return to their chosen way of life.

Sunflower had two big fears about being 'found out' as far as the baby's father's true identity. One was that she was off by about a month if anyone counted the nine months. The other was that Pastor

Elmore James was a white man, and August was a Negro. A colored baby would be hard to explain.

Well, sometimes God does work in mysterious ways.

Sunflower went into labor on her birthday August 23rd, 1850. Angel Alice was in attendance and squealed in joy when she saw the first baby boy be born, to be followed quickly by his brother.

The boys were very fair skinned (Grandfather Joseph watching over). Daisy was in attendance too. Her skin was also very light.

Plus because she had twins, no one would be surprised if they had counted the months. Twin always came early. Sunflower's prayers had been answered.

James and John were the names picked by Sunflower because she loved the Bible and especially the gospels according to St. James and St. John. She also picked the letter "J" for Jesus.

Sunflower's twin baby boys were happy and healthy.

Her new master and his wife were very kind, not only because of their love of the boys and their mother, but also because this master's wife had also been a victim of rape. Rose had told her brother and his wife all about Reverend Elmore James.

For the first four years, James and John had a life few Negro children would be fortunate to have. At this plantation the slaves were given more privileges than any other in the immediate area. This master did not believe in separating birth families. He and his wife enjoyed Negro gospels and attended the church services held at the small chapel that had been built on the property. It sat next to a beautiful weeping willow tree.

At the age of four, the boys began to sing gospel songs and also favorite songs of the south. The boys had the tone of little angels. Church services were always a joyous event filled with music, laughter, joy, and of course the highest glory to All Mighty God and his son Jesus Christ.

Sunflower's religious beliefs were very simple. You do right by people and Jesus will do right by you. She felt that even though she had lived a life many would call sinful, she knew Jesus loved her. Sunflower reasoned that if Jesus could forgive Mary Magdalene for her sins, then she too would be greeted in Heaven with welcoming arms.

Most of the slaves could not read. Sunflower could read at about a ninth grade level. Thus, Sunflower was asked to read the Gospel many times at the Sunday service. She loved doing this and looked forward to being asked to do so. She would gaze proudly at James and John as they listened.

Life for the Negro slaves was hard, but it also had meaning that centered on family life. So it was that freedom was a dream mixed with fear and hope.

It was now 1855 and the racial tensions in the city of New Orleans were heightened by the idea of the northern states to abolish slavery. To most slaves it was a dream that would reunite them with their families. However this dream was not without fear. The fear of suddenly having no home to live, and no work. Having never tasted freedom, some slaves did not want to leave their plantations. The fortunate few, like Sunflower, had led a life that was predictable and had some comforts. These slaves were of mixed emotions when freedom was whispered.

Some slaves at nearby plantations tried to escape and were met with death. Certainly this escape attempt would be met with the whip and other punishments. Most slaves just did what they had to do, and that was to obey.

For the slave owners the tension was unbearable. Not owning slaves meant a loss of income that would lead to bankruptcy. Another fear of the slave owners was that the freed slaves would retaliate for the atrocities that had been committed against them. The slave owners felt it was their right to own Africans. They would fight to the last man, woman and child before they gave up this right.

Rose had great fears for not only Sunflower, but also for but also for Angel Alice, James and John. Pastor James had killed Lily and vowed to Rose he would not have a problem killing another whore.

Especially that colored whore Sunflower who had deceived him. If ever he again saw her, then his would be the last face she would see. Rose knew he meant it. Pastor James did not know of Sunflowers pregnancy. That would have fueled his rage even more.

Rose feared for Sunflower but not for herself. She knew that Rev. James would do no harm to her. Although Rose could sometimes be a hard hearted Madam, she was also a woman of great compassion. Especially when it came to her "girls". Most especially when it came to Sunflower. Rose knew it was she, whom Joseph (Sunflower's master and father) was traveling to see when the horse accident happened and he met his death. She loved Joseph and missed him even though more than twenty five years had passed since she last held him in her arms. Rose loved Sunflower with a mother's love and commitment. Rose never knew that the father of James and John was in reality the slave August.

Thus Rose tried to arrange a better life for Sunflower and her twin sons. Through great effort she was able to work out a new life for them. One of Sunflowers wealthy clients had been asking Rose when Sunflower would return for years. This client traveled from his home in New York City to New Orleans, several times a year on business. He was also a patron of one of New York City's most successful brothels. He knew the Madam of this establishment well. Rose knew this connection could be the answer for a happy and free life for Sunflower and her sons.

With her southern charm and business skills, Rose told the man from NYC that Sunflower would surely be a wise investment. Rose also knew that this man was a reformist who detested slavery. "You can save her life and at the same time, she will make the NYC madam a wealthy woman. You will also benefit by being the one to bring her such good fortune. With your influence I'm sure, my dear sir, this could be arranged," Rose said with a tilt of her head and a wink. "Plus, I will include the beautiful Indian woman, 'Angel Trumpet', as a gift to the madam.

He told Rose to retrieve Sunflower, her sons and Angel. They would accompany him to NYC to work once again at their chosen profession. A profession that both women still loved and missed.

The best way to travel from New Orleans to New York City was via the ocean. Which is what James, John, Angel and Sunflower found themselves doing in the summer of 1855.

James and John were now five years old. Their features were now more African. Although their skin color was still very light, their heritage could not be denied. Getting the two boys aboard the ship would normally be very difficult. However the gentleman from NYC, being their guarantor for the journey, made the embarkation go relatively smooth for them. (If you could look the other way at the sneers from some of the sailors.)

Aboard the sailing ship, while on the sea, the twin boys thrived. Most all the other passengers were sea sick, including their mother. James and John, full of energy and quite healthy, sang sea shanties all the way to New York City. The boys received a special request from the captain of this vessel for a private show. Proudly the little sailors sang with all their hearts as the ocean breezes accompanied them. These songs were to remain in the minds and hearts of James and John till the day they died. Both boys loved the sea

MY TUTORIALS

"A shiny new city in Arkansas"

In October of 2009, we went to visit our daughter Crystal, her husband Matt and our three grandchildren, Kyle, Trinity, and Noah. They live about an hour's drive east of Little Rock. Our plan this vacation was to drive the winding roads thru the Ozark Mountains to Branson, Missouri. About a three hour drive.

Our drive took us through farm lands, valleys, and green meadows. It was so beautiful. If there is an Eden on earth, then this land might just be it.

As we drove along on winding roads through spectacular scenery, Matt, being the perfect host, would inform us about various historical facts. Just as we entered the Ozarks National Parkway we traveled through another city that looked much the same as all the others we passed. As we entered this city, Matt informed us that this city is perhaps one of the most controversial in Arkansas. I asked Matt why and he informed me that this city has had more than its share of racial turmoil. It still to this day is controversial. I looked out the window and saw the same McDonalds, Wal-Mart's, and pretty little white churches with a cross on the roof as I had seen all along the way. "You're kidding?" I asked Matt. "Sorry, no I'm not mom. Some things take a long time to change. Unfortunately this city "Shame" (not the real name) holds unto its dark history."

My thoughts went back to the 1950's when in this part of our country some of the most historical fights for civil rights took place. This was the epicenter. Was it possible that this city "Shame" still clings to hate in this year of 2009? I shuttered and made sure my door was locked.

We continued our journey through the Ozark countryside. Great natural beauty surrounded us from every turn on the highway. However my thoughts were never far from Shame.

On our return from Branson back to Little Rock, we once again entered the city of Shame. As luck would have it the grandkids were hungry as were the big kids. "Matt, drive on", I said "I don't want to stop in Shame". The grand kids were now even more persistent. "Not another city for about 30 miles, Mom," Matt informed me. He then announced he needed fuel and was going to ask the attendant to direct us to a pizza parlor. I sat in silence thinking about home. I did not like this place.

This is how John Lennon let me know how things do change. Sometimes for the better.

The attendant directed us to a local pizza diner that serves excellent home style pizza. The best in town! Great I thought, local flavor. I just hope I do not see a man in a pointy white hat behind the counter!

We found the little pizza parlor in a small strip mall facing the highway. Nothing especially scary I thought to myself. "Let's give this one a try," Matt said, as he parked the van.

As I entered the parlor my eyes feasted on a very large photo of John Lennon sitting at his white "Imagine" piano. The small pizza parlor had devoted a portion of their establishment to honor John. There were other Rock and Blues musicians who were honored also, but it was obvious who had the most honored position. John Lennon.

I walked to the counter to talk to the young man standing behind it. I asked him "who is the John Lennon fan?" In his very charming southern accent he told me "I am and so are many of my friends and customers. The owner is the one who picked out the pictures." I thanked him and went back to my seat. I took a couple of pictures with my grandson Kyle.

As I left the pizza parlor I thought to myself how things have changed for the better since the sixties. How back then, this city would have stomped on John's image for what he had said about Jesus and the Beatles.

Some might think, oh just a coincidence. Well, I don't. How many pizza parlors would have a wall dedicated to John Lennon? If we had not stopped at the gas station we would have not asked the attendant to recommend the pizza parlor in which he did. Nope no coincidence, we were directed. The timing, once again was perfect.

I got back into the van after having a delicious home style pizza, feeling so much better about well, everything.

I no longer refer to this city as "Shame"; I refer to it as a "Shiny New City" in Arkansas. I'm not so naïve as to believe that everything is perfect in "Shiny New city". I'm sure there are problems still just like just about anywhere in this world, however I am sure that there is at least one pizza parlor with employees and patrons who love John Lennon.

XOXOXOXOX

"My friend Robert B. from Newcastle, England"

Once again I've received a wonderful confirmation from a loved one on the other side. I have indeed discovered the name of Sunflower's lover. I know his name was August.

First I must introduce my friend Robert B. who was born in 1952 in Newcastle, England.

I met Robert on Eric Burdon's website. Eric had a discussion board where fans would leave messages. Robert had left an interesting message about life in Newcastle that I responded to. This was back in 1999 and it was the first of many letters to each other that continued for many years.

Robert was a student of English music and musicians. If you wanted to know anything about the music of the British Empire, then all you had to do is ask Robert and he would know the answer. No matter the decade.

Robert began to send me snail mail from England too. He would send me clippings, photos and magazines. He also sent me one of the most precious gifts of love I've ever received.

In one of our many letters we shared our "desert island' picks. What would be our top songs to bring if we were left on a desert island with only these choices? Little did I know Robert would record all my picks, along with other songs I had mentioned in our correspondence with each other?

Robert had recorded four cassette tapes, each with about twenty songs. All my favorites, and some of his too.

One tape was called "Made in England." All British artists.

The second tape was called "Mr. Lennon."

The third tape was entitled "Yer' Blue's", a wonderful selection of British artists who recorded songs that had a touch of American Blues.

The fourth tape I somehow misplaced and did not find it until just recently.

It was after I received these tapes, that I suddenly stopped getting emails from Robert. At first I just figured, like many online friends, we would reconnect in time.

I finally got a letter from Robert and he told me he was sorry for not writing but he had been very ill. I wrote back and wished him well. A few weeks later I was to receive another letter. This time he wrote to me telling me he had been diagnosed with the big "C". This was the last letter I was to receive from my dear friend Robert.

The love of his life, his wife, wrote to me to tell me that he had passed away. The year was 2004.

In 2011 I found the missing cassette tape. It was a sunny Sunday and I was home doing my Sunday chores around the house. I had spotted a stain in the carpet that needed attention. I took a pail of water and a sponge. As I was working on the stain I bumped the cabinet that holds our c.d. and cassette tape collection. When I did this, several tapes fell out and one hit me on my head! I picked up the tape and I was blown away when I realized it was Robert's missing cassette tape he had sent me many years ago.

Robert always printed a title for each cassette. The title for this tape was "AUGUST." Simply August. I have not a clue as to why he would name this tape August. The songs on the tape are a collection of English artists.

Once again I feel this is a confirmation from a friend on the other side of the looking glass. Because of you, Robert, I now know that his name was indeed "August."

Thank you Robert. I miss you.

XOXOXOXOX

"Elmore James"

I have only known one Elmore in this lifetime and he was a horse! I met Elmore when I had started riding horses as a hobby in 2007.

There was a new stable in our community and it was fun to get out and enjoy riding once again. Until I met Elmore, I thought I was a fair equestrian. Elmore was the tallest horse in this stable that included approximately twenty horses. Elmore was a black beauty with red eyes that would stare you down in defiance. He had a slight defect. Elmore was missing half of his left ear. Phil, the cowboy owner of the stable, said it was from another horse bite, but I have to say that to me it looked the size and shape of a human mouth.

I wanted to ride a challenging horse, so I requested Elmore. Phil told me that not many people could handle him, but if I signed the waver then it was up to me. I thought I was up to the challenge, so I signed away my life, so to speak. After all, I grew up on a horse ranch and knew how to handle tough guys like Elmore. Famous last words!

Right from the start I had my hands full with Elmore. He decided that he wanted to show me who was the boss! I didn't have a chance. Elmore bucked me off like I was a little bug on his back. I fell on my right side and broke my wrist along with my pride. When I got up I looked at my arm. That's when a very strange thought came to me. My arm was bent and twisted in a really strange way. I had fallen in some very dark soil which made my arm almost look black. For a moment a thought came into my head that "this is not my arm." Even though I was in pain, and a bit in shock, I giggled as I gazed at my arm. This is the arm of a person of dark skin color, not pale like my own.

As far as Elmore, well, let's just say he really could care less about my predicament. In my state of shock, I swear I saw him give me a very snicker of a smile. Then he trotted away and left me on the trail.

Eric Burdon sings a song called "Elmore James." It is a rock'n song with just a touch of blues. I like it a lot!

In this song Eric repeats this line over and over,

"No more Elmore! No more Elmore James! It's a shame, a dirty shame! No more Elmore, no more Elmore James!" Which pretty much describes my relationship with Elmore the horse after this day!

I cannot leave out one other person who mentions the great guitarist Elmore James (B. January 27th, 1918). His name is George Harrison. In his song 'For you Blue" George pays tribute to his mate John Lennon who plays a fabulous lap steel guitar while using a shotgun shell for the slide. In this song George sings "Go Johnny Go! Elmore James has nothing on this Baby." Nice and oh so perfect! Thanks George.

XOXOXOXOX

"A Dream within a Dream"

A few years ago I gave Eric Burdon a birthday card:

The greeting inside the card was from Edgar Allen Poe's masterpiece poem entitled "A Dream within a Dream" At the time

I thought giving this card was a bit strange, but now I know it is once again "perfect."

"Is all we seem or seem, but a dream within a dream?"

This poem was published in 1849. This was the year that Sunflowers sons John and James were conceived.

From the wonderful wacky and genius song "I am the Walrus" I am reminded of these lyrics:

"Man you should have seen then kicking Edgar Allen Poe." Maybe all of this was just a heads up and happy birthday from John to the Eggman.

XOXOXOXOX

"Who is Jesus?"

It seems to me, that John Lennon will be apologizing for his "We are more popular then Jesus" comment forever. My personal thoughts about John's statement are that he simply put his foot in his mouth! He was young and on top of the world. He may or may not have believed that the Beatles were more popular then Jesus at the time, does not really matter to me, he simply should have not said what he was thinking. How many of us can say this has never happened to us? I still giggle to this day when I see the old news reel footage of John being asked about why he said it? John replies that he said it, he's sorry he said it and he did not mean to offend anyone for believing In God or Jesus or whatever it is. I just have to giggle! His expression is priceless!

The next is from another reading with Reverend Arlene. During this reading she did indeed know by then that my special Guide 'John' was no other then John Lennon.

Rev. Arlene: "What would you like to ask John today dear one?"

Sherry: "John who is Jesus?"

Arlene: "Jesus;" Rev. Arlene says after taking about a minute before speaking. "Does he have a beard and long hair?"

Sherry: "Ha! Ha! Ha! John don't be cheeky! I'm being serious. I'm gonna repeat my question. Who is Jesus? You know John, Jesus Christ. Who is he? Is he God?"

Arlene: "Oh you mean the Nazarene."

Sherry: "Yes, John. Jesus Christ."

Arlene: "Ah, yes. The Nazarene. I will say this about Jesus, he sure knows how to keep and hold an audience!"

After hearing this statement both Arlene and I broke up laughing.

I must reiterate that Reverend Arlene knew very little about John Lennon and his personality. She is a country music gal and really did not like the Beatles at all when they first appeared. Telling me that she did not like their haircuts, their tight pants or even their music when they first came to America in the mid 60's.

She did not know about John Lennon's sarcastic wit. At least she did not at this time. She was to learn so much more in the coming years.

Rev. Arlene is a student of the Bible. She loves Jesus to the core of her being.

This statement about Jesus was not like her at all.

After our laugh, she reconnected with John's spirit once again. Then as if she were listening to an inner voice she could only hear, she tilted her head ever so slightly and said: "Yes John, I agree. Jesus is Love."

Nothing further needed to be said or asked.

From time to time I pull out this tape and listen to it again. I love it because it proves to me that there is humor in Heaven and that "Jesus" is smiling and loves each and every one of us, including John Lennon.

XOXOXOXOX

"Heroes"

Today is the 11th of November. It is Veteran's day in America. Today it is especially important to thank our veterans for their service to our country.

We all have our heroes, John Lennon is no exception. This next message has to do with three of his heroes.

Captain Richard Phillips was taken hostage April 8th, 2009. He was the captain of the ship Maersk Alabama. Captain Phillips volunteered himself as a hostage in order to keep his crew from harm. For five day's he lived a life of terror on the high seas. He tried to escape but was unable. He was finally rescued by Navy Seals after three pirates were shot dead.

On August 22nd of 2009 my granddaughter, Olivia, and I attended a concert by a Beatles tribute band called American English. In the audience was Captain Richard Phillips. The M.C. of the concert made an announcement that Captain Phillips was in the audience. At which time he received a well-deserved standing ovation.

The next day, August 23rd, Olivia and I decided to have Sunday brunch in the Grand Ballroom of the Queen Mary ship. As I have already revealed Olivia and I were seated at table # 9. Sitting directly behind at table # eight, was Captain Phillips. He is the man in the photograph with the lovely salt and pepper hair.

As a way of connecting Captain Phillips, John Lennon, and myself, I would like to point out that Captain Phillips was kidnapped on April 8th. John Lennon's son, Julian was born on April 8th. My father, whose initials are JML, was born on April 8th. So it seems all three of us have a connection with April the 8th.

I believe John wants to honor Captain Phillips for his bravery. That this was to happen on August 23rd is no coincidence. Nope no way.

Forrest Gump is my favorite movie. I believe the movie is one life lesson after another. Each time I view it, I learn a little more about humanity through the eyes of Forrest Gump. This brilliant movie stars Tom Hanks as Forrest Gump. Mr. Hanks is my favorite actor and I believe he is also John Lennon's.

I know some will say I have no right to speak for John, about something so special such as who his heroes are, but I feel much honored and do believe that I have been given this message about heroes from John and it is very sacred.

One scene opens with Forrest sitting on a park bench in Alabama reminiscing with a lady. Forrest told her about when he was on the Dick Cavett TV show. Forrest tells the lady about a nice man and lady he met while on this show. The man and lady were John and Yoko Ono Lennon. Forrest then say's that this nice man from England was on his way home to say good-night to his little boy, when a man shot him. The scene fades out with John looking very sad. It is a hauntingly beautiful scene.

I believe John was letting me know that he is very proud of his scene in "Forrest Gump."

Another of 'our' favorite scenes in this movie is the scene in which Forrest Gump and Lt. Dan (Gary Sinise) are aboard their shrimp boat 'Jenny' when the pair find themselves in a predicament by the name of "Hurricane Carmen." In this Scene, Lt. Dan is shown standing high up in the crow's nest on the Jenny. With clenched fists, Lt. Dan swears that he will not be defeated. "It's you or me, God" he repeats to the Heavens above. For those of you who are not familiar with this movie, Lt. Dan blamed Forrest Gump and God for saving his life and for taking his legs in battle. It was in this scene, with hurricane winds blowing and Lt. Dan screaming at God, that he makes his peace. Lt. Dan vs. the sea and God. Quite a remarkable scene.

I believe John, along with myself and many others, consider Tom Hanks and everyone associated with this immortal movie, our heroes.

I think we all have memories in our lives that if we could we would put them in a bottle to open and relive over and over again. I believe this next hero and message is one of those times in a bottle memories for John Lennon.

In 1980, John Lennon began to take up a new hobby. This new adventure involved the sea. John had decided to sail to Bermuda with four friends. The vessel was the "Megan Jaye" The captain was Captain Hank. The date of departure was June 6th, 1980.

It was during this adventure at sea that John Lennon discovered some hidden talents. The Megan Jaye encountered hurricane strength winds. Only John and the captain of the vessel, Captain Hank, were not below deck feeling the effects of motion sickness.

Captain Hank called on John to help him sail the ship. John stepped up to the plate and took control. Even though he had little experience.

Singing every Beatles and sea shanty song he could remember, he bravely took the helm. Captain Hank commented that John became a valued member of the crew.

I recommend the novel by Phillip Norman entitled "John Lennon," if you wish to read more about John's experience at sea.

This memory of John's reminds me so much of Lt. Dan's life changing scene at sea in Forrest Gump. Both men, Lt. Dan and John Lennon, coming to terms with life aboard a vessel during a storm at sea.

It was after this, while in Bermuda, John Lennon went on to write some of the most beautiful songs of his career. The songs we all love which are featured on his final album 'Starting Over'.

Captain Phillips, Tom Hanks and Cap't Hank are all heroes of John Lennon, men who love the sea as does John Lennon. As did two young boys, bound for the city of New York the year of 1855. John and James Wells.

As I finished this tribute to hero's, in perfect synchronicity, "Sweet Home Alabama", came on the radio. Perfect timing. I remember the scene with Forrest and Jenny dancing to this song. Jenny was trying to teach him to dance. It is so special. And yes, John, I know, Captain Richard Phillips was the skipper of the 'Maersk ALABAMA.'

XOXOXOXOX

Chapter 3

LIFE IN NEW YORK CITY

ENTERING NEW YORK HARBOR, SUNFLOWER gazed on her new city for the first time. In her mind she pictured a city of class and culture. Unfortunately reality is sometimes not what we imagine. Sunflower was greeted by several very dangerous looking men and women who were cursing her twin boys calling them "niggers" and telling them to go back to Africa. Although Sunflower was no stranger to this word, it saddened her to hear it said in New York City. After all New York was a city were the colored were a part of free America. It was at this moment of realization that Sunflower knew that she would continue to need all of her skills and more to endure, to survive, not only for herself but more important for her sons. She had no fear she could and would prosper. Thus was her resolve.

As the foursome made their way by hired horse drawn taxi to their destination, Leonard Street near Broadway, they traveled through the most dangerous and fearful area of the city, a slum which was known as "Five Points." Sunflower had been warned not to wander to this area of the city. Danger loomed on every corner.

When she finally arrived at her new home and place of employment, Sunflower was very pleased. This would be her home, along with James, John and Angel for the next nine years. New adventures, new clients, a new life in New York City, USA.

The taxi pulled in front of an immense Victorian designed house with an immaculate garden surrounded by a large white iron fence.

Sunflower glanced at the hand mirror she had brought. The image she saw was that of a very beautiful woman in the prime of her life at the age of thirty six. She straightened her hat, and smoothed out the wrinkles in her long velveteen dress of blue. As she stepped to the front door of the house, she held John's hand in her right hand; in her left she held her mother's butterfly fan. 'Angel Trumpet' Alice wore a native dress of beautiful color full weave. Her long black hair was braided and glistened as black and shiny as a raven's feathers. She held James by his hand and walked proudly behind Sunflower and John.

Before the door was answered, Sunflower opened her butterfly fan to its full glory. She was ready to meet face to face, with no fear, her new madam. Her name was Julia Brown.

Sunflower was soon at home and very comfortable in her new home located on Leonard Street. Madam Brown and Sunflower proved to be an excellent team. Both women were very ambitious and both women knew how to court high society. Julia's gala events were a welcomed invite for many "must know" persons of persuasion who wanted to be seen. There seemed to be no limit to the amount of money these two women could generate.

Sunflower's New York City clientele grew larger by the day. She was soon the most requested lady at Julia's brothel on Leonard Street. Sunflower was now thirty seven years of age, which made her one of the senior ladies at this establishment. Many would never guess her age anywhere near her actual age. She was very beautiful. In her prime.

Her skin was the color of light honey. Her long black hair hung around her shoulders with light wispy curls. Her eyes were dark as coal with dark eyebrows and full eyelashes that fluttered like the wings of a hummingbird. She wore a light dusting of pink on her high cheek bones with a light shade to match on her ample lips. She was about five feet four inches tall with an athletic figure. She was most proud of her teeth. All her life she applied soda three times a day. First she would rub her teeth with her fingers and then finish with a ruff cloth. She never lost a tooth and she often flashed a flirty smile to let everyone admire her teeth. She never lost a tooth and she often flashed a flirty smile to let everyone admire her teeth.

Sunflower would sometimes dress in Cajun attire. A colorful print cotton dress to her knees, bracelets on her wrists and her ankles. No shoes. This was a common dress request from her gentlemen friends.

Sunflower could also dress with the finest of ladies who resided in the west side. Long hoop skirted dresses of lace and velvet, cut high in back and low in front. Of course these dresses were not complete without a corset. This was required as an undergarment. This 'torturous' undergarment accentuated Sunflowers tiny twenty two inch waistline. The outfit required a matching hat with feathers, jewels and bows. Long gloves of lace and an umbrella for the sun or for New York showers completed the ensemble. Sunflower was a lady in the finest sense. A walking dream of feminine perfection. If there were names called at her as she walked the sidewalks of the west side, she never heard them.

As the years went by Sunflower continued to make known that she would not have any sex in the traditional fashion with her clients. Julia Brown understood this also. Both women were very manipulative and knew that "no sex" could be accomplished provided you were imaginative. Julia admired Sunflower for being able to do this and was relieved that she had one less woman to worry about replacing because of pregnancy.

Sunflower had also gained respect from men and women because of her communication skills. Another gift Sunflower had been given was the 'gift of the ear'. She would listen for hours to the problems and complaints of her gentlemen. Then she would apply compassion and try to help solve their problems. Many of her clients trusted her with their secrets and knew she would keep her word and not gossip. She was a trusted friend and confidant to many. Thus her reputation grew and her status at the house was never in doubt.

As was the custom of many brothels, the women would gather together in the parlor happily chatting with each other as they waited for a knock on the door. In time an eager gentleman would appear and then request a woman of his choice for that evening's pleasure.

While the women waited in the parlor for a client, they would play parlor games. One parlor game that was a popular choice was to pick a subject at random, then make up a story about this subject. Sunflower was a very good storyteller.

James and John were also very happy living in New York City at the brothel on Leonard Street. It was unusual for children to reside at a brothel such as Julia Browns, but because of Sunflower's very large clientele and her popularity, Julia made an exception and allowed the twins this privilege.

James and John would clean, sweep, help with the laundry and when asked by the gentlemen, would shine shoes and wipe off the dust from their clothing. From their first day of residence, the boys were schooled in proper house manners. They were also taught to read and write by their mother. The little boys were not allowed to play within the house, only outside in the courtyard. When it was a sunny day and Sunflower would allow them, James and John would play with the other children in the neighborhood. When asked who the ladies the boy's lived with were, they answered "Our aunties".

The rules inside the house were strictly enforced. James and John were expected to talk only when asked a question. "Be as quiet as a church mouse", Sunflower would remind her boy's several times a day.

The most common request was for James and John to sing. James and John would sing every song they could remember be it northern melodies, a sea shanty, or a song from their homeland. Everyone especially loved hearing the boys sing gospel songs. James and John's voices blended in perfection and everyone fell under their spell.

In February of 1859, when James and John were nine, a new song could be heard in the streets of New York City. In Walk a bouts from minstrels dressed in black face came a song of the south. A song which was first heard only a few blocks from the Leonard street residence at a theatre called "Mechanics Hall."

This song was called "Dixieland", or "I wish I was in Dixie". James and John learned the lyrics and quickly put the song to voice. This song became their "Trade mark" and their most requested song to perform.

On a cool and crisp October evening in 1859, Julia Brown and Sunflower decided to dine at Manhattans newest and most elegant dining rooms in the newly opened Fifth Street Hotel.

All heads turned as the two ladies were escorted to their table. Manhattan's number one madam and number one call girl.

As they sipped champagne and studied the menu a very large man, who was seated a few tables from the ladies, was laughing loudly and obviously did not have a problem with being the center of attention. "Who is that man?" Sunflower asked Julia. "His name is Isaac Singer. He owns Singer Sewing Machine Company and has made a fortune," Julia replied. Again a commotion came from the Singer table as Mr. Singer could be heard throughout the diner barking orders to his many waiters who were very busy trying to keep the large table of twenty happy.

Sunflower studied the large man. By this time in her life she had an uncanny ability to judge a man inside and out with just a glance, or just by the tone of his voice. She thought to herself that he was probably a sometime actor. He was also a man who had the ability to bend anyone to his way of thinking. Then Sunflower noticed the gentleman sitting next to Mr. Singer. There was something about the way he sat quietly sipping his glass of wine, dressed in a dapper grey suit with a small white carnation on his lapel. As she watched him his eyes met hers for a brief moment. Sunflower was intrigued. Again she asked Julia (who knew just about everyone who was anyone in the greater Manhattan area), "Who is the gentleman sitting next to Mr. Singer? He is a handsome man." "Ah, yes. Mr. Edward Clark. He is Mr. Isaac Singer's attorney," Julia answered followed by a wink to Sunflower. "He is a happily married man, my dear." Sunflower again looked towards the Singer table to see Mr. Singer's arms flying about while he gave instructions to anybody within ear shot. Mr. Clark was no longer seated and had left the dining room.

A few minutes later the Singer table was empty and Mr. Singer was making his way from table to table interrupting everyone's dinner. He finally stood in front of Julia and Sunflower. "My dear Julia Brown, how lovely you look tonight," Mr. Singer's voice boomed. Julia extended her hand and Mr. Singer kissed it. "Who is your lovely companion? No doubt one of your actresses," he inquired. "Mr. Singer, may I introduce you to Miss Sunflower," Julia replied. "I am indeed an actress in the theatre of life," replied Sunflower to Mr. Singer. "My eyes are feasting on your beauty. Do you reside at the Brown residence on Leonard Street?" Mr. Singer inquired. "I do indeed, Mr. Singer."

This was the beginning of a very challenging relationship. Sunflower had just met the man who would be her equal when it came to money, cunning, and survival.

Isaac Singer soon became Sunflower's most frequent client. He was indeed a wealthy man, a sometime actor, and he could and would convince the devil to convert if given the opportunity. He was also married (with some say more than one wife) and he was a womanizer. He also had a sex drive that could not be satisfied.

Isaac and Sunflower made quite the pair. Isaac was very determined to "de flower" the lovely Sunflower. It seems he wanted to be the first man to put a stop to her no sex rule. The cat and mouse game between them went on and on for over a month. Finally a very large sum of money was offered and Julia and Sunflower agreed that for the first time in her life, Sunflower would accommodate Isaac in his desire. Sunflower was to become a prostitute in the truest sense of the word.

In 1860 many people were very aware that a civil war over slavery was in the air. One presidential candidate that many people were interested in was a lawyer from Illinois. His name was Abraham Lincoln. Mr. Lincoln was to speak at "Cooper's Union", on February 27th, 1860. Sunflower felt quite passionate about the abolishment of slavery and because of this, decided to attend his speech.

For this auspicious occasion, Sunflower dressed in her finest, a beautiful satin dress of black with blue and white trim. A large blue sash fitted tightly which accentuated her tiny waist. She wore a small black hat tilted to the side that had a large white peacock feather and small blue bows. Her gloves were black satin. Her beautiful butterfly fan complemented her attire. When she floated downstairs from her room, everyone stopped to gaze at her. Julia Brown accompanied Sunflower and was dressed in her finest also.

When she stepped off the carriage at Cooper's Union, the first person Sunflower met was Isaac Singer. He was surrounded by many other colleagues. As usual Isaac was making himself the center of attention. However, he did stop his nonstop chattering when Sunflower walked by. "Miss Sunflower, you are a vision," he chimed in as he kissed her gloved hand. "Thank you, Mr. Singer, so good to see you here," Sunflower politely responded. Then her eyes once again met the man she had seen with Singer at the Fifth Street Hotel dining room. Mr. Edward Clark took her hand and asked Isaac to introduce him. "Counselor, may I introduce you to Miss Sunflower, a friend of mine. " Isaac said. "Miss Sunflower, what an unusual name. Have we perhaps met before? You seem so familiar," Edward asked. At that point Isaac put his head back and laughed much too loudly, "I don't think so, Edward. I'm sure you have not met Sunflower. I'm sure of that!" Edward ignored him and went on to say "Well, perhaps not, but hopefully we shall meet again. I am an attorney of law, as is Mr. Lincoln. I am most excited to hear what he has to say about the abolishment of slavery as it fits in law." "Yes, Mr. Clark. I fully agree. That is the reason I am here also," Sunflower replied adding "I have many friends in the south that will be affected if the union is to succeed with the abolishment of this inhumane treatment."

The crowd began to move forward toward the entrance. Edward offered his arm to Sunflower which she took. They walked into the doors together then separated when they were escorted to their assigned seating area. Sunflower thought to herself that she had just met a man who was a true gentleman. She wanted very much to see him again. Not as a business associate, but as a friend.

Mr. Lincoln's speech held the entire audience in rapture. He stood tall and erect in his black suit and tall hat. His demeanor was of a man who held great promise for the future. A sort of quiet realization hit the audience that this was history being made by the second. Some said the decision to end slavery was started right then and there. With that decision would come war. The audience quiet throughout the speech, roared their approval at its completion.

Sunflower could not shake the feeling that she had met this man, Mr. Abraham Lincoln. He seemed so familiar. However, she thought to herself, she had never been to Illinois, and no he never been a client! She would remember this man. She just could not shake the feeling however, that she had met him before. This feeling stayed with her from this day forward.

The year of 1860 was a presidential campaign year. In the summer of that year James and John decided to do what they could to help their hero, Abraham Lincoln. As a way to help with the Lincoln campaign, John and James would apply black face make-up, put on a hat and wear long sleeved shirts along with long pants in order to disguise their African heritage. Then the boys would go to the prestigious neighborhoods and sing "Dixieland", which had become known as one of the Lincoln campaign songs. By disguising themselves in black face, they commanded more respect, plus it was a dangerous time, even in New York City, to be African.

Sunflower was very proud of her sons. They talked nonstop about "Honest Abe," wanting to hear their mother tell true life stories of young Abe growing up in Illinois. They were fascinated that Mr. Lincoln was poor growing up and now he was going to be President.

James and John would walk the city streets singing Dixieland to anyone who had an ear to hear. One time they even sang in front of an outhouse when the moon was shining. James and John stood at the door shouting "Vote for Honest Abe!" The man shouted, "Go away, leave me alone and let me shit in peace you little heathens." James and John continued to shout back at the man sitting behind the moon. The man opened the door and fell to his feet with his back side shining in the moonlight. James and John ran away as fast as they could, laughing all the way back to Leonard Street and home. The man could not catch the tricksters.

Abraham Lincoln became the 16th President of the United States of America under a great cloud of fear. War was on the horizon. The south had declared its independence and eleven states succeeded from the Union. April 12th, 1861 the first shots were fired at Fort Sumpter in South Carolina. The great civil war of America had begun.

Sunflower's thoughts and prayers were for her family and friends who still remained in the New Orleans area. She thought of Rose and how kind she had been not only to herself but to James, John and Angel Alice. She also thought of her African family who still lived a life of slavery. Sunflower would awaken nights in a cold sweat. Hearing in her mind the cries of the women as their children we're torn from their arms. These helpless children were born into a very cruel world, their misfortune being the color of their skin. Whenever she would think how cruel and unjust war is, she would remember the children and pray that Mr. Lincolns Union would somehow prevail. The crying and dying might stop. She also thanked God every night that, James and John who were now eleven plus years of age, were too young to serve.

Life in and around the Leonard Street Bordello did not seem to be affected by war. Everyone knew it was going on, as there were very few men to be found between the ages of 15 to 40. However, there were still many influential "older' men who were in need of the services of the ladies. It seemed sometimes some men make a profit of war, which in turn brought more dollars into the house. Stress needs to be relieved in war and peace. The oldest profession continued on.

Sunflower was now into her early forties. Although still youthfull in appearance, she was now semi-retired from her profession. She would help 'advise' the ladies of the house. In turn for doing this she would receive extra pay from Julia Brown. Sunflower would respectfully refuse all but her most favorite, and generous, of gentlemen callers.

Julia was now very involved with the theatre. In years past, her ladies would perform in theatre. This was a way to attract new clients. Now Julia was once again involved with theatre only now, it was more legitimate. She especially loved children's theatre.

Because of Julia and her endeavors in the theatre, James and John quickly became local celebrities. Appearing in many plays and vaudevillian productions.

It was at a theatrical play off Broadway that Sunflower once again was pleased to be in the company of Edward Clark. While chatting together during intermission, she learned of Isaac Singer's escape to London, England. It seems ole Isaac finally got his rewards for his mistreatment of women. He was forced to escape the law and justice for his bigamist ways.

Sunflower and Edward had a good laugh about Isaac's troubles. Edward whispered into Sunflower's ear, "I can't stand the man, but one day I will make a lot of money because of him. You'll see." "I already have," Sunflower replied, then after saying this to Edward she felt herself blush, which she hardly ever did in front of any man. "It seems we have something in common Mr. Clark". "Call me Edward, please," Edward said as he gave her a wink in return. "Yes, Isaac thinks we both like him, when we both really dislike him thru and thru. Yet the man is profitable for both of us," Sunflower said while fanning herself to conceal a feeling of warm desire.

"You're very right my dear woman, he is profitable," Edward replied. Then he asked Sunflower if she believed in justice? "Of course I do Edward. Why do you ask?". "Well, there is a man who is now as we speak fighting for the Union and the liberation of the Negro men and women slaves. This man's name is Elias Howe. Do you remember this man, Sunflower?" "No, I'm sorry I do not," was her reply. Edward cleared his throat and shook his head. "Well, you are not alone in not remembering him. Many people believe he was the true inventor of the sewing machine. I find it an irony that the man who will be remembered in history as the liberator of women with his sewing machine is a most un-liberating and chauvinistic man, as far as women's right are concerned." "Sometimes, dear Edward," Sunflower replied as she smiled and lowered her eyes "we are not meant to under- stand. Hopefully Mr. Howe will receive his rewards when he stands before God and the final justice is served." "So true, of course God will be the final judge, but I as an attorney wish to see my fellow men and women realize just how important Elias Howe was in helping women move out of the drudgery of hand sewing. Hopefully justice will prevail."

Edward at that point, bent over to kiss Sunflower's cheek for the first time.

Sunflower soon realized she was falling in love with the tall and handsome Mr. Clark. She had never felt this way for any man.

She smiled when she would think about August. His beautiful brown body. His long black hair in tangles hanging to his shoulders. Mostly she remembered his smile. His smile made her feel all was well with the world.

She realized her desire for August was lust. Her feelings for Edward were the same, but also different. She loved the way he talked, how smart he was, how she felt protected when she was with him. He was also a very handsome man. He was always dressed in only the finest of suits. His tall hat tilted a bit to the side and his hands were never without gloves. She also had to admit she loved the attention she received as they walked down the boulevard together. He never had an unkind word for anyone, well except for Isaac, but that was understandable and both Sunflower and Edward would have many a laugh at his expense.

Sunflower asked Edward if he was concerned with what people might say about his relationship with her. In his gentle way, he answered, "I have nothing to hide nor any concerns with anyone's opinions when it comes to our friendship. Caroline knows about you. She is happy that I have such a beautiful companion. Caroline is a captive of her health. She can never leave our home as this would bring on pneumonia. She loves me and trusts me".

Sunflower never knew such a love could exist. She also knew she was in love with Edward mind, body and most important his soul.

In the spring of 1863, Sunflower finally moved out of the Leonard Street brothel and retired. At the age of forty four she was able to, for the first time in her life, rent a small flat in mid- town Manhattan for not only herself to live but also James, John and Angel Alice.

John and James were also very talented artists and were both beginning to draw portraits in Central Park. John loved the medium of ink. James loved charcoal. Both boys were also very talented in oil. The boys were most industrious and their mother was surprised at the amount of money the two young artists brought home after a Sundays work.

James and John were regulars at the age of 13 in musical theatre. They were able to read lines, not because they had ever attended public school, they had not, but because of the loving teachings they had received from the ladies of the Leonard Street address. Also the devoted teaching from their mother and their God Mother who was Angel Alice.

Through the encouragement and connections of both Julia Brown and Edward Clark, James and John were becoming little celebrities in the Harlem and Midtown areas of the city.

Life was good

MY TUTORIALS

"Julia Brown"

It took me some time to realize the name of the Madam who employed Sunflower in New York City upon her arrival in 1855. I was able to connect the dots to her identity with help from a wonderful book I purchased in 2008, called "City of Eros", by Timothy J. Gilfoyle. New York City, prostitution, and the commercialization of sex, 1790-1920. I wanted to find the name of Sunflower's madam when she moved to NYC, and found this book which included the time period in which Sunflower did indeed live and work in NYC. I found a few names of well-known Madams in this novel. When I read about Julia Brown, I felt I had found Sunflower's boss, friend, and madam.

Julia was very well known and in some circles actually very respected in New York high Society. She did indeed own a brothel on Leonard Street. There is not a huge amount of history about her on the internet, but there is enough for me to be in little doubt that I had found her. As I read "City of Eros," I discovered Julia's name and slowly began to put the puzzle pieces together. This is how John Lennon led me to this conclusion to verify my discovery.

Twelve years ago I went to a concert in Mesquite Nevada to see Eric Burdon perform a show. He was to appear at a casino by the name of Casa Blanca (White House). After the show I was able to meet Eric and get an autograph. After giving me his autograph he noticed my John Lennon pin I was wearing. He mentioned to me that the following week he had a show in Brownsville, Texas, at a park that was named "John Lennon Park." Eric then told me that he was working on a tribute song to perform for this show. The song he had chosen was "Yer Blues." He proceeded to sing a few lines from the song to me. When he did this "I felt John's presence as if he were standing next to me."

A week or so later I was at work alone in the shop before we were to open for business; I turned on the radio to listen to "Breakfast with the Beatles." The station was not coming in clear, so I reached for the retractable antenna to adjust it for better reception.

When I touched it, I felt a surge of electricity pass through me. Not like a shock, and it is hard to explain, but best I can describe is it was like a surge of energy. I could feel the hair on my arms and back of my neck stand up. The moment of this surge the radio came in loud and clear. The familiar opening of "Yer Blues" along with the 'energy' was thrilling.

I once again felt John's presence and really expected to see him standing in the corner of the room! He did not appear, at least that I could see, but I can say that if he did appear at that moment in time I really would not have been scared or surprised to see him standing there!

I had a picture taken of Eric Burdon and myself the day he told me about his wanting to sing "Yer Blues" to honor John. The shirt I wore was a U.S. Army shirt I had purchased from a second hand store. I had purchased it about a month before this picture was taken. This was almost ten year before I had discovered my past life in which I was Sunflower. The owner of this shirts name is imprinted on the reverse side of the collar. The name is "Brown."

As for Eric's concert at John Lennon Park in Brownsville, Texas— well it never happened. The band had flown to Brownsville only to find out the event had been cancelled… Interesting to me because it feels like it was all meant to help me find Julia Brown (s—ville).

This morning, as I finished this message, I took another look at this U.S. Army uniform shirt that I wore that day back in 1998. I had not looked at it for many years and I wanted to make sure that Brown was indeed imprinted on the inside of the collar. I was right. However, not only was Brown imprinted but the persons initials were there also. "Brown E. J."

Time simply does not seem to matter on the other side.

It took me over twelve years to discover Julia E. Brown.

XOXOXOXOX

"Ladies in Waiting"

I have had many moments of de ja vue in my lifetime. This Next experience felt so real that I felt if I closed my eyes, and then re-opened them, I would be back in the year of 1857.

It was during a Sunday worship service I attended at a beautiful oasis called Nu-Vu. This is also Reverend Arlene's home.

There were nine ladies at this service, no men. It was a very amazing and uplifting service.

During this amazing day, Rev. Arlene was able to channel one of her guides "Grandmother Devereaux." While she was in contact with Grandmother she gave me a couple of words of advice. Amazingly her advice to me was spot on. She held my hand and started to rub my wedding ring. She looked at my ring and told me that this ring is not from who people think it is from. That it belonged to another before me. How could she know this, I thought to myself? The diamond in my wedding ring was actually given me from my first husband. The diamond was his great grandmothers! There is no way Arlene could have known this.

It was while Grandma was holding my hand that I took my voyage back in time.

There was a knock on the door. I felt a huge "this has happened before" feeling. One of the ladies answered the door. It was my husband Randy coming to pick me up. I excused myself from the group and left. I felt like it was time to get back to work!

When I got to the car, we started the engine and the radio came to life. The song that was on was John Lennon's "Strange Day's indeed."

As if planned, and I believe it was, I heard John sing—

"Most peculiar Mamma".

Absolutely PERFECT TIMING.

XOXOXOXOX

"Dyno"

I believe all of us who love our animal companions hope that when we step to the other side of the mirror we will be greeted by our loyal furry, feathered and scaled family. In my life I have been given quite a few messages which lead me to believe that when we are sad and grieving the loss of a pet, either the pet or a loved one on the other side will send messages to us to help us through the pain and sadness.

Dyno came into our lives in 1997 only days after we had moved to our new shop location. He came to our front door crying for help. He never left the shop after that night. Dyno worked at our bicycle store for over 13 years. He never missed a day of work, nor did he ever complain about working conditions.

A cat must have a very special temperament to be a working cat. He must be very calm, yet at the same time loving. He must be able to judge the humans who come in, and decide to be either friendly or just be invisible.

Dyno especially loved children. Every day he could be seen following the youngsters around in hopes of getting a pat on the head. He was as gentle a cat as ever lived. I had witnessed babies pick him up by the tail, and he would just hang there! I don't think he knew how to hiss!

Dyno had a cute kitty trick he would do over and over again on command. I would ask him "Dyno who loves you?" and he would answer me with "Meow Meow", except it sounded more like "Mau Mau."

In June of 2010, Dyno became very ill. We took him to the veterinarian who diagnosed him with late stages of renal failure. There really was not much we could do for him. In his last few weeks he could hardly walk any longer. However we were able to go outside the shop sit together and watch the birds. He had not been outside for over thirteen years, so it was special for both of us. I think he liked it.

We tried to make him as comfortable as we could, but after two months of good days and bad, the bad finally won. Had to do what we knew was right. It was very difficult.

Randy and I cried as we both held him as he took his last breath after the injection. Dyno crossed over to the Rainbow Bridge very peacefully.

Randy and I were very sad on the drive home. I told Randy I was confident that Dyno would give us a message as soon as he could. It came only an hour after arriving home.

I believe that somehow on the other side, spiritual beings have the ability to look into the future. Here is an example in the message I received from Dyno.

It was a Wednesday night September 22, 2010 when we lost Dyno. Out of habit I turned on the television to watch Ghost Hunters as I always do. Sometimes doing the familiar can be comforting. That night's episode was a world premier and I had not seen it before. The Ghost Hunters, Jason and Grant were investigating a light house. It was during this investigation that Jason and Grant heard an audible disembodied voice say "Ma Ma." Grant asked Jason if he heard someone say "Ma Ma". Jason said he heard it too, but to him it sounded like it was saying "Mau Mau." The way Jason said it did sound like Dyno when I asked him who loves him.

I knew this was my message from Dyno. Telling me he is O.k. and is now on the other side at Rainbow Bridge. It made me giggle that sad night.

As a side note—Mau Mau is Egyptian for cat. I miss you Dyno—we all do at the bicycle shop.

Update

Today is September 22nd, 2011. It is exactly one year since we lost Dyno. There is not one day that goes by that we do not think of him.

Today we had a visit from him. First I need to explain. Eight weeks ago our dear friend Mike and my husband Randy rescued eight kittens and their mama from disaster. This dear sweet kitty was left behind to fend for herself. Mike and Randy found her in a sewer with her kittens near death. The kittens were about a week old at the most. Mike scooped up the kitties and their mama and took her to his house. Mike has way too many cats already as do Randy and I. However, what could we do? Turn our backs? That was not possible. So Mike took them home.

I put a "free kittens" sign on our counter at our bicycle store. Until today, we were not getting any takers. Until today—one year to the day that we lost Dyno.

Today a lovely couple came into the store looking for a bicycle. She picked out a green bicycle and put it on lay-a-way. While we were doing the paper work, she noticed my "free kittens" sign. Her husband told us that their daughter and grandson had asked him to be on the lookout for kittens that need homes! He got on his cell phone and called their daughter who said she'll take two kittens.

We were so happy! I knew, just knew, this was a message from Dyno. It was confirmed a minute later when the lady presented me with her credit card to put a deposit on the bicycle. The credit card had a huge Sunflower on it! I have never seen one like this ever! I was amazed! Mike, Randy and I shared a few tears of joy and thanked Dyno.

XOXOXOXOX

Our beloved kitty "Dyno". Just another day of work at the bicycle shop.

"Story Ville"

As I researched the brothels of New Orleans and New York City during the mid-1800, I discovered a bit of history. There actually was a red light district in New Orleans called "Story Ville".

I discovered this after I had written about Sunflowers story telling ability.

XOXOXOXOX

"Dixie Land"

Several years ago I had a dream that felt so real, I was actually surprised to wake up! I will elaborate more on this dream in a later chapter. At this point in Sunflowers story I only want to share one part of this dream.

As I was dreaming I was shown in big numbers the year of "1859". I was sure that Sunflower must have died in this year. I was not correct in this assumption. This is how I discovered the importance of the year of 1859 and what happened to make it such a memorable one in the lives of Sunflower, John, and James Wells.

It was a year or two after having this dream, in 2008, that I discovered what happened. I was at my local laundry when once again I thought about the year of 1859. Suddenly as I was about to leave, I got a huge urge to view the movie "Gangs of New York."

I was writing about Sunflower and I had a feeling that something within this movie was going to help me continue with her life story. I finished my laundry and headed to our local video store to rent the movie. I was absolutely driven to watch it! Sure enough the time period was correct. I watched every scene in anticipation of discovery. Two things felt very familiar, the slum "Five Points' and the "Draft Riots."

I enjoyed every moment of the movie, but nothing really connected as far as the year of 1859.

I finished the movie and almost gave up my search for anything specific about 1859, when I noticed there was a short interview with the director Martin Scorsese.

In this interview, Mr. Scorsese told of his fascination with this time period. How he discovered "The Gangs of New York," written by Herbert Ashbury in 1928. This novel inspired him to direct the movie.

At the end of this interview Mr. Scorsese told his audience about how life in NYC in the 1800's was centered on music. Songs were often sung in the streets of NYC during walk-a-bouts. How people would sing while walking, doing work, shopping or just for the joy of song. Then Mr. Scorsese told of a little known fact about a song of which many Americans know and love. "Most people think this song was first introduced in the south," Mr. Scorsese went on to say, "however it was not. In the year of 1859, 'Dixieland,' was first heard in New York City.

When I learned this, I knew this was at least one of the reasons I was shown the year 1859 in my dream. I also know I was shown this by my mother, "Dixie."

Dixieland was the song that brought happiness to Sunflower's twin sons. It was a pivotal year for other reasons also, which I will reveal in later chapters of Sunflower's life.

XOXOXOXOX

"New York City 2001"

This next message was given me in the summer of 2001. I did not know about Sunflower's existence at this time. I did however believe that John Lennon was a part of my life and was communicating with me in spirit.

I really did not know why. I thought one reason might be because he wanted me to convey a message to his friend in life whom he called "Eggs," Eric Burdon, whom I had grown to love and admire not only his music but his incredible "truths" he tried to live.

I had not, to this date, been to any Spirit Medium. The only people who knew of my belief that John Lennon was communicating with me were some of my online friends who also believed he was active in their lives.

In the summer of 2001 my husband Randy and I decided to fly to New York City to not only see the Big Apple for the first time, but to also attend a concert that Eric Burdon had scheduled at BBKings on 42nd street.

My first stop after arriving in New York City on August 12th was to visit the Dakota on 72nd and Central Park West.

When the subway stopped at 72nd street, I got off and climbed the stairs to get my first view of the Dakota. From the hustle bustle of the subway station I stepped out into a brilliant blue sky that was interrupted by the silhouette of gray stones and bricks along with pointed spires. My first thought was how the Dakota reminded me of a fairy's castle. However this was no castle, this was John's house, the Mighty Dakota in all its splendid gothic beauty. Stepping out a little further I saw the familiar archway that I had seen so many times in newsreel footage, the same arched driveway, the same little guard house that witnessed John meet his fate and travel to the other side of reality. It is hard to describe how I felt at this moment, but I suppose awe would be the best word, followed by a moment of sadness.

I took a couple of pictures and then silently said a prayer for John and for his family. In this prayer I also thanked God for the beauty of the Dakota and the city of New York.

After leaving the Dakota driveway, I asked very humbly if it were possible I would forever be thankful if I could receive a message from you (John) to take home with me. I knew it was asking a lot, but I also believe John would come through.

So off I went with high hopes to visit Strawberry Fields Park and the Imagine Memorial Mosaic. Right across the street from the Dakota.

The Imagine mosaic had one flower on it that day. It was a very large Sunflower. The Sunflowers center pod was in the shape of a heart. I did not realize it at the time, but I now believe this was a Hallmark gift card from John. For I Am Sunflower.

I sat on one of the little benches that circle the mosaic, watching the tourists and locals come and go. People of all ages, races and amounts of hair. Each taking pictures in all kinds of positions of themselves, lying down, sitting down, with just about everyone flashing a peace sign to the camera.

I thought to myself how lovely, so many people love John. I was about to leave when the message I was hoping to receive from John arrived. Here it is, given to me from John arriving in a magical wonderful envelope of hope and love.

I do not know if I've ever met an Angel or not in this lifetime, but I would like to think that maybe I did on this summer day in New York City at Central Park.

There are many people who do believe that Angels exist and walk amongst us. That these Angels come to us in times of sadness, pain, happiness and when we are in need of help. I like to think that maybe they come to us to deliver a message. At any rate the last thing I had on my mind were Angels that beautiful sunny day at Central Park.

Just as I was about to leave my park bench seat at Straw- Berry Fields Park, an elderly gentleman tapped me on the shoulder and asked if he and his friend could join me on the bench? "Of course," I said as I sat back down happy to have some company.

"I'm Frank", the taller of the two men said to me. He smiled and I thought how happy he looked. I noticed the 72nd street sign in the background behind him. The shorter man quietly sat down after telling me his name is Nigel. After he sat down, out of nowhere a small dog was at his side asking for a pat on his head. Nigel bent over, kissed his nose, and then the dog took off to find his human.

Frank was the more talkative of the two gentlemen. We first exchanged small talk about the weather and the lovely park surroundings. Frank asked me if this was my first time to New York City. I told him yes and where I was from. Nigel sat listening and never said a word.

Nigel finally commented to Frank that the park was a little busy for a Tuesday morning. "Yes," answered Frank "it's always good to see the young ones (children)." An Asian couple came up next to have their picture taken in front of the mosaic. These lovely couples were all smiles while taking pictures of each other. I got up at that point and asked them if they would like me to take a picture of them together? Although they did not speak English they got the idea and I took their camera in my hand. The young couple took their position in front of the mosaic, both of them smiling and flashing the peace sign to the camera. After the picture was taken they bowed to me and said "Thank you."

I went back to the bench to visit again with my new friends Frank and Nigel. "That was nice of you," said Nigel. "We see so many Asian people visit John's Imagine". Frank at that point mentioned that he and Nigel were also musicians. That he and Nigel played in a jazz trio. We chatted a bit more about our mutual love of music. How music has no age or race barrier. It's all good.

"I loved John Lennon very much," Nigel said with a smile which brightened his face and magically he looked twenty years younger. "I loved his music." "You know my dear," Frank said to me, "John lived in that building right behind us, at the Dakota." "Yes", I said, "I know", telling my two friends that coming to New York City and visiting the Dakota and Strawberry Fields Park, was along with a special concert, the reason I had traveled across the United States.

Frank pointed to the building on the other side of the Dakota. "My dear friend Nigel and I live in that building. We have lived there for over twenty five years." "Oh, my gosh! You must have seen John and Yoko strolling along the sidewalks from time to time!" I replied. "Why yes, we did indeed," smiled Nigel. "Many times," chimed in Frank. I just had to ask at that point if they ever had the chance to speak with him "Nope," just a casual hello and a nod," replied Nigel adding that Yoko and John were a stunning couple.

Then the mood seemed to change and Frank looked very unhappy. He looked down at his feet then crossed his arms and sighed. I thought I noticed Nigel shift his position on the bench and shudder. It seemed the clouds had suddenly appeared from nowhere.

Frank then looked me square in the eye and said "We were home that cold December night in 1980." I then knew why the mood had changed. "I was reading a book in my bedroom when I thought I heard a backfire from a car," Frank said to me. "Nigel heard it too. It came from the direction of the Dakota so both Nigel and I looked out the window and saw a police car speeding away a few minutes later. I saw no ambulance. I could not make out what had happened but we both knew and felt that a great loss had occurred. I did not know it was John Lennon, but I knew someone had been shot. We heard the news reports on the radio a few minutes later. John was gone. We would no longer see him strolling the sidewalks. It was a sad and very cold night."

Nigel mentioned the fans and how moving it was. The singing, the signs and pictures of John. "Never forget the fans; they still come after all these years." "Yes, they do," replied Frank to his ole buddy. Both men at this point looked in silence at the fans who stood around the Imagine mosaic. "They come to see John every day, rain or shine. They come with a pocket full of hope for the future," Nigel said.

Silence seemed the appropriate communication after Frank and Nigel finished their memories of December 8th, 1980. Both men now sat with their heads bowed in quite tribute to John Lennon.

I thanked my newly found friends for sharing their thoughts with me. I then tried to think of something else to talk about in order to bring back the festive mood of this spectacular setting. "Nigel," I asked "have there been other famous celebrities who have lived at the Dakota besides John and Yoko?" "Well," Nigel replied, "there have been many." He looked at Frank, who by now was looking happy again, to "help" him remember. Frank smiled and said, "The only person who pops into my head at this time is the man who invented the sewing machine. I'm not sure if he lived at the Dakota but I do know that it was his vision and his finances that were responsible for its construction. This man was also the head of the Singer Sewing Machine Company. He is the only person who comes to mind," Frank finished with a smile and I thought I saw a look of satisfaction.

When Frank responded with this information, my mind went into overdrive. I knew this was my message from John I had been hoping for. I was one big goose bump! I was a very happy Sherry! Smiling because I knew at that instant that "I GOT IT."

At this point, I told Frank and Nigel I had to leave as it was getting close to show time and I needed to get back to 42nd street. Both men expressed how much they enjoyed our chat and bid me farewell. I wished Frank and Nigel a happy life and turned to take one last picture of the Imagine Mosaic with the single sunflower still in place. I took a close up of the sunflower. I turned to wave farewell to Frank and Nigel, however they had vanished! I was really surprised these two quite elderly men had left so quickly! I looked east, west, north and south, and although it had been only a matter of seconds, they were gone!

Here is the meaning of the message I received via Frank and Nigel:

In 1965, the Beatles made their second movie called "Help." This movie tries hard to make a statement on religion. However, at least to me, it is sort of like a Marx Brothers, or the Goonies, trying to make this statement

To me, this is the basic plot of the movie. It is also about a huge ring and a religious sacrifice. The person who wears the ring, in this case Ringo, "will be sacrificed." Thankfully Ringo escapes and sticks the ring onto the finger of the high Priest. "Here's your bloody ring back, go sacrifice yourself", Ringo says, "I don't subscribe to your religion anyway." I just love this line! The movie is really fun and it really does have its little statement on religion. Great music too by the way!

At the very end of the movie there is something that appears that had puzzled me for over 35 years! At the very end of the movie just as the credits start to roll is this message, but first a huge Singer

Sewing machine appears on the screen. Then a rolling text appears which reads:

"Respectfully dedicated to Elias Howe who, in 1846 invented the sewing machine."

I have always wondered what the heck a man who invented the sewing machine has to do with the Beatles movie, Help.

Well now I know, and it makes perfect sense to me. It had to do with the construction of the Dakota.

After reading about Elias Howe I learned that he did indeed invent the sewing machine, but he did not own the Singer Sewing machine Company. The owner was of course Isaac Singer. His attorney was indeed Edward Clark who Singer later promoted to President of his company. It seems that way back when the sewing machine was first invented by Elias Howe, Singer did all he could to steal away the patent from Howe. A mighty battle of patent pending rights! The great sewing machine wars of the mid 1800's. An agreement was finally reached with Singer by Howe. In 1856 the Singer Sewing Machine began to be mass produced with Edward Clark at the helm.

So it seems to me that John was making a statement. Elias Howe should have been given the credit for this remarkable machine that liberated women from the drudgery of hand sewing.

Why would John Lennon want to do that? Because of his love for women and equal rights. John's way of getting back at ole Isaac Singer, who defiantly would not have agreed with the women's movement. Elias Howe was the true inventor not the womanizer Isaac Singer! The only good thing Isaac did was to hire Edward Clark who was the most influential person behind the building of the Dakota.

John and Yoko moved into the Dakota in 1973. The movie Help was made in 1965. Did John know about this sewing machine message and the building of the Dakota eight years before he moved into the Dakota? I believe he did, at the deeper subconscious soul level.

Our next two nights in Manhattan were filled with great music, dear friends, and a whole lot of fun.

Randy and I had traveled the subways, seen the Dakota, walked in Heaven in natures beauty in Central Park, had a great time rockin with the band at BBKing's, went to the top of the Empire State building to look at the city in all its glory then looked down on the street to see a sea of yellow cabs flowing like a river. One last thing to do before we go home, "tour the World Trade Center."

Today is September the 11th, 2011. These are my memories of that glorious day ten years ago. It seems like yesterday.

We first took a ride on the New York Staten Island Ferry, and looked across the bay to see Lady Liberty. I must admit, I was thinking of John Lennon and the wonderful picture of him standing under her flashing a smile and a peace sign.

After the ferry ride we walked to the Trade Center.

When we arrived at Tower II the first thing that I can remember of the lobby is how huge it was and how many world flags I saw hung in the lobby. It was very moving. Made you proud to be an American.

We walked a little further to see the line. One of those Disneyland round and round lines. There must have been a thousand people I would guess. It took about forty minutes to finally enter the elevator to the top.

It was a very quick ride to the top, one hundred and seven floors. Once at the top we joined the hundreds of other tourists.

The first thing we wanted to do was to get to the very top of the building. We spotted a sign that read "to the top" so off we went to the escalator to the top one hundred and tenth.

I remember thinking that once on top we would be able to lean over and look straight down. Nope. Thankfully it was not like that. There was a glass wall in front to protect. If you did manage to climb this wall it was only two stories down. The edge of the world could not be reached.

However the sea wind that greeted us renewed and invigorated every cell of my body.

We went back to the escalator to return to floor #107. We then went to the Windows of the World diner to have a bit of lunch, which by now we welcomed. There were many chairs to sit and just soak in the view. One view saw the city in all its glory. Skyscrapers that stood fifty stories or more seemed so small. I could see Central Park in the distance and knew where the Dakota and Strawberry Fields Park was located. I blew a kiss. On the other side was the Hudson Bay and once again I could see Lady Liberty. No words are adequate. We noticed on the wall were pictures of New Yorkers of the past and present, beautiful portraits of not only these wonderful people, but of the New York City they were a part of.

We saw that a virtual ride was available in a theatre and although I get motion sickness quite easily, I decided it was worth going on this tour. I'm so glad I did. Although I will say my eyes were closed on most of it. The tour took us on a virtual helicopter ride through the skyscrapers and majesty of Times Square, Central Park and then returning through the skyscrapers back to the World Trade Center.

When we got off the ride we noticed a small built to scale model of the city. We took a picture of me standing in front of this model. I look like the hundred foot woman!

We finished our World Trade Center tour with a fast ride down on the very smooth, fast and efficient elevator.

We walked a few blocks to Saint Peters Church. We noticed the small cemetery. Glancing at the headstones I saw that many of the dates were in the past century. I felt a feeling of "been there" come over. The inside of the Cathedral was spectacular. I felt humbled.

We next stopped at a small pub. Finished our tour talking to some fantastic people.

One month later everything changed.

My first thoughts when I awoke to see the Trade Center building on fire, was of the tourists who would be on the top floors. Then I remembered that the tours started at 10:00 a.m., one small thing to be thankful for on this sad day we will all remember forever.

The reason we went to New York was because we wanted to attend Eric Burdon's shows on August 11th and 12th at BBKings on 42nd street.

The other reason was my desire to the Imagine memorial.

I will never forget my tour of the World Trade Center nor will I forget the Two Angels I met in Central Park.

XOXOXOXOX

"Lincoln and Lennon"

Once again at a reading with Reverend Arlene she was able to connect with John's spirit. Arlene is very serious when it comes to her spirituality and her abilities to help people thru her readings. No matter the subject, nor how 'silly' it may seem at the time, it is special and we both feel blessed to have been able to connect. Once again as a reminder I do have all of my readings on cassette tape.

From the reading:

Arlene: Sherry was John extremely thin before his death?

Sherry: Yes, I believe he was.

Arlene: Well, I'm seeing a skeletal man standing before me. He is very thin. He is walking towards me (as she says this she seems to be looking within herself. Then she'll tilt her head slightly while looking up, next she'll turn her attention back to me).

Arlene: Oh, great! Now he's walking goofy. (At this point she is laughing as she speaks). He is walking with big long strides. Did John have an unusual gait to his walk?

Sherry: I don't think he did.

Arlene: Oh, now I get it! He is trying to look like and walk like President Abraham Lincoln. Did he have a fascination with President Lincoln?

Sherry: I really do not know.

Arlene: Well, he is definitely trying to appear as Lincoln.

That was all that was said about President Lincoln, but I knew I had to get more information regarding John Lennon and President Abraham Lincoln. What was the connection?

I was able to find out that John was indeed fascinated with President Lincoln and had a collection of biographies about the great man.

I figured that John admired Abraham Lincoln because of his fight for peace and his fight for equality for all. So for now I was satisfied. However I did find out more.

XOXOXOXOX

"Lennon and Lincoln"

I believe John Lennon and Abraham Lincoln are two of the most passionate men who ever walked this earth as far as their concerns for humanity and world peace.

There are far too many quotes from each of these two men, whom I consider to be genius, for me to list here. However these two quotes sum it up for me:

President Lincoln: "A house divided against itself cannot stand."

John Lennon: "War is over, if you want it."

In my opinion both quotes are the same. Peace is indeed achievable if we stand together and desire it.

XOXOXOXOX

"Trick or Treat"

This next adventure in the afterlife, happened in October of 2002. Right before Halloween, I went to visit Reverend Arlene to have another visit with our friends. After a very pleasant reading, as I was about to leave, Arlene asked me one final question. This was after our reading was over, so I do not have it on tape, but I promise it happened.

> Arlene: "Sherry, has John ever knocked on your bathroom door while you were sitting on the toilet and caught you by surprise?"

> Sherry: "No", I answered a bit embarrassed by this question. "Not in this lifetime for sure and I don't think he has in spirit either. I've wondered about that though, but I don't think so, at least that I know of!"

> Arlene: "Well, I know it is a strange question, but his nagging little voice in my head prompted me to ask you this question anyway. He really can be so persistent!"

At this point we both just giggled and shrugged it off. We hugged and said good-bye.

On October 31st, Halloween night of 2002 I got a little surprise as I was sitting on the toilet. I heard my husband, Randy, from the other room calling me to come out. It took me a few minutes to get to the front door. When I did he exclaimed to me "you're too late. You missed him!". "Who?" I asked. He then proceeded to tell me that a trickster had just left who was dressed as John Lennon! He was dressed wearing a long hair wig, round granny glasses, a Beatle type suit complete with a peace sign necklace! At that instant my mind went back to Reverend Arlene's toilet question. John Lennon had knocked on my door and caught me by surprise as I was sitting on the toilet. It had come true! Amazing!

By the time I had realized all of this the little trickster was gone, never to be seen again. Randy knew nothing of Arlene's message. Nobody knew except Arlene and me. Well, maybe one other person who has a very cheeky sense of humor even if he is on the other side of reality!

XOXOXOXOX

"Elias Howe"

Someone did honor Elias Howe for his wonderful invention of the sewing machine. John Lennon along with his friends, Paul McCartney, George Harrison and Ringo Starr.

XOXOXOXOX

Chapter 4

THE NEW YORK CITY DRAFT RIOTS

A T TIMES THE WAR WAS of little concern to the citizens of New York City. It was far away and except for the newspapers or the black ribbons that hung on the door handles, life continued as usual. Not much was said about the war in the south other then everyone wanted it over. Some people had even forgotten what the fighting was about. Nor did they care any longer.

Then suddenly the city erupted in chaos and the New York City draft riots started on Monday the 13th of July 1863.

The violence began in the slums of the Five Points area in lower Manhattan. On the first night, the sound of terrified horses pulling the fire brigades throughout the city could be heard. The fires could be seen glowing with an anger that could be felt and seen all over the city.

The next day gunfire could be heard along with the never ending crying of terrified sea gulls.

The anger was over the unfair draft system. For the sum of three hundred dollars the rich could avoid the draft. The poor had no choice and were thus drafted into a war that many did not support. Sunflower knew that soon the violence would spread. She also knew that soon the violence would affect the Negro citizens. The hate was coming. She felt frightened and knew her sons were in real danger.

On the third day of the riots the violence was all over Manhattan. There was nowhere to hide and no police force to protect the innocent. The police were in fact a part of the violence.

By the evening, Sunflower was hiding in a small room at the Leonard Street House along with John, James and Angel Alice. Sunflower felt they would be safe there because the men would not want to destroy a place that brought them relief from all their sorrows! However the thought that at any moment the building might be torched or looted was a horrifying reality. Many Negro boy's had been beaten or killed.

The only comfort was Angel Alice's voice in prayer. After she had spoken a prayer she would put a small amount of lavender scented powder into her palm and blow it into the air for protection. In her arms she held a small white terrified kitten whom the ladies had adopted as the house kitty.

The sound of breaking glass terrified James and John. John started to cry asking his mother "Mammy, why do men make war?" Sunflower looked into her son's terrified eyes and answered that she did not know the answer to his question. She then told him that in Heaven there is no war, "In Heaven, all you need is Love." John continued to cry. James held his brother's hand and told him "Don't be scared Johnny, we'll be all right." John looked in his mother's eyes and told her "I DON'T WANNA BE A SOLDIER, MAMA. I DON'T WANNA DIE."

My Tutorials

"Five Points"

I'm not sure why, but I have gotten more than a couple of messages from Spirit while I'm at the laundry mat! Maybe it's all the water filling up in the tubs as I've read that water is a conductor for spirit. Or maybe it just happens? Anyway it was while I was at this laundry mat that I spotted a gentleman outside who was busy throwing some bread crumbs to the many sea gulls flying like acrobats overhead. While he was doing this, he would whistle at the gulls.

He informed me he did this act of kindness every day. He also told me he found the gulls fascinating and was in awe of their intelligence. He then proceeded to walk out further into the parking lot and empty his bag of bread crumbs. It was fascinating to watch him communicate almost telepathically with the gulls.

I went back to my wash. I thought about the sea and the gulls. As I was thinking about the gulls, the movie "The Gangs of New York" came to mind as I have stated in a previous message. As stated, I had a huge desire to go and rent the movie to watch. This is what I did when I finished my laundry.

One scene in the "Gangs of New York" features the lead character, Amsterdam, walking along the side of the docks in the slum area of New York City that was referred to as 'Five Points'.

As I watched this movie, three things felt very familiar. First was the time period. Second were the New York City Draft Riot scenes. Third strangely enough, were sea gulls!

That night after watching the film my mind went back in- time and I remembered an adventure I had at the age of fourteen with my Beatle Buddy Bonnie.

Bonnie and I had met a couple of boys at a movie theatre during a Saturday matinee. We were fourteen. We met the boys in the balcony. That day I received my first real kiss from a boy, as did Bonnie. We of course fell immediately in love! After the movie was over I asked the boy (I think his name was Bob) where he lived. He told me he lived in Five Points.

A couple of days later, Bonnie and I rode our "English Raleigh three speed touring bicycles" the fifteen miles to the Five Point area in our city of Riverside. Yes, we did indeed have a Five Points. It was an older and slightly run down part of the city and it was quite frightening to us at the tender age of fourteen.

When we finally reached Five Points after riding our bikes for over an hour, I remember hearing, before we actually arrived, the cries of hundreds of sea gulls. The gulls were flying every direction, reminding Bonnie and I of the Alfred Hitchcock move "The Birds." The gulls were everywhere! Screaming and darting at us almost like they were soldiers on the attack!

Bonnie and I quickly gave up the idea of finding our balcony buddies and peddled our bicycles home like we were racers in the Tour De France. We never returned to Five Points again.

XOXOXOXOX

"Leo's Place and Leonard Street"

If I am to believe each of us have lived many lives and will continue on forever, then I am also led to believe that we will all from time to time channel former past life memories. Some of these memories turn into real life adventures in this reality.

When I discovered the name of the Madam whom Sunflower was employed when she moved to New York City, I also discovered the name of the street this bordello was located on, Leonard Street.

Which brings me to a song that Eric Burdon recorded called "Leo's Place." As I listened and then read the lines to this song, my thoughts returned to New York City in the nineteenth century and also to Julia Brown's bordello on Leonard Street.

"Leo's Place" tells a compelling tale of a young man who works at a pub just a few blocks from Piccadilly Street. Looking through his serving hatch he is able to view all forms of humanity on parade as they walk by. The young, the old, the straight, the rich the poor, all races.

There is more to this song, much more. It's a great song with a terrific message.

It all seemed to fit so perfectly. After I read the lyrics I thought to myself how these lines could have been the thoughts of a young man living at a bordello in NYC in the 1800's. How he would look through a window at Julia Brown's establishment and view all forms of humanity as they entered the front door. A young man by the name of James Wells.

XOXOXOXOX

"Judy"

Judy left us on our wedding anniversary which is October 26th. Judy was a beautiful white kitty with several black spots that looked like islands on her. One of these islands was shaped like a heart.

Judy lived for many years in our bedroom. She seemed content. Her world consisted of four walls, a bed, and a couple of dressers, her cat box and her meal dish.

Judy was quite happy right up to the night we lost her. In the middle of the night I heard her fall off the bed. I arose to find her wheezing for air. It is a sound I'll never forget. I awoke Randy and told him Judy needs help. He immediately went to her. He took her in his arms and held her. He kept telling her it was alright. That we loved her. Holding her tenderly as she took her last breath. I don't think I ever felt more love for my husband in my life then in this moment of compassion. In the darkened room, I saw her little limp body in Randy's arms.

Behind Randy was a tee shirt that hangs in the corner of our bedroom that features a photograph of John Lennon in NYC. It was almost as if John was a silent Angel watching over this sad and touching moment.

The next morning we wrapped Judy's body in her favorite smiley face blanket and took her to the vet's to have her body cremated. Neither Randy nor I could go to work. We were exhausted and fell asleep at 9:00 a.m. We awoke around noon and decided to go to lunch.

By the time we got to the diner it was around 2:00 in the afternoon. Odd time to eat so we were the only ones in the diner. Which was a relief because I looked like I had lost one of my best friends, and I had. There was a TV monitor across from where we were seated. The TV was tuned to ESPN and the show that was on was Sports Nation. The show had four experts who were commenting on football plays. I never watch these shows, as I'm not much of a football fan. One of the commentators had a John Lennon t-shirt on. It was the very same John in NYC tee we have hanging in the corner of our bedroom. It was surreal to suddenly see John's face appear on a sports network.

I felt so much comfort seeing him. I know this was John's way of coming through once again to let us know Judy is OK, and like our other precious pet kitties at Rainbow Bridge.

No coincidence. We had to be at that diner at that exact moment in time, the TV had to be tuned to that channel and of course there are many John Lennon t-shirt choices. This was perfect timing and it was also John's way of wishing Randy and me happy anniversary to help cheer us.

XOXOXOXOX

Olivia (age 12) reading "John Lennon: in their
own write" by my friend Judith Furedi

"Carol"

In 2005 a friend was diagnosed with stage four breast cancer. Her name is Carol and she will forever be the most

Courageous woman I have ever known.

Carol had cancer in one breast, however she decided to have a double mastectomy because the probability of her developing cancer in her other breast was very high.

I will never forget the morning of her operation. Carol was so upbeat and just ready to get it over with. Her optimism was unbelievable. When it came time to be wheeled into the operating room, the last memory I have of her is that of Carol giving me the thumbs up! The operation went well, although it took much longer than we expected.

Three days after the surgery I returned to the hospital to visit her and to give her a gift to hopefully cheer her up. On that morning before I drove to the hospital I heard "All You Need is Love", on the radio. Although I have heard this song countless times, on that morning the song was exactly the message I needed to hear. I printed out the lyrics of "All You Need Is Love" to give to Carol. It just felt right.

I had decided to give Carol gifts of lavender. I've always felt that the scent of lavender has healing qualities. So I picked out a candle, some skin lotion, bubble bath, along with other lavender items to give to her. Just as I was about to finish my purchase I spotted a small stuffed "Angel Bear" collection. I noticed there were about twelve of these bears in various pastel shades. I picked the lavender Angel Bear and put it in Carol's gift bag.

When I arrived at the hospital I noticed that the Angel Bear had a tag. This little tag informed the customer of all of the bears in this collection. Each Angel Bear had a name with a positive message. Names such as Love, Hope, Happiness, Charity etc… The lavender Angel Bears name was-----"Imagine"-------

I really do not have words to express how moved I was when I read the name of this Angel Bear. I know it was not just a coincidence. I know it was John's message to Carol and her loved ones of hope and comfort.

I gave Carol my gift and explained that it came from not only myself, but my Guardian Angel whose name is John Lennon. I did not hide his last name this time. No way!

It has now been over five years since Carol was diagnosed. I am happy to say that as of 2011, she is fine and doing very well.

XOXOXOXOX

"I Don't wanna be a Soldier, Mamma"

Along with the sea gulls and over all feeling of de-ja-vue I had while I watched the "Gangs of New York" was a very strong feeling of terror while I watched the scenes from the New York Draft riots. It felt very real to me.

I felt a mother's fear for her children.

Before I fell asleep that night I could hear in my head John's voice singing to me "I don't wanna be a soldier, Mama; I don't wanna die". This is of course from John's brilliant antiwar chant that was featured on his Imagine album recorded in 1971, the year of my son Franks birth.

Eric Burdon uses John's "I don't wanna be a soldier Mama, I don't wanna die", war chant in a song called "Red Cross Store", to perfection. It is very moving.

I felt this fear as I wrote about John and James who were in total fear as they heard the riots outside their home on Leonard Street.

"War is never the answer, love is."

XOXOXOXOX

Chapter 5

WAR IS OVER

A FTER THE DRAFT RIOTS, THE war became more than just what was read in the newspapers. Long gone were the days and nights in which people could be heard singing patriotic songs while taking a walk. No one felt much like singing anymore.

Each day that went by meant that James and John were getting closer to becoming eligible for the draft. Sunflower was in great fear for her sons. Not only that they would have to fight in the war, but also the racial anger could not be ignored. Hate was everywhere with no escape.

While taking a walk one day with John and James, Sunflower was angrily approached by a white man who spat at her sons, saying to them "damn you niggers, you're the reason for my son's death." It seemed everyone had forgotten the reasons for this horrible war. The abolishment of slavery really did not seem to matter to most people. It had gone on too long and the cost too high.

Then a sweet wind came in from the Heavens and war was over. It was April 9th, 1865 and a beautiful sunny day in New York City.

War was over! "Glory be to our President Lincoln." War is over! "Glory be to the Union and the United States of America." War is over! "Glory be to God."

Then, just as fast as war was over, a terrible injustice occurred.

On April 14th, 1865, just five days after the announcement that the war was over, the world lost President Abraham Lincoln to an assassins hand gun.

Tears streamed from Sunflower's eyes as she read the news to James and John. President Lincoln, a man who desperately wanted peace, who had just fought a long and terrible struggle to end the worst war in American history, was gone. The horrible irony was that President Lincoln was about to enter a wonderful time of life. Then his life was over. A man of about twenty six years of age was last seen jumping off the booth where the President and his wife were seated while at Ford's theatre. The man landed on the stage, shouting a line from a poem, as he ran away.

"This will be remembered for all eternity as one of the most heartbreaking days in history," Sunflower told her sons. Too sad to say anything more to her boys, her thoughts turned inward as she thought about Mrs. Lincoln. She thought about how Mary Lincoln had been witness to seeing her husband being shot point blank. Horrible. Then Sunflower thought about Mr. and Mrs. Lincoln's two sons. They would now have to live a life without their father. Unbelievable. It made no sense at all.

Sunflower held her sons a little closer that night. Angel Alice and Sunflower said a prayer not only for Mrs. Lincoln but for all humanity that sad April night in 1865.

The next few years were happy ones for Sunflower and her sons. Peace was finally a reality and it seemed that everyone was excited for the future.

James and John were getting more and more offers in the entertainment profession. The boys were very popular with their minstrel show that they performed at various cabarets in the city. Whenever the boys were not singing they were perfecting their skills as artists. Busy painting portraits in the newly opened Central Park.

It was during this time that John began to be interested in masonry. John loved to work with brick. At times Sunflower would notice John staring at a building for hours at a time. John would detect small details in the mason work, noticing how bricks were laid in ways that made the creases hardly visible.

He also liked to chase both his brother and his mother with his hands full of clay and mud.

Edward Clark was by now a very successful attorney and had many friends in the entertainment business. Sunflower and Edward would meet at least once a week to not only attend a show, but also to catch up on the goings on throughout the city. They had become very close friends. Edward Clark's wife, Caroline, could not attend shows, go for walks in the park or even visit a museum as she was quite fragile and would fall to ill health and influenza quite easily. It was for this reason that she was a prisoner of her home. Edward would take Sunflower's hand and hold it from time to time. When they parted company he always kissed her on her cheek. Sometimes he would hold her in his arms in a good-bye embrace. Nothing more.

The year was now 1867, and Sunflower had moved with her sons to a small flat in the area of known as Harlem. At the age of 48, Sunflower had retired from her chosen profession. She would visit the Leonard Street address from time to time to chat with her friends and of course Julia Brown.

Christmas time in New York City turned the city from various shades of gray and browns to a festive sea of red and green that was complimented by a covering of white snow.

Sunflower loved this time of year for many reasons. She loved hearing John and James sing Christmas Carols most of all.

It was during the holidays that Julia Brown called on Sunflower to ask her for a favor. She asked her if she would come out of retirement in order to entertain a very special client. Julia explained that her client was a world famous author from England, a man who had wrote an incredible Christmas story. "It is called A Christmas Carole," Julia informed Sunflower. "The Author's name is Charles Dickens."

Sunflower knew that Julia would only ask her to do this if this man were of great importance to her and to her reputation as New York City's leading madam. Sunflower replied "yes, of course I will give Mr. Dickens only the best of company and comfort I can offer."

The date was December 8th. Julia asked Sunflower to bring James and John with her to hear Mr. Dickens read from his new Christmas story. Julia also asked if Sunflower would ask her sons to sing a non-religious song for the occasion. She suggested a song from Mr. Dickens' homeland, England.

The Leonard Street address on this night was filled to over flow. Sunflower had chosen a gown of red with golden trim to wear for this auspicious evening. She wore her hair, which was black with a few stands of silver, up with a small golden comb to keep it in place. She looked absolutely radiant. James and John were now seventeen, becoming more men than boy's every day. They had chosen to wear their suits of gray wool, topped with fashionable derby hats. They each wore a red carnation in their lapels along with a matching red bow tie to complement their mother's attire.

The guests surrounded the small and very frail man as he read his story of Christmas Ghosts- past, present, and future. His manner and accent were very "British." Before beginning his reading he requested a cup of tea with a slice of lemon. He sat sipping at the tea all the while looking over his round glasses at each of the guests. His manner was most curious and for a few it was an uneasy moment. Sunflower flashed a smile towards Mr. Dickens. He felt like an old friend.

James and John sat next to Mr. Dickens in utter hypnotic fascination. Every guest that night knew they were in the presence of a genius.

The story of Ebenezer Scrooge was not only a story of redemption; it was also a story of great truths mixed with mysticism. As Mr. Dickens read some say that it was so quiet you could hear the snow falling in the background.

After the reading was finished, the guests were so enraptured that no one commented. There was only silence. Mr. Dickens himself spoke up and asked if someone would please comment! The guests in the room broke into applause and cheers.

When the cheering stopped Julia announced to Mr. Dickens that she would now like to present a little entertainment for him. "I would like to introduce two very special boys." She then motioned for James and John, who stood up on shaky legs and bowed to Mr. Dickens.

The song they had chosen to sing was "Good King Wenceslas." It was a new song they had learned and had chosen because they felt it represented Mr. Dickens homeland. They also liked it because it was about a kindly king.

James and John sang with angelic voices clear and pure. It was a perfect complement to the reading of a Christmas Carole." When the song was finished James and John led the guests into a very moving rendition of "Silent Night."

After James and John finished singing, it was Mr. Dickens turn to be amazed at perfection. He thanked the boy's for the wonderful moments of peace through music. James and John shook his hand and told him how glad they were that "Tiny Tim," was doing better. "Does he live near your home in England?" John asked. Mr. Dickens smiled and told them that "Tiny Tim is a boy who lives in many countries. Not only in my homeland but all over the world. When you see a crippled boy, remember to be kind and never cruel." "I promise, Mr. Dickens," James said. "Me too," followed John. "Sir," asked James "Do you believe spirits can and do indeed connect with us in our dreams?" Mr. Dickens smiled and replied, "That is up to you to decide. If my Christmas story brings anyone closer to the spirit of God and our Lord Jesus, then I did well." "You did well sir", James and John replied in unison.

After this, James and John left with Alice to return home and dream of Angels who come during the night. Sunflower escorted Mr. Dickens to a private room where he fell under her spell.

The next morning, Mr. Dickens met with James and John for breakfast. The three men talked for hours about many subjects.

Mr. Dickens was very passionate about the problems of the poor. He loved the working class heroes. He also was very interested in spirituality and felt a kinship of sorts with both James and John. Many philosophies were discussed that morning. Never to be forgotten.

Christmas time of 1867 was over and Mr. Charles Dickens went home to England after spending a few weeks in NYC. He was not to return to the U.S.A.

He never forgot James and John and often requested Good King Wenceslas be sung at the Christmas parties that he would attend. He also remembered, with a gleam in his eye, the mother of James and John who called herself "Sunflower." He smiled as he also remembered that the Sunflower is the flower of "Peace."

My Tutorials

"Transition"

As I was writing about the death of our beloved 16th President of the United States, I noticed that there were quite a few similarities between two very passionate men of peace. President Abraham Lincoln and John Winston Ono Lennon.

I have asked John, through Reverend Arlene, what his thoughts were about his assassin. The next is what I was told during a reading with Rev. Arlene:

"I do not dwell or think about it much. My advice to others is to do the same. Don't let the bullet stop in midair then bounce back the other way."

I think he was telling us, "Don't let it affect your life." or maybe he was referring to Rubber Soul. He can be very cheeky.

President Abraham Lincoln and John Lennon lost their lives at a time of transition. President Lincoln was on a pathway to peace and happiness for his family and his country. John Lennon was on a pathway of happiness and peace within not only himself, but his family. He was also on a pathway to recommitting himself to his second great love of his life, music.

I think John wants us to think positive and of only peaceful possibilities and then make it happen.

XOXOXOXOX

"Brick and Mortar"

Many years ago, before I began to put the puzzle pieces together of the life and times of Sunflower Sarah Wells, I received a gift from a friend I had met online. This friend had gone to Liverpool, England on vacation.

This friend was kind enough to send me a gift. When I opened the envelope from my friend, who lives in Spain, I was quite surprised at what he had sent me. In my hand I held three tiny bits of red brick. My friend, Dr. Rios, had sent me these chips of masonry from John Lennon's boyhood home "Mendips." At the time I thought it strange, but it now makes all the sense in the world to me.

I put these tiny pieces of red brick in a heart shaped pendant that I proudly wear all the time.

Thank you Dr. Rios

XOXOXOXOX

"Good King Wenceslas"

Tonight is Christmas Eve 2010. I have just been given a very lovely message from John Lennon that is so wonderful!

Every year about a week before Christmas, I listen to the annual Breakfast with the Beatles Christmas special with Chris Carter on our local radio station KLOS.

This annual Beatles Christmas show always features the Christmas messages the Beatles recorded for their fans. These seven zany messages are very funny and to be honest a little strange! I love em! The messages highlight the incredible humor of the loveable lads from Liverpool.

The very first message was recorded in 1963 and starts out with John Lennon singing a song that I never could figure out its name or what it was about. John starts blabbing about a king and Betty Gable. I gave up trying to figure it out many years ago and just figured it was John's wacky sense of humor.

Now before I get into the heart of this message, I need to explain one bit of information. When I learned that Julia Brown was the Madam of the New York Bordello that employed Sunflower, I tried my best to find out more about Ms. Brown. There is scant little on the internet about her. However one thing I did learn is that she claimed that Charles Dickens was a guest of hers at her Bordello in NYC. I thought this was very interesting but because I had no messages that Sunflower had indeed met Charles Dickens so I let it go. However before I fell asleep that night, I asked my Guides if at all possible I would like to be given a message about Charles Dickens and the holiday seasons of long ago in my dreams.

I did indeed receive a message in dreamland. Just not my land, the land of Charles Dickens.

Two nights later on December the 22nd, after a very busy day at the bicycle shop, I turned on the television hoping that a Christmas special might be scheduled. I was delighted to see that the "Christmas Carole," was airing. This particular telling of this revered story starred one of my favorite British actors Patrick Stewart.

I had been watching the movie for about ten minutes when the message I was hoping for came to me loud and clear.

In a scene from this movie several boys are shown singing Christmas Carols in their neighborhood. The boys walked from house to house while singing. In this scene the boys had just finished a Carole when they were given a few shillings from a kind neighbor. The next house was the house of Ebenezer Scrooge! One of the boy's say's to his friends "Forget it!" and they start to walk away. Another brave and determined lad walks over to the front door of Ebenezer's home and starts singing as loudly as he can.

It was at this instant I realized that I had just been given my Christmas Message. The melody of the song the boy is singing is the same mystery song John Lennon sings on that zany Beatles Christmas message. The one about Betty Grable. The song I could never figure out!

This was my message. John was telling me that he had met

the great author Charles Dickens in his former life, and it was at Christmas time.

The name of the song I could never figure out is "Good King Wenceslas."

This song was published in 1853 by John Mason Neal. It is a Carole written about a king who ruled in the country of Bohemia. Wow! My ancestors are from Bohemia! I am a Bo Honk!

Everything made perfect sense to me. Even when I thought about Julia asking John and James to sing a Christmas song that was from his homeland. Well, John and James did not fulfill her wish. The song was not from Mr. Dickens home land but from mine! Bohemia! Awesome!

I received all my requests for a Christmas message. If I am to believe I once was a lady by the name of Sunflower who lived in the 1800's in NYC, then I have to believe I did have a brief encounter with Charles Dickens of England and so did my sons, James and John.

Update

Tonight is December 8th 2011. It is thirty one years ago today that the world lost John Lennon. It is also almost a year since I received my wonderful message that confirmed my beliefs that James, John and Sunflower had met Charles Dickens. Today I received another wonderful confirmation.

My little sister Vicky has given me three antique coins. All three are dated from the nineteen century. For this message I will explain the meaning of the date on one of the coins.

It is a three cent nickel that is from the year of 1867. This is the year that Charles Dickens was in New York City for the Christmas holiday. I believe the exact date to be Dec. 8th, 1867.

I asked Vicky why she sent me a coin with the year of 1867. She told me she had no idea why! She told me that while she was searching for another year, the year of 1867 kept popping up. She said that she felt 'compelled' to buy a coin from that year for me.

I received this 1867 three cent coin on December 8th. I am 100% certain that Vicky had no idea the meaning of this date. Those one hundred and forty years ago her sister met Charles Dickens at a Christmas party. At this party he read aloud the incredible novel "A Christmas Carole".

Also thirty one years ago the world lost John Lennon on this night.

My little sister Vicky is an amazing woman. I love her very much and adore how open she is to my beliefs.

Happy Christmas everyone!

XOXOXOXOX

"Spill the Wine"

In 1970 a new song called "Spill the Wine" was performed and recorded by Eric Burdon and War.

I have heard Eric perform this great classic many times in concert. It is a crowd pleaser and it always brings out this question by fans "What is the meaning of Spill the Wine?"

I went to the internet and did a search. Asking—"What is the meaning of spill the wine? "The answer was not War's song "Spill the Wine", but Charles Dickens book, A Tale of Two Cities.

Charles Dickens published "A Tale of Two Cities", in 1859. As I have revealed, 1859, was a very pivotal year for Sunflower, and her sons James and John.

Her life was a tale of two cities, New Orleans then New York City.

The first sentence in the novel "A Tale of Two Cities", book one, Chapter five is entitled "The Wine Shop"......

—A large cask of wine had been dropped and broke in the street.—

Many people through the years have asked the same question about this Dickens's classic:

What is the meaning of the spilling of the wine?

Some scholars interpret the Dickens spilling of the wine as the spilling of blood (war) and the rise of the peasants.

After reading more about Charles Dickens I truly believe that John Lennon's life was very much influenced by the incredible genius and spirituality of Charles Dickens.

I also believe this of Eric Burdon.

All three men were always searching for answers. Looking for the truth, the meaning of life. Passionate for world peace. No more spilling of the wine.

We are the lucky ones as we get to reap the rewards of these incredibly talented men who were passionate about Peace and the human Spirit.

XOXOXOXOX

Chapter 6

A Perfect day in my Life

Saturday the 11th of May, 1868, was an absolutely beautiful day in the city of New York. Sunflower started the day with a walk to the Fifth Street Hotel with John and James.

She met Edward Clark near the Fifth Avenue address. Together the two of them discussed the latest news of the city as they walked together arm in arm. As they conversed a 'velocipede' lumbered by. Edward made a comment to Sunflower that he had recently read about an idea that someday it may be possible that the hobby horse may lead to a form of transportation in which people will be able to ride in a horseless carriage. Incredibly this ridiculous contraption may lead to a way of transportation that only dreamers can make a reality. "Really Edward, do tell", Sunflower said as she positioned her umbrella in a way to deflect more of the very warm spring sunshine. "There are some very intelligent men I know who believe someday we will be able to sit in a horse drawn coach without the help of our beasts of burden," Edward replied. Sunflower smiled and asked if perhaps this coach might be propelled like the hobby horse? That would be exhausting she giggled. "No. It will somehow be propelled by energy" Edward replied. At that instant a rather obtrusive word was heard from behind. Sunflower and Edward turned to see the fellow who was riding the hobby horse on the ground in a heap. Sunflower and Edward laughed at his misfortune. "This new form of transportation will never happen in our lifetimes", Sunflower said adding "at least I hope not. Maybe in theirs", she said with a nod towards John and James.

Her sons had taken the day off from their usual weekend of portrait sittings as they wanted to visit an art exhibit that day. The boys were fascinated with any art work that featured either maritime ships or marine life, which is what this particular art exhibit featured.

One piece in particular held the attention of James and John for some time. The boys had a wonderful imagination when it came to art. They would stand together and gaze at a painting until in their minds, it came to life. This painting featured an underwater scene that depicted an octopus gliding thru the water with various sea urchins, star fish and a variety of sea plants in the background. James and John stood giggling in front of the painting. John turned towards his mother and exclaimed, "Look Mammy, how the ocean tide moves the plants and how the octopus glides in the current amongst them. This is an octopus garden in the sea."

Sunflower smiled at John and thought to herself how wonderful it would be to have an imagination like her seventeen year old sons have. The boys were fascinated with any art work that featured either maritime ships or marine life, which is what this particular art exhibit featured. "What an incredible creature the octopus is. Look it has eight arms," James commented. John put his arms around his mother and looked down at her (James and John were now over six feet tall and towered over her) "If I were an octopus I would have eight arms to hold you, Mammy", John said and then kissed his mother tenderly on her cheek. Sunflower hugged her boys then watched them walk off together to look at another painting. Sunflower smiled a mother's smile to herself, thinking how her sons were becoming men right before her eyes.

Edward and Sunflower continued their walk together. They were to have lunch at the new Fifth Street Hotel. James and John trotted ahead of them. Edward took Sunflower's arm into his as they walked the tree lined sidewalks. When they were about to enter the lobby, Sunflower felt a rush of emotion which took her by surprise. She knew she could seduce any man. Every man wanted her it seemed, but this man was different. She longed to feel his body against hers. To kiss him as a lover, not as a friend.

Edward took out a small box from his pocket and placed it in Sunflower's hand. She opened the box to see a beautiful gold ring with a very large red gemstone in the center.

"I give this ring to you as a token of my love and admiration. I will never find another friend such as you in this life, or any that may follow. You are as beautiful as the flower you are named for" Edward whispered into Sunflower's ear, and then kissed her ever so lightly on her lips.

Sunflower put the ring on her left marriage finger. She looked at Edward who stood so tall and handsome that morning in his dark blue suit with a matching tall hat. She took his hand and looked into his eyes and said something to him that she had never said to another man. "I love you, Edward, and I want to marry you."

Edward was taken by surprise, but ever the gentleman, he handled the situation with honesty and compassion. "I love you too Sunflower. I also love James and John as my own flesh and blood. However I made a promise to God many years ago. I promised to love Caroline and honor her as my wife, till the day I die. I will keep that promise. However, I assure you, that if circumstances were different, my love, I would have married you years ago."

This could have been an uncomfortable moment for both Sunflower and Edward, but because of their friendship and love for each other, nothing more was needed to be said. The lunch was lovely. Again they walked arm in arm back to Sunflower's apartment.

When they reached her apartment Edward held her in his arms, then kissed her first on her forehead then her cheek, his voice low soft deep whispered, "May the Angels of the night protect you until we meet again my love". He stepped back and blew a kiss to her and then he was gone

Sunflower went to her bedroom and warmed a cloth to sponge off the day's dust. The warm cloth caressed her and felt good. She stood naked before the mirror of truth and examined herself with a critical eye. She was now forty eight years old, but the mirror projected an image of a much younger woman. Perhaps half her age.

She went to her dressing table and took out the pin that held her black and silver hair. Her hair tumbled to her waist. It was soft and still had a faint smell of lavender. She next applied the warmed scented oil she had received from Angel Alice, applying slowly, caressing her soft supple skin. She thought of Edward as she did this. Releasing the tension she felt. Again her thoughts turned back to Edward. She knew she could seduce him. Then they would join in a joyous union. She would no longer have lonely nights alone dreaming of him. She would awaken in the morning and he would be next to her.

Then she remembered what he had said to her earlier in the day. She knew how much he loved his own sons. She also knew in her heart, how much he loved his wife, Caroline. He loved her more than life. If she succeeded in her seduction, his family would be pulled apart.

The moonlight shown through her bedroom window. A beam rested on her finger and the red gemstone winked back at Sunflower. "I will never remove this ring," she whispered to her angels. That is when she realized that she must sacrifice her love for Edward, because she loved him too much to go any further then their friendship for each other.

She kissed the ring, and then put her hands together in prayer. She thanked God for all her blessings as she did each and every night before she fell asleep. In this nights prayer she finished by thanking God for bringing her friend, Edward Clark, into her life.

She then blew out the candle, and one of the most perfect days in her life came to an end. For James and John, their perfect day came right before their eighteen birthdays in August.

Over the years the women of the Leonard Street address would come and go. One lady, who was known as "Shoe'sy Sue," was a sassy Irish lady with long curly red hair, freckles, and a very large bosom. Shoe'sy Sue, loved to make' em laugh. Her motto was "If you don't have a good laugh and a good time, feel younger when you walk out then when you walked into my room, then I'll refund your money". She never refunded a dime.

Sue, along with her saucy humor, also had a rather unusual obsession with shoes. She had a closet full of shoes. However, without a doubt, her favorite type of shoe was the western boot. Not just any western boot. These boots were styled with rhinestones and other jewels. The boots also featured tassels and elaborate western scenes burned into the leather. She had boots of every color of the rainbow.

Rumor had it, that when you entered Sue's private room, she would greet her guest with nothing on except a pair of cowboy boots and a western hat that matched. Then she would smile and tell a joke.

Sue was twenty two years old when she came to work at the Leonard Street address. She only worked at this brothel for a year. It was during her employment at this residence that she met James and John Wells. She took a shining to the "shy and handsome" twin boys.

One night, after entertaining at the Leonard Street address, Sue invited John and James to her private room. "Welcome to cowboy Heaven," she said then closed the door.

Two innocent boys walked in, two very happy, men walked out. A perfect and happy day in the lives of John and James came to an end.

Two weeks later Sue left to be with her new man, a shoe company executive who lived in Chicago. James and John took Sue to Grand Central to catch her train to the windy city. With a good bye kiss and a joke, Sue said so-long to her very "Happy" friends. Giving them both a pair of her beloved cowboy boots with which to remember her.

James and John would never forget "Shoe'sy Sue".

Another day in the life of Sunflower which she would relive, if she could, happened the day when she met Neko.

For most of her life, Sunflower kept her spiritual views to herself. She did not attend any formal church services and if asked her religion she would simply answer "I believe in a loving God who does not condemn." She realized that her profession would be frowned upon by most and did not want to hear that she was bound for Hell because of it.

Every night before falling asleep, she would read a few verses from her King James Bible which was given her from her step mother. This Bible was her only gift given to Sunflower by her.

Sunflower would try her best to understand what she was reading. For all of her life she loved Jesus.

Another way that Sunflower gave thanks and connected with God was to take a walk at least once a week in Central Park. At the park she would take time to meditate and feel closer to the plant and park animals. Then she would take the time to just be thankful for all her blessings.

It was during one of these morning walks in the park that she met Neko. She was a very petite Asian woman who many people were afraid of because she was different. Many thinking her possessed by Satan because she talked to invisible spirits.

People referred to her as the "crazy cat lady." Sunflower always thought that this was cruel. Even though most the people calling her crazy, would seek her out to have their tea leaves, flowers, or palms read. Her specialty was numbers. Apparently the crazy lady was able to predict the future with some accuracy. She was also able to connect with departed loved ones. Because of this ability the little woman was able to provide for herself.

No one really knew where this woman lived. Some whispered that she was homeless. No one really seemed to care, as long as they could have a laugh at her and get their fortunes told.

On a sunny day in October, Sunflower saw this lady sitting alone under a huge elm tree. As Sunflower approached her, she could hear she was indeed talking to someone whom Sunflower could not see. This did not frighten her, not at all. Sunflower noted that she was perhaps ten years her junior. It was difficult to see her face, because she wore a veil and a large hat, however when Sunflower did get a glimpse she thought that she was quite pretty. Her complexion was flawless except for one small birthmark, which was on the side of her left eye. It was a small ruby colored birthmark that was shaped like a heart. She was surrounded by several cats, who seemed to protect this woman most people ignored.

The two ladies sat for almost an hour without one single word exchanged. Finally Sunflower asked her what her name was. "My name is Neko," she answered quietly. "I'm Sunflower." Nothing else was said that morning. This was the start of what was to be many morning visits.

On the next visit, Neko told Sunflower of her voyage to the "Imperial Palace" on the other side of this life force. How at an early age when she lived in Japan, she had become very ill and fell into a deep sleep. From that day forward she has been able to not only talk to those in Heaven, but she is also able to see them in the physical. She also understands the language of cat.

Together the little gypsy from the Orient and the call girl, Sunflower, shared the secrets of life both on this side of reality and on the other side too. In all the years the two ladies shared their beliefs. Sunflower saw no evidence that she was dependent on opium or any other drug.

Neko was fascinated by Sunflower's birth date being the same as her sons. She studied the number 23, and together she and Sunflower explored its meaning for her in this life and the next.

This beautiful quiet lady simply talked to cats, and Angels. Sunflower saw nothing wrong in this and often wondered why "people of other religions"—thought it wrong when they professed to praying themselves to God and other Saints? Who are after all unseen Spirits.

My Tutorials

"Eight arms to hold you"

I think we've all had days in our lives in which, if we could, we would return time and time again to relive. One of those days for me was the day Reverend Arlene held a special service to celebrate life and to honor our Creator. This service was held at her home, Nu Vu Oasis.

It was a sunny crisp February Sunday. I was outside her home when I spotted a large labyrinth of stones. I asked her what its meaning was. She told me "Sherry, just start at the beginning and keep going until you find the opening at the end. While you are doing this clear your mind and let anyone who would like to connect with you, do so."

I walked the labyrinth of stone and was surprised to find it more challenging than I thought it would be. It was an awesome experience, but I really did not hear anyone "Call my name," or so I thought.

I caught up with Reverend Arlene who was talking with a lady by the name of Sharron. They were deeply involved in a discussion about the meaning of 'Spiders' in American Indian folklore. These spiritual messages have been passed from generation to generation.

It was at this point that I blurted out (actually I rudely interrupted this very respectful conversation) with my thought. "Yeah, but don't forget, the spider has eight arms to hold you!" I have to admit, this was quite rude of John!

Thankfully, Arlene got it and knew it was John speaking thru me.

She giggled and said "Sherry, I think your walk thru the labyrinth did indeed connect you with a special friend!"

It was after I blurted this "eight arms," announcement that I found myself in an utter state of euphoria. I felt as happy as a kid at play. I felt wonderful! Alive!

I am sure that Reverend Arlene has never watched the movie "Help."

It is a known fact that the Beatles were going to call their second Technicolor move "Eight Arms to Hold You."

For some reason the boys changed the name to "Help."

John Lennon and Paul McCartney went on to write the title song for the movie. The rest as they say is Beatle history!

$$XOXOXOXOX$$

"The Ring"

I have received many messages from John Lennon in which the movie "Help" seems to be a focal point. The next message was once again at a reading with Reverend Arlene. It took me almost two years to realize what John was trying to tell me. I now know the ring message was meant to help me remember my love affair with Edward Clark.

Once again these next few lines are from a tape recorded session with Arlene dated two years before I began to write about Sunflower.

> Arlene: "There is something about a ring (she asks me this as she is rubbing her finger), my finger is itching. Did John wear a lot of rings?"

> Sherry: "No, I don't think he did. However Ringo did."

> Arlene: "John is now showing me a ring. It has a very large red gemstone. Did John have such a ring?"

Sherry: "I have no idea."

Arlene: "John is now telling me that this ring is a clue for you".

There was much more to this reading but this is where we ended "the ring" discussion.

Many years later I realized what the meaning of the ring was. This next line is from the Beatles second move "Help". This line is repeated several times during the movie. This is the line:

"He who wears the ring shall be sacrificed". The ring had a very large red gemstone in the center of it. The ring, once placed on the victim's finger, could not be taken off.

John was helping me to remember the sacrifice that Sunflower made by not pursuing Edward Clark. 'She who wore the ring sacrificed." This memory is now very real to me.

Authors note: I must refer back to my perfect day when Rev. Arlene was channeling her spirit guide Grandma Devereaux in message "Ladies in waiting." Grandma was very fixated with my ring. I did not realize it at the time but Grandma was also referring to the Gemstone ring wore by Sunflower giver her by her beloved Edward.

XOXOXOXOX

"My friend Sue loves shoes"

I do indeed have a friend whose name is Sue. I met Sue in 1998 at an Eric Burdon Concert. She is an amazing friend whom I've had many fun adventures with. Most of these adventures were at concerts where the two of us would clap, dance, sing and just have too much fun for ladies of our age. We cared not what anyone thought. When the music hit us, well let's just say "The girls can't help it!"

Sue is the only person to this date who has read all nine chapters of Sunflower's life story. I chose Sue to read my work because first of all she is open minded and second because I know she loves me!

After my friend Sue read chapter six she asked me if she, and another friend of ours, Kathleen, were the inspiration for Shoe'sy Sue… I told her perhaps, that I also believe Shoe'sy Sue was a real person who lived, loved and laughed in the city of New York in 1800's. She really did exist! Then Sue asked me, "Was I Shoe'sy Sue?" I told her that I am not sure. Hopefully someday I will know the answer.

This I can say with certainty. My girlfriend Sue does have a love for shoes! I received this next message just a day or two after I started writing about a gal who went by the name of Shoe'sy Sue.

This lovely message came to me right after I sent Sue the chapter about Shoe'sy Sue. I was cleaning out a box at work when I discovered the box I was about to throw out was not empty. I picked up the box and heard something inside of it when I shook it. I opened the box to find about fifty small square shaped rub -on tattoos inside the box. I have no idea where these stickers came from! The timing was, once Again, perfect!

One of the little rub on tattoos is a pair of disco shoes. This little sticker says "ITS FUN BEING A GIRL.' I gave one of these stickers to Sue a couple of days later when we met once again at a concert Eric Burdon was having. We danced the night away, my friend Sue and I in bliss, just like we were seventeen.

This is a perfect motto for Shoe'sy Sue's philosophy on life! She did love being a girl, and oh yes, she did indeed have fun!

There was another sticker I found that day. The sticker is of a beautiful butterfly. Perfect.

XOXOXOXOX

"The Imperial Palace"

As I was reflecting and meditating about Sunflower's friend Neko, I realized that when she told Sunflower she had been to the "Imperial Palace" she was telling Sunflower that she had a near death experience.

I too had a near death experience at the "Imperial Palace" except that my Imperial Palace was located in Las Vegas, Nevada.

In 1995, George Harrison, Ringo Starr and Paul McCartney presented us with a new and exciting production called "The Beatles Anthology."

The excitement for this production started at the end of summer with advertisements "Here come the Beatles," CBS presents!!! The Beatles!! Etc. etc. etc...The show was scheduled to be aired in November.

It was exciting and felt almost like it was 1964 and Beatle mania was happening all over again. At the age of 43, I felt like I was 12 again. Well almost.

As a way of celebrating this event, Randy and I decided to book a flight to Las Vegas and get a room at the Imperial Palace. This was where we could watch the telecast in style and comfort.

We arrived in the bright light city around noon. Problem was we had about eight hours to party before the big event. So we did what we love to do. We found a cozy corner at the Sand's casino and started to play video poker. We were having some luck and having a whole lot of fun. Yippee! We were also getting complimentary Crown Royal and Coke cocktails. One after another. Yippee! We also forgot that we had not eaten anything that morning, nor afternoon for that matter.

Around six thirty p.m. I began to feel, well weird. To say that I felt drunk is not exactly the right adjective. I felt, strange, out of touch with my body is the best description. Anyway I excused myself from my poker machine and went to the ladies room.

Now I am not proud to say this, but I know how it feels when you've had way too much alcohol. I've been there and I'm sure many of you have too. That horrible dizzy feeling, then of course you get sick. This time was different.

I went into the stall and looked at the toilet, thinking that I probably will get sick. How stupid I thought to myself. I really did not feel nauseated though. I stood looking at the water in the toilet, and then I flushed it. Round and round the water went. Then nothing. Lights out! Next thing I heard the door open behind me and looked up to see a paramedic. This young man asked me if I was alright. First thing I thought was "How the heck did he get into my stall," plus, what the heck am I doing on the floor?"

I was next brought out of the stall and stood looking at the five or so paramedics who were asking me questions. My name, age, where are you, etc.? Which to the best of my memory I answered correctly. After about fifteen minutes a wheel chair was brought in and I was wheeled out to the casino floor. First person I saw was Randy, who had a strange shocked look on his face. Was I really this inebriated? I sure did not feel like I was.

I was wheeled out the casino by a big angry looking guard who acted like he just wanted me out of there. Can't really blame them. Not really good for business. I sat in the chair, still not really fully comprehending what the heck had happened.

We were wheeled out the door and onto Las Vegas Blvd. All the way I kept asking "What is going on, what happened?" I know everyone just wanted to answer "You're drunk", but no one said anything.

I got to the property line where I assume the Sands ended and the Imperial Palace began. So the big angry guard passed me to his twin, who worked at the Imperial Palace, to continue my ride. Into the hotel I was wheeled, next into the elevator, then into our room. I'm sure everyone was glad to see me gone.

When I got to my room things started happening fast. I cannot say that the room started to spin. It did not. Nor did I feel sick. I lay on the bed and the best description I can give is this, I had a strange feeling of "shutting down." I was not struggling. I was very relaxed. I knew I was about to leave my body. It felt very familiar.

I could hear Randy's frantic voice telling me to wake up. He was asking God for help. Asking me to come back. I cannot reveal all that I heard him say, but I will say that at this moment I really knew just how much he loved me. As for me, I was just curious. Once again, like I was, when I was seventeen.

The feeling was amazing. Very light. A floating feeling. I loved it—it was not scary at all, like my first experience.

Randy kept pleading for me to come back "Don't leave me, "I heard him say. I felt his love pull me back into this reality. There was also another voice I could hear.

Just as I was about to look back onto the bed to see myself, I heard a very familiar voice who spoke with a very familiar "Liverpudlian" accent. All this voice said was, "Not Now. Go back" With that I was back." No more floating feeling.

I sat up on the bed, grabbed the remote and turned the volume up. The Beatles Anthology was about to begin! Randy sat next to me with a very shocked expression. I next asked him "Let's get room service, I'm starving." I grabbed the phone and ordered some food. I turned to ask Randy what he wanted and noticed my dear sweet man had passed out on the bed!

I watched the Anthology from start to finish alone. I ate the delicious room service food. After the Anthology was over I thought about the whole experience and how refreshed I felt. No ill effects at all.

I do believe I overdosed on alcohol that night and just like the time before, when I was seventeen I heard John's voice bring me back to reality. Only this time he was speaking not singing.

Just like the time before I learned a very valuable lesson. I have never drunk this much since nor will I ever again. The experience I had that night was not at all fearful like the one I had at the age of seventeen. However, I was not ready to leave Las Vegas forever!

Because of this experience I do not fear the moment of death. I do not believe it will be painful. Just the opposite.

I have often thought about people who have these near death experiences and come back to say it was pleasant. I've often thought, well if it's so pleasant, then what is keeping you here in this existence? For me it is this reason.

I believe we are here for a purpose. This purpose is to learn, to love, to enjoy not only the good but the bad things in life. We are also here to learn from others. Even when horrible atrocities occur, something good will come. This is the only way I can understand tragedy. For some souls, their sacrifice teaches and guides the rest of us.

"Why?" I've come to the conclusion that "It's just the way it is and always will be." We really don't need to know any more than this. As for me…I thank our Creator each night for this gift we call life. In this existence and in the next.

XOXOXOXOX

Chapter 7

A WALK IN HEAVEN WITH A FRIEND

I N THE YEAR OF 1868, the lives of Sunflower, James and John were about to be changed forever. One woman was responsible for setting in motion these life changes.

Her name was Marianne Le Soleil Levant. She was born in the French Quarter of New Orleans in the year of 1838.

Her father worked in the hotel industry. He was fluid both in

English and French. He worked as a concierge at various hotels in the city. He was able to earn a decent living and provide for his large and growing family.

Marianne's mother never worked outside her home. She was responsible for the care of six children. Marianne was the eldest. She helped her mother with many tasks at home. Although she helped her mother day and night she never felt as though her mother had a life of her own. Even as a child she vowed to herself that she would not live a life like her mother. She would rather remain a single woman than a married woman who lived only for her husband and children.

Every chance she got, young Marianne would work alongside

her father at the hotel, as she did she learned many valuable lessons from him. She soon learned the English language and quickly made herself invaluable to the French speaking patrons at the hotel.

Marianne was amazed at how her father was able to assist his wealthy clients and keep them happy when they were angry at some indiscretion. She learned the value of customer relationships and how to woo and keep the customer happy.

With her pretty brunette hair, large brown eyes, high cheek bones and fine porcelain skin she never had a problem finding friendly men to assist her. When she grew from a young girl to an adolescent, she began to find men more 'interesting'. However, she was not really in need of a boyfriend like most of her girlfriends were. She did like the attention she received and realized quickly that she could lead both men and women in just about any direction she chose to.

She loved to toy with people's opinions. By flirting around with them, she could quickly mold just about anyone, man or woman. Soon people she hardly knew would come to her for her advice. If there were a disagreement, she would use her biting tongue and the disagreement would be over, in her favor. She liked this ability.

One day she met a woman who was to set in motion her course in life. Marianne had long ago sat in the various lobbies of the hotels her father worked at and watched the whores of the area try to attract customers. Most of the girls, although pretty, were very unkempt in appearance.

One night a particularly pretty woman caught Marianne's attention. This young lady wore an ill-fitting dirty dress with holes in it. Marianne noted that she also had way too much blush on and a horrid perfume that could only attract the most desperate of men.

Marianne watched this young lady escort her client out of the hotel lobby. She then followed the couple. Just as other ladies would do, this young woman led her date to a dank and darkened street. She watched as the young lady closed the door to a small shanty. Fifteen minutes later the man walked out the door and into obscurity.

The girl finally emerged and started to walk back to the hotel.

Marianne noticed that the girl now had a bruised and broken lip. Her blush was smeared, her hair in tangles her dress torn.

Marianne followed the girl back to the hotel lobby where she noticed the girl was now leaning up against the wall. She was in distress. Her eyes were red as the blood trickled down her lip.

Marianne did not know why, but she knew that she wanted to help this girl. She felt as though in doing this she would also be helping herself. She took the young girl by the arm and escorted her to her room that her father had reserved for his daughter to use when she wanted some privacy.

In this room Marianne and the girl talked for hours. The girl was only seventeen. She had been a working girl for only a year. Marianne noted that this year had made her look much older than her actual age of seventeen.

Marianne requested a bath for the girl. The girl cleaned up nicely. After several more hours of discussion, Marianne came up with an idea.

"Use this room to conduct your business, it is mine to use as I choose," Marianne explained to the young girl. Then she eyed the young woman and realized they were about the same size and weight. "Here you can wear one of my dresses," Marianne said handing the girl a pretty party dress. "Now brush your hair and arrange it in a pretty style. Your hair is beautiful, use it. Do not put on too much blush. Just enough to brighten your face. No more no less. Never use that horrid perfume. Instead keep yourself clean. Bathe every day and let your natural aroma attract men."

"How can I repay you?" asked the girl. At first Marianne thought it not right to ask for payment, then her business sense kicked in and she told the girl "You owe me one half of your payment when your business transaction is concluded." Marianne then asked the girl how much she would receive. The girl proudly replied "I try to get a dollar. Usually it is two bits." "That's horrid," replied Marianne. "From now on, you will accept no less than ten dollars. If the man will not accept, then decline. Keep your dignity. Make them want your more." The girl laughed at this and said that she will have no customers. "You will, and if you don't, then I will pay you at the day's end five dollars. How- ever, I demand honesty or we will not be business partners." The girl accepted. She had many ten dollar dates; many times it exceeded that amount.

This arrangement continued for some time. Marianne's father had no idea that his sweet and innocent 18 year old daughter was using the room he had procured her for this very corrupt reason. Marianne was very clever. She soon had four girls working for her and every kept her secret. The maids knew what was going on, but they were easy to bribe. Besides, everyone was frightened of Marianne and did not want to tell on her.

It was about a year later that Marianne decided to rent her own apartment. A swanky apartment in the French Quarter. It had four bedrooms which were each decorated by Marianne. She soon became, at the age of twenty, known by the name of "Madam Marianne."

The girls were required to be discreet, loyal, charming and most of all; their hygiene would be checked and rechecked. If any girl were found to be unclean, she would be asked to leave.

The war years, although hard, were actually a boom time for the young Madam and her business. The young and the older confederate soldiers made the young madam a very rich woman.

Madam Marianne soon needed a larger establishment and in 1862 she found a beautiful French Style building on Esplanade Avenue that was to her liking.

She named her new residence "The Rising Sun." She chose this name because of her last name, Le Soleil, which translates from French to English to "The Sun." Marianne was very pleased.

The House of the Rising Sun soon became the busiest and respected brothel in the city of New Orleans from the year of 1863 until it was closed in the year of 1872.

In the winter of 1868 Marianne was invited by Julia Brown to attend a gala New Year's Eve party at the Leonard Street brothel. Julia was looking to sell her establishment and Marianne Le Soleil Levant had expresses some interest through mail correspondence. Marianne reasoned to herself that she could conduct business and have a holiday. All paid by Julia Brown. So she accepted her invite.

Marianne took only one person with her to New York City. Her hand maiden, "Alvina."

On her arrival at Grand Central station she was met by several prominent citizens. "Welcome to our fair city and to the golden Age," Julia said as she took Marianne's hand into hers.

It was the first week of December and the city was dressed once again in white with green and red bows.

Marianne shopped at the best of stores and dined with style at Manhattans finest. She was indeed the toast of the town, enjoying each moment to the fullest.

One of her first stops was at the Leonard Street Address of Julia Browns establishment. Marianne admired the décor. She met the ladies of the house with the eye of a race horse owner, thinking to herself of each lady's assets and of each lady's flaws. She would do a lot of rearranging. These women did not have near the allure of her southern belles. Marianne also knew the minute she walked into the Leonard Street brothel that she was not interested in becoming the new owner. This was not her city and not her people. She would "Miss New Orleans" horribly along with her "Rising Sun" establishment.

However, she would play the game as long as possible. What lady would not like the attention she was getting, she reasoned with herself.

One of the first ladies Madam Marianne met at the Leonard street address was Sunflower. Marianne did what she always did when meeting someone for the first time, she critiqued them, her critical eye once again appraising her for her worth or lack of it. She had heard from several people the legacy of Sunflower. How she managed a large and very influential clientele for many years. How she was able to do this with no sex. Marianne thought to herself that this was impossible. Just a myth.

However upon meeting Sunflower she changed her opinion. Marianne's first impression of Sunflower was that she could have been either Alvina's sister or her mother. Both women had a special quality about them. Most people could not guess their ethnic heritage. Sunflower and Alvina had features that represented many races. At times they could look African, then at other times Italian, Caucasian, American Indian, Asian, and sometimes they had the features that made them appear to be mid-eastern. It was almost like Sunflower and Alvina had no race. As if they had ancestors from all over in the world.

From a distance Marianne would have thought that Sunflower was a prominent wife of some city father. A "society" middle aged woman of some means. Sunflower's beauty was a beauty most women of her age had long since lost. Her smile caught Marianne by surprise.

"Hello, Madam Marianne, my friends call me Sunflower. Welcome to our home and welcome to New York City," Sunflower said as she held out her hand in friendship. Marianne put her hand in Sunflowers and kissed her three times on her cheeks. The two ladies exchanged small talk for a few minutes, each of them thinking of how they had just met their equal. Both women were very determined and had learned how to play the game of life very well.

John and James were also at the Leonard Street house that day. James never talked to or hardly noticed Madam Marianne. His eyes only saw Alvina. His breath was taken away. Alvina was the most beautiful girl he had ever met. She was a natural beauty. Not a single brush of blush was needed. She was innocent and perfect. Alvina was charmed by the sweetness of the shy James. The rest of the day the two young people sat in the corner talking for hours. If there was or is a possibility of "love at first sight," then this was a classic meeting.

On this same day Julia asked James and John if they could be hired for the entertainment festivities for New Year's Eve. James and John asked their mother who agreed to the employment opportunity.

Almost every day for the next two weeks James would find a way to meet Alvina at a secret place.

They fell deeply in love with each other.

On New Year's Eve of 1868, the snow fall was deep and heavy.

Inside the bordello on Leonard Street on that New Year's Eve of 1868-69 the atmosphere was warm and festive. Marianne charmed the party with her wit and her sassy French accent... She was the belle of the ball.

Sunflower was very proud of James and John as they sang holiday Carole's once again to perfection. It was a perfect way to bring in the New Year of 1869. When the New Year was ringed in she was the second woman James kissed. The first was his love Alvina. Sunflower knew at that instant that James had found his love of this lifetime and she was very happy for him.

New Year's Day arrived. Marianne and Alvina had their bags packed for their return to New Orleans. They were scheduled to return that day via train. James and Sunflower met the two ladies at Grand Central. This was not a happy day for James and Alvina.

"It seems my James is in love with Alvina," Sunflower smiled as she greeted Marianne. "I suppose I will see her again in the arms of my son. I do hope that you can find a suitable replacement for her. She is a sweet and charming girl indeed," Sunflower commented to Marianne.

At that point Marianne turned to face Sunflower. Her face was contorted in rage. Her French accent was suddenly not quite so cute, nor sexy, it was very matter of fact and angry. "Alvina will not be returning to New York City. I have plans for her and they do not include James. However, I can see that I must play the game, as Alvina is in "puppy love" with your son. I will send James a ticket to New Orleans along with a promise of some meaning less job in a few weeks."

Sunflower felt her knees buckle. She found it hard to find her voice. "Madam Marianne I do not understand," she pleaded.

"Don't be so naïve. I have groomed and prepared Alvina to work at the Rising Sun. She will make a small fortune, not only for me and the Rising Sun, but for herself. Alvina will be the most desired woman in New Orleans." Marianne then pinched Sunflower's chin, "She will replace your legend, Miss? Oh dear I've forgotten your name. Oh that's right, it starts with an 'S', I remember now, Sunflower, that's your name," she said with an evil laugh. "I will send your precious James back to your arms before the next New Year's day. He'll come back to you I promise with a broken spirit and a broken heart. Which I'm sure you'll be able to mend. After all that's what mothers do best, is it not?"

"How can you be so heartless?" Sunflower asked.

This time Marianne looked Sunflower square in the eye and almost spit her reply, "You of all women should know the answer. How can you be so stupid? Men are a necessary nuisance. Your James is no more and less a man and a nuisance to me and my Plans." With that, Madam Marianne said "Adieu" and turned her back to enter the train, home for New Orleans.

Sunflower could not find her voice. She had no reply. She knew in her heart that this was a war she could not win. Gold would be the victor and love would be the loser.

Sunflower watched as Alvina and James held each other for one last long embrace. Tears were flowing from each other's eyes.

Alvina rolled down the train window to say one last good- bye to James. In a clear and determined voice James shouted to his love "I WILL BE WITH YOU AGAIN."

The train pulled out and slowly rolled away. Sunflower watched as it disappeared into the angry blood red New York sky. Then she saw James running after the train. He fell, cutting his lip. His blood and tears were left on the tracks. James was overcome and collapsed into his mother's arms.

On the morning of February 9th, 1869, James found his mother quietly reading a book in the parlor of their tiny apartment. The book she was reading was the new novel by Charles Dickens entitled "A Tale of Two Cities."

James informed his mother that he was leaving the next day for New Orleans. He was going to ask Alvina to marry him.

James also informed his mother that Madam Marianne had graciously offered him a job helping with security at the Rising Sun. Sunflower's heart ached for James when she heard this. How could she explain to James that the plan was in motion for his destiny? This destiny would break his heart and his spirit. Sunflower knew very well how determined a woman of power can be, for she only had to look inside and see her own dark side. Money, power, and fame can be a powerful motivator.

Sunflower told James she would not give him her blessing. Telling her son that she feared for him because New Orleans was still a very racially divided city and he would be in danger. "Don't be ridiculous, Mammy," James replied, and then added that President Lincoln made the south a safe place to live for all people, colored and white. Besides I am a man now. "It's my life and I'll do what I want to do!"

Sunflower then pleaded with James, "What about your brother? Have you given any thought as to what this will do to him? James was now very angry, his voice boomed as he furiously shouted at his mother, "I am not my brother's keeper! Don't let me be misunderstood, I love Johnny very much! However he will be fine without me. We are not your little boys anymore." At that he slammed the door as he left.

Sunflower was very hurt and angry too. Her emotions took her to a sad and helpless state of mind. Painful tears flowed. She walked over to the table where her book laid. Looking down at the title, she remembered Mr. Dickens. Then she noted the title of the novel, "A Tale of Two Cities," appropriate. New Orleans where she was born of pain, sorrow and then victory, New York, the city she adopted as her and her son's new home. A tale of two cities. Now it seemed New Orleans was calling her son home. A new and dangerous home.

She ached when she recalled Madam Marianne's words. She was also very upset that James would not be able to love and adore his Alvina. That Marianne would make that impossible. All she could do it seemed was cry.

It was then that John walked into the parlor to see his mother in pain. "Mammy are you all right?" he asked. Sunflower quickly wiped away her tears. She knew she was going to have to tell John about James and his plans to leave the next morning. She also knew she needed some time to approach John with this revelation in just the right way. It was going to devastate him and change his life.

"John, let's go to the Fifth Street Hotel and have dinner tonight, just you and I," Sunflower said with teary eyes, her voice shaky. "We can ride the elevator once again to the top floor and enjoy the view of the city. It should be lovely tonight with the new snow covering."

Sunflower kissed John and then imagined that perhaps she would wake up and this would all be a bad dream.

Sunflower loved the Fifth Street Hotel, for many reasons. This grand hotel was inaugurated on her, James and John's birthday August 23rd. The year was the same year, -1859- that she had first heard the song "Dixieland." This song had meant so much to not only her, but to her sons.

1859 was also the year she had met Edward Clark, the love of her life.

Sunflower dressed in her prettiest dress which was sky blue with yellow and white trim. As she glanced at herself in the mirror her thoughts went to a sunny day with white clouds and a large yellow sun. She chose this dress because it was a dress to wear to a party. She did not want to look at all solemn. She knew that she would have to tell John some devastating news and wanted to look her best.

John and Sunflower walked hand in hand to the Fifth Street hotel. Before the pair entered the lobby, John stopped across the street to admire the masonry. The bricks were crystal white and were gleaming in the early evening moonlight. John told his mother all he knew about this particular masonry.

When the pair entered the lobby, Sunflower spotted the new elevator to the top floor of the Fifth Street Hotel rooftop. "Let's take a ride on the lift," Sunflower said to John "it's almost sunset and it will be so beautiful right now." John agreed and together they walked to the cab.

Inside the elevator cab were four paintings of various areas of Central Park. The doors of the elevator were of dark stained oak, beautifully ornate in their carvings. On the ceiling was a glass chandelier light. Attached to this chandelier were eight covered candles, soothing to the eyes. A very light scent of lavender was in the air.

The elevator operator bowed to the twosome as Sunflower and John entered the cab for the smooth ride to the top floor and the city lookout area.

John and Sunflower stood together gazing at the city they both loved very much on this very cool February evening. Sunflower sighed as she gazed upon the city. "Do you remember the last time we stood in this spot John?" John thought for a moment then answered, "Yes, I do Mammy. It was when I was nine years old and James was with us too". Sunflower continued, "It was the grand opening of the hotel, August 23rd, 1859. It was your ninth birthday and my thirty-ninth. I remember that was the night that the sky was painted with lights of blue, purple, yellow and white. The lights swayed with the wind." "The night that we thought Jesus was coming home", John reflected. "It was a night like no other," Sunflower replied.

On this February night the snow glistened on the rooftops as the moon stood witness. The stars filled the blackened sky like pearls. "Simply beautiful", sighed Sunflower. "Yes, you are my Mammy," John whispered into his mother's ear.

Sunflower knew the time was right to tell John about James and his plans. She knew how difficult it was going to be for him. Since birth, James and John did everything together. The boys performed, laughed, sang, lived and played as one. On every Sunday the twin boys would be sitting in front of their easels, singing tunes in Central Park. By now they had a large following and were loved by many.

Sunflower took a deep breath and took John's hand in hers. "John, your brother is leaving tomorrow morning to live in New Orleans. He wants to marry Alvina," Sunflower heard her voice break when she heard her words that were going to pull John's world apart. John bowed his head and took a deep breath of his own. "I want to go home now, Mammy, I want to talk to James." "Of course," Sunflower answered

John and Sunflower waited for the door of the elevator to open to take them, along with several other guests, back to the lobby. When the door of the elevator closed, Sunflower felt the floor drop out beneath her. She felt she was falling at great speed. Her first thoughts were that the elevator was overloaded and was plunging down the shaft. Then, the fall slowed to a gentle drop. Slowly it stopped falling.

Sunflower opened her eyes and saw the chandelier on the ceiling above her. The light from the chandelier candles were now a very bright white. Glowing brighter by the second. The chord that held the chandelier in place seemed as though it were a lifeline. The lights from the candles began to grow in length.

Soon the lights began to resemble the arms of an octopus. A memory flashed before her eyes of Edward and herself at the art exhibit were she told him that she loved him and wanted to marry him. She remembered John telling her how the painting looked like an Octopus Garden.

The Octopus, now with its eight glowing arms embraced her, shimmering and shining arms of light glowing like diamonds.

It was then that she looked to see John below her kneeling. She could see that he was crying uncontrollably. "Who is John holding in his arms?" Sunflower asked herself. Then Sunflower could see it was herself. Then Sunflower knew that her heart had ceased to beat and that she was no longer in the physical.

She felt herself being pulled toward another bright light. She felt and saw the presence of white everywhere as she looked to the Heavens, white light, white stars, white moon, snow, and thousands of white feathers falling everywhere around her.

"Simply beautiful," Sunflower whispered into her son's ear, as she left for Eternity where she saw a familiar face beckoning her towards him. A person she had somehow known but could not figure how or when they had met. She just always knew. President Abraham Lincoln smiled at Sunflower as she stepped into her new reality. "I have something to show you lovely Sunflower Sarah Anne", Mr. Lincoln said as he took her hand in his.

Sunflower turned to see a much younger Abraham Lincoln than when she first saw him standing before her. She felt the course fabric she was wearing. A tattered dress with a single tie holding it in place. Her feet were bare. She was once again eleven plus years old.

Mr. Lincoln put his hand on Sunflower's shoulder, then on her forehead. He took her back to the year of 1831 and a beautiful April morning.

"Sarah, when I was twenty two years of age I made a voyage to the city of New Orleans with some friends of mine. Look Miss Sarah do you recognize this hotel, this room, and this stage? She could now see New Orleans, the hotel, the room and the stage.

She could also see a very young and very frightened girl. Sunflower had long forgotten this morning, the morning of the slave auction, but now with the help of Mr. Lincoln, the memory was now like it happened yesterday. "I remember Mr. Lincoln," Sunflower said in a soft voice. Mr. Lincoln took Sunflower's hand once again "On that stage stood the bravest girl I've ever known. You, Miss Sunflower Sarah stood on that stage, eye to eye with the monsters and took them on. This was the bravest thing I've ever seen with these two eyes of mine.

"With all the atrocities you had witnessed, you were able to do this at the age of eleven plus. It was after this, Miss Sarah, that I made a vow to my friends that if I ever have the chance, I will put an end to this evil and peculiar practice we call slavery. I could watch no more. I walked away and prayed that this brave girl will somehow find compassion. My heart ached for you."

Mr. Lincoln now had tears in his eyes. "Because of this memory of you and your bravery, many times I was able to go on during the hardest moments of the war. When things were at their worst, and fear clung to me like a cloak, I would go back in time and remember you on that stage. How brave this young girl who, was not quite a woman, was. Then I would remember why this war was just. You, Miss Sunflower Sarah helped to change humanity for the better. Thank you Miss Sunflower Sarah".

Once again the fabric of her life changed along with the dress she was wearing. Long ago lost, but not forgotten, was the beautiful dress of black satin with blue and white trim. Her blue butterfly fan a perfect complement. Her hat adorned with a single white feather which was tilted ever so slightly to the side. She was once again at her prime ready to attend the speech of Abraham Lincoln at Cooper's Union in the year of 1860 on a very crisp and sunny February 27th.

Sunflower could only think of four words to say:

"Thank you, Mr. President"

On the evening of February 9th, 1869, President Abraham Lincoln and Sunflower Sarah Anne Wells were greeted by a small woman of African heritage. Her smile was the smile of an angel in human form. "Hello, Sarah. I am your mother. My name is Daisy," she sang the words which were not quite as angelic sounding, but who cared!

Together Abraham, Daisy and Sunflower walked towards the White light, love and eternity and "YES" there were many white feathers.

My Tutorials

"The House of the Rising Sun"

The author of the American folk ballad, "House of the Rising Sun," is unknown. There have been many versions of this song including a version by Jody Miller, Dolly Parton, and the punk band Frigid Pink.

The best known version is, without any doubt, at least by me, the Animals version which was recorded in 1964. The song reached number one on the American charts on September 11th, 1964.

I have heard Eric Burdon perform this masterpiece many times live at his shows. The song is a tapestry of sound that encompasses rock, blues and spirituality into one incredible experience in music. To this day, I hear it with a new ear each and every time Eric performs it.

Eric once said, in an interview, that sometimes when he is performing, something truly magical and mystical happens. He tells of a space between the artist and the audience. It is a special connection he feels that helps him keep performing all these many years. I have felt this connection and it is very special.

The House of the Rising Sun in the city of New Orleans was a magical, mystical house indeed.

A few years ago I received a flyer, from my friend Sue that was an advertisement for a future show in our area starring Eric Burdon and the New Animals.

Somehow I think Johnny Lennon was behind this once again. This flyer had a typo. Eric and the New Animals would perform the hit song: 'House of the rising SON."

Rising son, very funny John. Perfect timing.

Was there a brothel in New Orleans that was called "The Rising Sun?" Many opinions, but no one really seems to know. The Rising Sun may or may not have been a brothel according to historians. Some say it was a gambling hall. Some say it may have been a convent. Perhaps the Rising Sun was a metaphor for either slave pins or for the plantation itself.

According to Wikipedia, one theory is that it was indeed a brothel at 1614 Esplanade Avenue in the French Quarter of New Orleans. Doing business from 1862 until 1874. The Madam was Marianne LeSoleil Levant, whose name does translate from French to English as Rising Sun. Not much more is known about her or the House.

In June of 1999, my husband and I traveled across the USA to New Orleans, Louisiana, to attend a concert by our favorite band "The New Animals" starring Eric Burdon.

The concert was to be held at the House of Blues. Once again it was a fabulous show.

The venue was standing room only. When the band and Eric broke into House of the Rising Sun the loud audience went silent as it was performed. When the song finished, the applause was ear shattering.

The next day, Randy and I decided to try to find the location of the Rising Sun brothel. So who better to ask then a taxi driver? We asked the driver who confirmed to us that it seems no one really knows for sure, but that he had been told that it may have been on St. James Street.

It was a rainy and foggy morning. The drive through the streets of New Orleans brought forth mystery and de ja vue for me. The narrow streets felt so familiar.

We finally arrived at where the taxi driver had been told was the area where the House of the Rising Sun may have been. We pulled in front of a large black iron fence that stood guard in front of a white wall. I could not see a house but I could see that the wall stood in front of a large rooftop. I really could not see much, but again it felt familiar.

After we had our little adventure we asked the taxi driver to take us to the New Orleans Hard Rock.

We pulled up a stool to sit at the long bar inside. We ordered our Bloody Mary's. Then just as I was about to take my first sip I heard the familiar opening guitar chords to 'The House of The Rising Sun' by the Animals. There he was, just like he was the night before only now he was on the TV monitors all over the Hard Rock, Eric Burdon and the Animals from 1964. The coincidence and timing was perfect. Even my skeptical husband was amazed.

I asked the bartender if this song was played all the time because after all, we are in New Orleans. She surprised me and said "No, I've worked here for many years and I've only heard it played a few times before". I laughed and asked her again. She promised me she was right. She was not kidding.

I grabbed my disposable camera and took a picture of Eric singing the song on the TV. Monitor.

So did we find the Rising Sun location? I'm not sure. Perhaps we found the location of the brothel operated by Madam Rose. That would explain why the location felt so familiar to me. Perhaps Sunflower worked at a brothel on St. James Street. The taxi driver had taken me home.

XOXOXOXOX

"Snow Fall on New Year's Eve"

Is it possible to channel the energy of someone who has passed on? I know there are many claims it is possible. As for me I've had two experiences where I really felt like I was viewing the world through another person's eyes.

The first time I felt as though I were looking through the eyes of John Lennon happened in the year of 2000. Randy and I had flown to San Francisco to attend a new movie in which Eric Burdon appeared. The movie premier was to be held at the Castro Theatre.

The movie was entitled "Snow Fall on New Year's Eve," which was directed by the German director Thorsten Schmidt.

When we arrived at the beautiful theatre we were greeted by a young lady whom we had met at Eric's New Year's Eve Millennium show in San Juan Capistrano. Her name is Gina (not her real name) and we were pleased to see her for this event. She waved to us to follow her asking us to sit beside her and her friend.

The theatre, once inside, had that old Hollywood feel. Everything from the concession stands to the restrooms had that turn of the century aroma. A very familiar scent. Inside the theatre were several ornate columns. There was an enormous stage with floor-to-ceiling curtains that surrounded a large screen. In the pit, in front of the stage, was a huge organ. The chairs we sat on were lush and felt as though we were sitting on chairs of red crushed velvet. There was a touch of Cuban flavor everywhere.

I sat next to Gina, a gorgeous young woman with long brown hair and a sassy way about her.

I asked her how long she has known Eric. She surprised me with her answer. "I've known him for many lives," she said with a giggle. Her companion smiled and agreed with her. I was not sure how to answer her because I was not sure if she was being serious. After a few seconds of silence she added, "We knew each other in ancient Egypt." I did not say anything, as I was trying to process the answer when the lights went down and the movie flickered to life on the giant screen. After a few minutes into the movie, I noticed that Eric had taken the seat next to her.

The movie started and I soon got caught up in the zany plot. Eric's character in the movie reminds me of Peter Seller's brilliant character, Inspector Clouseau , from the Pink Panther movies. Eric plays a detective in the movie also. A detective who flies about in a hot air balloon searching for his suspect.

It was quite surreal to see the fellow on the screen, then to look over and see Eric laughing at himself. We made eye contact and he grinned at me. I gave him thumbs up and then reached over Gina to squeeze his hand.

After I did this I felt a huge feeling of joy and laughter building inside my being. I felt like laughing in pure joy! I wanted to get up and dance or sing or do something. It's hard to explain, but I did feel like John Lennon was inside me. I knew that John was really happy for Eric and I got the idea that he liked the movie. This feeling only lasted a few seconds and then it was gone. It was a wonderful moment and I felt like I was a Goonie!

The other time I felt as though John was somehow inside my being was when I was in New York City on February 9th, 2002. It happened when I was walking to 42nd Avenue. As I walked the sidewalks of Times Square I had a feeling of been 'here done this'. I thought about John Lennon and how he had walked these same streets. The feeling was so strong that I asked my friend Sue, who had accompanied me, to take a picture of me at that moment.

XOXOXOXOX

Authors Note: I have no idea who the mysterious half man in the upper left corner of this photograph is. The camera used was one of those one time use cameras and did not have a strap.

"New year's day"

We attended Eric Burdon's New Year's Eve Millennium show that was held at The Coach House in San Juan Capistrano, California. I knew it was going to be a very special night.

The band was exceptional that night. Each of the members of the New Animals has become friends. Each man is a talented and gifted artist. The members of the New Animals on this memorable night were: Martin Gerschwitz, Dean Restum, Dave Meros and Ainsley Dunbar.

The audience that night was in a very festive mood. After all it was New Year's Eve and it was the New Millennium!

Randy and I were thrilled to see that Eric was wearing our Christmas gift we gave him. It was a shirt that featured Polynesian pin up girls in various poses. He looked fabulous in it.

Eric's voice and stage presence that night was perfection.

When the clock was about to strike midnight, the whole audience went berserk. Everyone was blowing those cheesy New Year's Eve horns, throwing confetti, whooping, hollering, dancing, standing on the tables; the place was in utter chaos!

My first kiss went to Randy, my second to Eric Burdon. What a night!

The last song Eric sang after everyone got through the excitement of bringing in the New Millennium was U2's "New Year's Day". Eric and the band covered this song brilliantly. My head was in Heaven. It just doesn't get any better!

What a way to bring in the New Millennium! I felt very blessed to have been able to share it with Randy along with many friends whom I love very much. My buddy Sue sat next to me.

The next morning we went to brunch with our friends including Eric and a friend of his by the name of Gina (not her real name).

Everything was going great until Eric cut his lip on a glass bottle of mouth freshener. It was a nasty cut that was bleeding profusely.

I felt badly for him and actually followed him to the men's room to help stop the bleeding. He was pretty worried, and I did not blame him for it. Luckily it was not too deep and he came back into the dining room and finished his meal.

This all happened way before I knew anything about Sunflower. I remember getting that feeling again of de ja vue, thinking to myself "this has all happened before!"

XOXOXOXOX

"My dream"

We've all experienced dreams in which we wake up and are glad to come back to this reality. These dreams are so real; you remember them for the rest of your life. Some dream experts say that these dreams are just our minds trying to work out difficult situations we experience in our day to day journeys. Others say these dreams are more spiritual, that these dreams are actual encounters with loved ones on the other side of reality. There is also another explanation for these very lucid dreams. These dreams reflect memories from a past lifetime. I believe this dream combined all three elements.

MY DREAM:

I am not sure if I am standing or sitting. I do know that I am in a very crowded space. I feel the space I am in is not very large and that I am surrounded by several people. It is a little claustrophobic, but not overly so.

I do feel that I have a person whom I love very much next to me.

In my dream, I begin to fall. At great speed. Once again, I am in an enclosed area. As I fall, I become extremely fearful. I know I am trying to scream but nothing comes out.

I next see a jellyfish or upside down umbrella shape, that is above my head. It is just a few inches out of my grasp. I am in desperate need to grab it. I feel it is a life or death situation and that I must reach this object or die. The Jellyfish, object has a lifeline attached to it. I must somehow reach it! Suddenly the Jellyfish object begins to glow. Shimmering, beautifully with white lights that glow like tiny diamonds. I must reach it to live!

I continue to free fall. I am absolutely terrified. I wake up before I reach the ground in this dream. However just before awakening I see in my mind's eye in huge print the numbers '1859'. The dream is over.

I awoke in such a state of terror that it took me a while to fall back to sleep. Then the thought occurs to me that this dream was a premonition of a future event.

I made an appointment with Reverend Arlene to discuss this dream with her. I told her why I thought it was a premonition of future events.

I was scheduled to fly back to Arkansas to visit my grandchildren in a couple of days. This was to be my first time to hold my newest grandson Noah.

Here is how I interpreted my dream. I felt the space in which I was sitting in was in the cabin of an airplane. I was seated next to my husband. I convinced myself that the plane was going to crash, thus my feeling of falling. The object I was so desperate to reach to stay alive was the air flow devise that is shaped like an upside down umbrella or if you stretch it a bit, a floating jellyfish. It even has a lifeline chord that is attached to it. I was convinced I should cancel my vacation plans. I really felt bad doing this.

Reverend Arlene smiled raised her eyebrow and shook her head no at me after I told her about my dream. "Sherry, you have nothing to fear. I see you living a long lifetime. This dream is not a dream of doom, but is a dream of hope and spirituality. The object you see in your dream is white light. White light is always hope and love. Never doom. Have a safe journey and kiss Noah for me."

I left for my vacation and boarded my flying ark to Arkansas to see my two month old grandson, Noah. I had a wonderful time and not once did I have any fear of an air disaster that trip nor any in the future for that matter.

After I came home I went to visit Arlene once again. She asked me if I happened to see a clown while I was there. I had to think. Then I remembered Noah's clown socks.

I felt a bit foolish about my dream and Arlene and I had a good laugh about it.

After my safe flight home I told myself to forget about this dream. However the memory of this dream would not go away. I felt there was more to it, much more.

Then one afternoon the thought came to me that the enclosed space in my dream was not an airplane but the cabin of an elevator. Of course, I thought, that is why I felt like I was falling. It was not an airplane disaster, it was an elevator!

I began to forget about the dream. Well, I say forget, but it would be a better description to say, put it aside. Until in the winter of 2010 when I began to form Sunflower's life and times into this novel.

When I got to chapter seven, my dream came back to me in vivid recollection. I began to obsess about elevators! I researched the internet for anything that involved elevators in New York City in the late 1800's.

I found very little concerning any accidents. It seems the elevator is a very safe invention. I did find out that Otis Elevators had its start in New York City. At the Fifth Street Hotel—the opening day ceremonies was August 23rd, 1859.

XOXOXOXOX

"A tale of two men"

If you have been reading my life's journey then by now you've probably figured out that if I were asked to take only two artists music with me to a deserted island, my choice would be John Lennon and Eric Burdon. Most people would assume that I am a walking encyclopedia of Lennon and Burdon trivia but I am very far from that.

When I first started attending Eric's concerts in 1994 I had no idea nor did I think about him having a friendship with John Lennon. I went to his shows because I love his music, that simple.

In 1998, before attending a show of Eric's at the House of Blues in Hollywood, Randy and I went to a used book store on Hollywood Avenue. I was, as always, looking for 'In His Own Write'', by John Lennon. As I was looking for this book, and this really did happen, another book fell off the shelf! It was the 25th anniversary issue of Rollingstone magazine. I saw that the 1971 Jann S. Wenner interview of John Lennon was included so I purchased the special edition of Rollingstone.

First I need to explain that at the time I found this book and interview, I did not realize that John and Eric were friends. I do not know how close they were back in the sixties. The only people who know that for sure are John and Eric. Finding this interview made me feel good. Best I can describe how I felt when I read this was like a mother's relief she feels when her kids stop arguing and realize how much they love and need each other. Strange.

This interview occurred January of 1971. I would like to add that the iconic picture of John Lennon on the cover was dated January 21st, 1971. This would make it my, Nineteenth birthday. It is also the year of my son Frank's birth.

'John Lennon', The Rollingstone interview
By Jann S. Wenner January 1971

Q: What was it like, say, running around discotheques With the Stone's?

A: (John Lennon) (condensed) We were all just at the prime, and we all used to go around London in our cars and meet each other and talk about music with the Animals and Eric (Burdon) and all that. It was a really good time. That was the best period, fame wise; we didn't get mobbed so much. I don't know; it was like a men's smoking club, just a very good scene. We created something, Mick and us, we didn't know what we were doing, but we were all talking, blabbing over coffee, like they must have done in Paris, talking about paintings… me, Burdon and Brian Jones would be up night and day talking about music, playing records and blabbing and arguing and getting drunk. Its beautiful history

When I read this part of the interview I felt happy that John held this particular time and place so dear. I was happy to read Eric was a part of this memory.

In this interview John mentions Eric once again. As a professional musician, poet, and artist, I believe John gives Eric the highest compliment and respect he could. My respect and admiration for both men was renewed once again.

(From the 1971 interview)

Q: Why do you think the impact of the Beatles was so much bigger in America that it was in England?

Answer (John Lennon) (condensed) we felt that we had…that the message was listen to the music. It was the same in Liverpool, we felt very exclusive and underground listening to all those old-time records. And nobody was listening to any of them except Eric Burdon in New Castle and Mick Jagger in London. It was that lonely. It was fantastic. We came over here and it was the same: Nobody was listening to rock & roll or to black music in America. We were coming to the land of its origin but nobody wanted to know about it. (End)

I just love this last paragraph! This is the stuff that changes history. In this case musical history!

XOXOXOXOX

"Dixie"

My mother's nickname was "Dixie." I miss her each and every day. In every way.

XOXOXOXOX

"Sticky Fingers"

I was at a session with Reverend Arlene many years before I started writing about Sunflower when she asked me this next question: (this was before she knew my Guide John's last name was Lennon)

First she told me that she was seeing hands that were covered with a brown sticky 'substance. Then she asked me if John was an artist? I told her that he was a very talented musician and poet, and that yes he was also a talented cartoon artist.

I was not sure what the sticky dark substance was at the time. However after many years of reflection, I believe the sticky substance on his hands was clay.

XOXOXOXOX

"1859 and the great solar flare"

Today is January 1st, 2012. Today is the beginning of a year that is mixed with hope and fear.

I do not believe that we are entering the end of times. The Mayan Calendar ending on this year of December 21st, 2012 is not a prophecy of doom, but one of hope for a new beginning.

However, I have been given a divine message that I feel compelled to share.

As I have mentioned, I had a dream in which I was shown the year of 1859. I revealed how this year was a year of great joy for Sunflower.

There is one other reason I was shown the year of 1859.

Please understand I do not want anyone to live in fear. That is not the reason I give in this prophecy. I give this message to you for a reason and that is—to live a happy and a safe life!

Many scientists believe we are entering a time in our Mother Earth's history in which we are going to witness an event that has happened many times. Our sun is going through changes which are natural. We call this event a solar flare. The biggest solar flare in recorded history was in the year of 1859. It is referred to as the Carrington event.

I am not writing this to frighten anyone. I only write this because I think it is my responsibility to share, to be prepared. We all know we should anyway. There are many natural events in every part of this globe which will continue throughout history in which we should prepare for disaster.

So if a solar flare happens, and perhaps we are without electricity for a few days, weeks maybe longer, be prepared. Perhaps you'll never need the extra food, yours and your beloved non-human family, but what does it hurt? Again do not live a life of fear live it in love, hope and peace. Be prepared, physically and spiritually to meet challenges.

"We all Shine On" Very cheeky John Winston Ono Lennon!

XOXOXOXOX

"White Feathers"

John Lennon once gave his son, Julian, a special message. In this message he told Julian that if he should die, that he would try to return to him and give him a message from the other side, letting his son know that he was O.K. and to let him also know that he, Julian, would be alright too. He told Julian to look for a white feather. This would be his sign.

Time went by and Julian did receive a white feather after his father's death. Julian took part in an ancient ceremony with an aboriginal tribe. He was handed a white feather by a tribe elder. This feather had great spiritual meaning for this tribe and Julian was much honored to have been given it. He also knew this was the feather his father had promised to give him as a sign of love and hope.

This happened while Julian was in Australia for the filming of "Whale Dreamers."

We all know of John Lennon's love of the ocean. John and James were also very fascinated with the ocean and sea life, or as John Wells put it "The Octopus Garden".

In 1995, after Paul McCartney , George Harrison, and Ringo Starr finished recording "Free as a Bird," they posed for a publicity photo. As they were outside the recording studio about to finish the photo, a white peacock appeared and wandered into the shot.

Paul said "That was John, spooky eh."

Many friends, family, fans etc., have since told me, about the white feather they've received from John. Each is very special.

I have three feathers of my own.

First feather I found at the shop beside the side door. The night before I had a discussion with some online friends who knew about John's message about white feathers. Perfect timing.

The second white feather I found at the golf course. I kept it and put it on my golf bag. A few steps further I found a black crow feather. I looked at it laying in the grass and thought to myself how beautiful it was. I put it next to the white feather.

A few months later, I went once again to see Eric Burdon in concert. After the show I went backstage to say hello. Eric greeted me with two kisses on each of my cheeks. How Euro! What he did next blew me away, it was very surreal. Eric picked up a black crow feather someone had given him, and put it behind his ear! All I could do is giggle to myself and think about John being represented by the angelic white feather and Eric the black crow.

Perfect though because:," She talks to Angels" by the Black Crows crossed my mind and I thought of all the love we can receive, if we just listen, then take a deep breath and believe.

XOXOXOXOX

"The Lovely Bones"

A few nights after I wrote of Sunflower's transition into Heaven I rented a movie called "The Lovely Bone's." It is a story of a young girl who is able to communicate with her family after she had been killed. Explaining to her loved ones, what it is like to be alive on the other side of reality, or as I like to say, 'the looking glass'.

I will never cease to be amazed at how incredibly clever those on the other side can be! In the movie, Suzie finally decides to go forward and into the light. When she finally sees the light and all the love within she say's two words which are "Simply beautiful." Those were the last words Sunflower said to her beloved son John, when she saw many white feathers floating across the universe before she also stepped into the light and love of our Creator.

I had not seen this movie before I wrote Chapter Seven.

The actress who portrays Suzie in the move is Dakota Fanning.

Well, I think you can see the coincidence of her first name. Her last name, "Fanning" was a bit of a mystery to me until I started to think a bit more about it. Of course, Sunflower's butterfly fan she held as she transitioned.

XOXOXOXOX

"Sunflower and President Lincoln"

I have tried to be as honest as I possibly can in every word, every thought, every memory I've written in this novel. To not be honest would do a terrible injustice to not only myself but to my friends, family and those on the other side who have lovingly walked with me through this life's journey.

With that said, this is how I came to believe that Sunflower Sarah was met by President Abraham Lincoln when she stepped through the veil.

I first learned of John Lennon's interest in President Lincoln when Rev. Arlene saw John walking towards her trying to look like Mr. Lincoln. It was funny at the time. When I got home to the internet I began to discover many Lennon/Lincoln connections, as I wrote in earlier chapters. However I did not connect Sunflower and President Lincoln until I had finished writing my thoughts as expressed in chapter seven—"A Walk in Heaven with a Friend."

It was after I had written about Lincoln being the person to meet Sunflower on the other side that I began to question why? How could I dare to write such an account? I had no messages to back up my thoughts. However, I always felt that somehow Sunflower met him. I knew she had been to Cooper's Hall where she was enchanted by the man, as were many others that day. After hearing his passionate anti- slavery speech. I just could not shake the idea that he and her had met.

After I wrote of Sunflower being met by President Lincoln in Heaven, I decided to investigate a bit further.

I began to wonder if President Lincoln had been to New Orleans. Perhaps that is where he met Sunflower?

So I went to the internet and searched—President Abraham Lincoln and New Orleans—this is what I discovered.

I learned that he had indeed been to the Crescent City twice. At www.mrlincolnandfreedom.org I found this next excerpt from Lincoln in New Orleans.

In New Orleans, for the first time Lincoln beheld the true horrors of human slavery. Wrote Mr. Lincoln's legal colleague, William H. Herndon ,"Agains(t) this inhumanity his sense of right and justice rebelled, and his mind and conscience were awakened to a realization of what he had often heard and read, "Herndon wrote from Hanks" memories,"One morning in their rambles over the city the trio passed a slave auction. A vigorous and comely "mulatto girl" was being sold. She underwent a through exam at the hands of the bidders: They pinched her flesh and made her trot up and down the room like a horse, to show how she moved, and in order, as the auctioneer said, that "'bidders might satisfy themselves whether the article they were offering to buy was sound or not. The whole thing was so revolting that Lincoln moved away from the scene with a deep feeling of 'unconque- able hate'. Bidding his companions follow him said "By God. boys, let's get away from this. If I ever get a chance to hit that thing (meaning slavery), I'll hit it hard".

This incident was furnished me in 1865, by John Hanks. I have heard Mr. Lincoln refer to it himself.

After I read this, I knew I had been given a divine message and one that I hold very dear and very sacred. I know that Sarah's description of the auction is a bit different than the description given to John Hanks then later William H. Herndon. I wondered why? Then it came to me and the answer is simple.

Lincoln and his companions left just as Sarah began her dance of seduction. Mr. Lincoln could take no more. Mr. Lincoln's last memory of Sarah was when she met eye to eye the monster with no fear. He walked away and Sarah did what she knew she had to do, seduce the men. Have some control of the situation. Perhaps then she would be able to at least have some say in who was going to purchase her. She had her eye on Rose. Women can be seduced also. Sarah knew this and at the age eleven plus she did what she had to do. Rose won the bidding while the men howled in delight and sexual desire for Sarah. Mr. Lincoln had left.

Another reason President Lincoln did not go on to describe Sunflower's dance is because he was a gentle- man first and foremost. That may be the real reason. I'm not sure. I just know it affected him to his core.

Again, I learned of this event in President Lincoln's life and times, long after I had written all of Chapter Seven.

In conclusion, Abraham Lincoln often referred to slavery as "the peculiar institution." John Lennon wrote a song 'Strange Day's Indeed.'

In this song John' writes

"Strange day's indeed

Most peculiar Mama".

I like to think this is John's tribute to Mr. Lincoln and his mother, Sunflower.

XOXOXOXOX

"Another message from Abe"

Today is the 24th of June, 2012. As I stated at the beginning of this novel, I continue to receive messages from unseen friends and family to this day.

These messages help me continue with my desire to finish this novel and get it published. I need this. I've been more than a little ready to give up.

Today on a drive to have a go at our local casino, we decided to stop and grab a quick hamburger. Just before we pulled into the parking lot, I finished reading a short article in Parade Magazine about a new movie that is about to be premiered. The movie is called 'Abraham Lincoln-Vampire Hunter.'

What caught my attention was the last paragraph which reads:

The Inspiration

"Lincolns anti-slavery sentiments were likely stoked by watching a slave auction during a trip to New Orleans at age 19."

I smiled to myself after reading this as it was just another confirmation of what I knew. I was there.

In perfect synchronicity as we pulled into the hamburger palace another man was walking out the door. He was wearing a tee shirt that read:

Abraham Lincoln Vampire Hunter

Production team

This time I was able to share my message with Randy. Even he was amazed! This is not an easy task!

XOXOXOXOX

"February 9ᵗʰ, 2002 in NYC"

In 2002 I turned fifty. My birthday wish was to return to NYC to not only celebrate my 50th, but to also attend a show at BBKings once again on 42nd street starring Eric Burdon and The New Animals. Two shows were scheduled for February 8th and 9th. A reminder once again, I did not know of Sunflowers existence at this time in my life.

Our good friend Sue went with us.

On February 9th, we made our way to the subway and to 72nd and Central Park West—The Dakota.

It was a very beautiful crisp February morning. The sun was shining as I once again walked across the street from the Dakota and into Strawberry Fields Park and to the Imagine Mosaic.

I was very optimistic that something was going to happen and I told my friend Sue, "I'll get a message from John, I just know I will!" I felt so sure of it.

We took pictures and once again I the tourists come and go, flashing peace signs. Happiness was contagious.

I kept waiting. Where is my message? Nothing. Finally I gave up and we went to visit the Tavern on the Green. Maybe my message would come from this location. After all John and his son Sean Lennon celebrated their birthdays at this venerable establishment in 1979.

The Tavern on the Green was beautiful. We took several photos as we stood next to the topiaries. However, no message.

I was somewhat miffed. Was I going to get the message I hoped for?

As we walked from the Tavern on the Green to 'Lincoln' Center to have lunch, I chastised myself for being so big headed. I said a silent prayer to John telling him how sorry I was that I had tested him. "How can I be so conceited," I said scolding myself. "How can

I, expect John Lennon who is known all over the world, to send me a message on command?"

We walked a few "big' New York City blocks until we arrived at a nice looking pub to have lunch.

Sue, Randy and I took our seats at the counter to order pub grub along with liquid refreshment, Long Island Iced teas, of course!

As I was sitting at the counter, I noticed that a young lady kept looking my way. She was seated a few seats from me and it was pretty obvious that she wanted to ask me something. She finally came over and sat next to me at the counter.

"Excuse me," she said in a quiet New Yorker accent, "I feel I know you." "Well, I'm sure we have not met, as I am from southern California," I informed her. "You just look so familiar," she apologized, then started back to her seat. Then she stopped. "I was in southern California on 9/11/2001," she said. I then asked her what city in southern California? "The beach," she told me. I informed her that I live near the desert. Then I asked her what city. "Dana Point," she answered. "Oh," I told her, "I have a friend who lives in that city. In fact he performs at a tavern in Dana Point on Sundays." Then she snapped her fingers and said "That's it! I remember you! Does your friend have long hair and play the keyboards?" She just described our friend Martin Gerschwitz who does have long hair and does play the keyboards! "Yes, I do have a friend as you described," I replied in complete shock. "I was there," she told me! "It was right after September 11th on a Sunday. You were there; I remember the pants you were wearing! They were awesome bell bottoms! You were also wearing a John Lennon NYC tee shirt. I was there! I wanted to ask you where you purchased your pants."

This was a completely surreal moment. I was thousands of miles from home, sitting at a pub in Lincoln Center, at this exact moment a woman was seated next to me who shared a special day with us. What are the odds?

In an instant I realized that I had received the message from John I had asked for. I'm not a no where girl. We are all special wonderful beings that are connected. We all make impressions; it's just that we don't always realize it.

The young lady went on to say how special that day was. She was very far from, and because of the events of 9/11/2001 she had to remain in southern California a little longer then she had wanted to. She missed her home and was concerned for friends and relatives.

She told me how sharing this day of music with Martin had helped her with her homesickness. She remembered Martins rendition of "Imagine."

After my experience at the diner we returned to our hotel room to get ready for the concert at BBKings starring Eric Burdon and the New Animals.

Eric was fantastic as always. He looked happy and very healthy. His voice was strong and commanding. The band, our friends, was perfection.

Just before Eric began to break into a fantastic song called "Hey Gyp," he made an announcement to the audience. Eric looked down from the stage to our table and pointed at me, then he said "happy birthday, Sherry Baby. You made it! You made it to 50!" Then the band broke into "Hey Gyp." As Eric sang the song, he inserted my name into the lyrics which are: "I'll buy you a Chevrolet—Sherry" "I'll buy you a Chevrolet".

He sang the complete song and inserted my name where it fit. I was in heaven. I cannot explain how happy I was.

After the show, I thanked Eric and he again smiled and said to me "I can't believe you made it to 50."

It was a few weeks later that I discovered that February 9th had one more message for me. February 9th, 2002 was the 38th anniversary of the Beatles first appearance on the Ed Sullivan show. Thirty eight years right to the minute! I made it to fifty. Sunflower died at age 49.

XOXOXOXOX

"Imagine"

Before I explain the incredible image I see in the photograph below, I would like to explain what was happening when it was taken. This was taken on the same day that the young lady I met in NYC on February 9th, 2002, remembered seeing me that I wrote of in the previous message.

The date was September 16th, 2001. We closed our shop on this Sunday morning as it just felt right to do so. Our dear friend, Martin Gerschwitz, was performing that Sunday at a pub in Dana Point. It is a very intimate setting outside in the patio. Martin has become a very special person in our lives. He is an incredibly talented musician and song writer.

After about an hour, Martin announced that his next song he was going to perform is going to be dedicated to the people of New York City. The song was "Imagine." Martin's voice and musicianship on the Hammond was beautiful. Very moving. It was while Martin was singing Imagine, a friend took a picture of Randy, a dear girlfriend of ours and myself.

A few months later I developed this photograph. That is then that I noticed a large orb within the photo. I enlarged the photo and started to see something within the orb. I see John Lennon's image inside the orb. I also see what some UFO believers call "A Grey" or a classic looking shadow of an alien with large cat like eyes—Hint— the little guy is almost in the middle of the orb at the bottom of the photo. I see the image of John that was featured on the cover of Rollingstone Magazine 1971. The same photograph that was taken of John on my birthday January 21st, 1971. I admit it's hard to see, at any rate, I luv how the sun beams kiss the afternoon sky.

XOXOXOXOX

Pictured from left to right myself, Randy White, and our friend Kristyl Adams.

"Peggy"

My friend and soul sister, Sue's mother lost her battle with Cancer on February 9th, 2007.

Sue was with me when we went to New York City in 2002. I treasure the memories and am so glad she was with me to share the wonders of John Lennon and NYC.

Sue's mothers name is Peggy. Peggy is a gifted song writer and poet. I had only met her once, but the memory of her is still fresh in my mind.

XOXOXOXOX

"Pappy and room # 9"

John has such a special way of letting me know he is near in times of need. This is another example:

In January of 2010 my father in law, Ralph, had a heart attack. He was diagnosed with heart disease and needed double bypass surgery immediately.

Ralph was transferred from a community hospital to a cardiac hospital a week after his diagnosis. We were very worried.

When Randy and I arrived at the cardiac hospital, the day of surgery, I received my message from Dear John. Ralph's hospital room number was #9. I would like to add that this is a large hospital with only one room #9.

I smiled and gave daddy Ralph a kiss before he was wheeled into surgery. "You'll be fine dad," I told him then added, "I mean it dad. I received a message from my Guardian Angel telling me so and he is never wrong. No reason to doubt him now! I'll see you later." I could see in Ralph's eyes that we had connected and he gave me a smile and we hugged.

It is now over a year since Ralph surgery. He is doing fine and is enjoying life as a loving husband, dad and Pappy.

He is also enjoying one of his many passions and that is entertaining. Pappy is a singer and he is singing his songs with renewed joy.

XOXOXOXOX

"Franks race of a lifetime. Oct. 9th, 1994"

On October 9th, 1994, on what would have been John Lennon's 54th birthday I once again felt John's presence and I believe, along with our son Frank, that I received a wonderful gift of support.

Our son Frank was diagnosed with epilepsy in 1986 when he was 15 years of age. Along with medication, a very strong will to overcome this medical condition and bicycle racing, he was able to conquer this very difficult medical condition. Through years of dedication, hours and hours of time spent on the bicycle saddle, proper nutrition and just plain old "I can do this," attitude, he began to build on his bicycle racing skills. This sport, I would like to add, is one of the very hardest and cruel of any. You have to have the heart of a lion to succeed. Frank does indeed have this heart.

Franks race of a life time was held in La Jolla Beach, California. It is called the La Jolla Grand Prix Criterion. For those who do not know what a criterion (crit) race is I will try to explain.

It is a lap race that encircles approximately one to two miles of city streets that are traffic free. The length of the race can vary. This particular race was 40 laps, or a little over 40 miles. The pace is usually constant. In this case around 35 miles per hour and just a bit over one hour in time. A reminder, the pace is constant; the racers never stop, except if they are unlucky and have a mechanical issue, drop out, or crash.

As we got ready for the race to start, I scanned the competition. This Crit was for pro and elite racers only. Pro, or Category 1 and 2 amateur racers. Only the best could compete in this race which included Steve Hegg. Mr. Hegg won the Gold Medal in the summer Olympics in Los Angeles. He won the Gold Medal in the 4,000 men's individual pursuit. He also won the silver in the 4,000 men's team pursuit. In road racing, Hegg was the first three time winner of the USA National time trial championship.

Our son, Frank, was now a category two amateur racer. This is an extremely hard accomplishment that many amateurs never accomplish. Just to be invited to compete in this race was an honor. We are very proud of Frank.

There were approximately 120 racers at the start line.

I will now try to explain what it is like to watch a race such as this. First word that enters my mind is "Terror!" These 120 racers, pull as hard as they can, bump, mussel, yell and curse, crunch, grunt and sometimes, to the horror of the loved ones watching from the sidelines, crash in a heap of blood, sweat, ripped shorts and jerseys, bent wheels and finally tears. All they have for protection against the pavement is their helmets and maybe gloves. It is horrific to watch, and crashes can and do happen at any given moment. All you can do as a spectator is walk the course and hope to see your loved one still in the race when they spin by. It is absolutely magnificent terror at its best.

For the first part of the race, Frank was in the middle of the peloton (racers), holding on and I could tell by his body language, peddling for all he was worth.

The favorites were all there at this point as far as I could see. Frank was riding Steve Hegg's wheel. Good place to be.

As we approached the 20th mile or so, the pack began to break up. As it usually does. This split the race up into three groups. The riders in the last group began to drop out one by one. The second group was packed with talent and off the pace by about 15 seconds. The first group, the leaders, was hanging tough. Frank was in the first group! Along with, I might add, Steve Hegg, Gold Medalist.

Then it happened, around mile 33. Three amateurs, which included Frank, broke away from the leaders. This was viewed as a suicide decision. These three would be gobbled up and swallowed to failure by the more seasoned athletes. My heart was literally in my throat. I was terrified something would happen. All I could think to do was to pray to God and as silly as it might seem, to John Lennon! "Please, God, and you too John, take care of Frank. Please don't let him Crash," I said to myself as I paced around and around the city block.

We made it through the crowds to find a spot at the finish line. I heard the comments from the announcer, "Here come the three amigos! They are still in front!" The pack was approximately 20 seconds behind as the racers approached 35th mile. "The three Amigos might just do it!" Then as we got to the final laps, the leaders began to lose just a bit more of their lead. Now the three amigos are only about 15 seconds in front! Oh God, I am beginning to think that this will come down to a pack sprint and this can and often lead to a horrific crash and broken dreams. "Please John! I know it's your birthday and you're probably busy, but please give Frank a big push and keep him safe."

The final lap approached and everyone can now see the three young amateurs approach the finish line and that one of them would win the race. Now the only question was, "who of the three amigos was going to win?" shouted the announcer.

I saw the helmet, I know his riding style, and Frank was out front with room to spare as he raced to the finish line. With his arms raised in victory he crossed the finish line. I know I jumped about six feet into the air (or so it felt). Incredibly Frank has won a very determined group of America's best cycling champs. Including, I might add, an Olympic medalist.

I ran to Frank and we hugged, cried, and laughed all at the same time! I watched in extreme pride as the other racers, which included Steve Hegg, congratulate the champion.

Then, the reporters, photographers and officials guided Frank to the winner's podium on which Frank stood on the top in the middle, light bulbs flashing, reporters asking him questions about the race, Steve Hegg giving his respect to the young lion. Our Champion, our son, Frank.

When we were finally able to really talk about the race together alone, Frank told me that although it took everything he had within, he felt he had an invisible helper. It was then that I told him that today is John Lennon's birthday. "Maybe it was John who was helping you a bit." I felt funny telling him this, but to my surprise he just said "That's cool Mom, really cool".

XOXOXOXOX

Chapter 8

FAMILY

THE FUNERAL AND MEMORIAL SERVICE for Sarah Anne Wells, who was at the time of her death 49 years of age, was held on February 12th, 1869. This would have been President Abraham Lincoln's 60th birthday.

The clouds that hung over the New York skyline that day were dark and angry. These clouds seemed to be crying tears from a mother who stood as a silent witness and could do nothing to stop or calm John and take the demon hate out of his soul. She loved her sons with all her heart and soul. Sunflower wanted desperately to tell James and John that she was fine. That she was now with Grandma Daisy and that both of them would be waiting in Paradise for them. However, although she tried to connect and give a message of hope, James and John could not hear her.

John stood cold faced and solemn at the funeral service which was held at a secret location where Sarah Anne Wells would receive her final request to be cremated. She had long ago discussed this wish with her two friends whom she considered her sisters, Angel Alice and Lily. Angel's ancestors were from native America and practiced cremation in order to purify and protect not only their own soul but those of their surviving family. Lily, whose roots were from the aboriginal peoples of Australia, cremated their loved for basically the same reason, even though thousands of miles separated the two cultures. And so a secret place was selected and a funeral pyre was built.

No birth certificate for Sarah was in existence and no death certificate was issued. Because of her "profession", she never was recorded in the census. Sarah Anne Wells, also known as Sunflower, simply did not exist.

Only a handful attended her remembrance service. James, John, Angel Alice, Edward Clark, Madam Julia Brown, a few of lady's from Leonard Street.

Neko was also in attendance. She was dressed in a beautiful kimono that featured butterflies and sunflowers. Neko led the service in prayer. One prayer was said in English the other in Japanese. Her life was also changed forever after this day. Sunflower had been the only one who loved her and accepted her. She could never repay the debt she felt she owed her.

It took many hours until the fire died. Then Sarah's ashes were collected.

There were no words that Neko could say that would comfort John. He held back his angry tears that bore down to his soul. He kept his head down and did not look at anyone. When he did look at James an evil sort of smile appeared, his eyes piercing as though looking through James

James tried to approach his brother. John would only walk away. When finally they met face to face, John's anger could no longer be contained. His voice was shrill, as he spat these words when he spoke to his brother James who was bent over in grief. "You killed our Mammy," he screamed at James. "She hardly had a sick day in her life. You broke her heart into a thousand pieces. Because of you, her heart ceased to beat. From this day on, you have no mammy and I have no brother. I never wish to see you again."

John took the urn that held his mother's ashes, walked away, and did not look back.

James was ill with grief and guilt over his mother's death. However, his love for Alvina beckoned him to go to New Orleans, there was nothing or anyone left for him to stay any longer in New York City.

James did indeed leave for New Orleans five days after his mother's death. This was February 14th of 1869 and Saint Valentine's Day. James felt this was at least one good omen.

At first life went well for Alvina and James in New Orleans. She continued working for Madam Marianna at the Rising Sun as her personal maid. James worked as a handy man and also helped with security when issues came up.

Then the requests started coming in from the patrons asking for the lovely Alvina. At first Alvina resisted, then large amounts of money was offered and she could no longer resist.

James, at first, did not have an issue with Alvina's decision. After all his mother worked in the same industry and she was well respected. James reasoned with himself that it was just a job. Alvina reassured James of this, telling him that she loved only him, no one else. It was just the money she could not resist.

On a sunny Sunday morning James received a message from Madame Marianne that she wanted him to meet with her in her study. James walked in to see that Alvina was sitting next to the Madame with a new look. Her hair was pulled up in a style he had only seen on some of the more seasoned girls. He knew the routine. Pull the pin out and let the hair fall. He had never before seen Alvina with blush and lipstick. She wore a very silky dress that left little to the imagination. It was obvious where this was going. "James, Alvina has changed her name. She will be known as Alvenia. You can be her room steward. Nothing more," Madame Marianne informed James with a sly snicker and a gratified smile.

Alvenia soon became one of the most requested girls at the Rising Sun. She had more money than she ever thought possible. She enjoyed the company and attention she received from her men. Soon she began to change and started finding excuses for not wanting James around her.

With his heart broken, James left to try to start a life on his own without his beloved Alvina. He knew that it would be impossible for Alvina to be happy with just one man. James never stopped loving his beautiful Alvina.

The year was now 1871. Sunflower was right when she warned James about the difficulties he would have living in New Orleans post-Civil War. The war had only been over seven years and many citizens of the city blamed the "darkies' for their heartbreaks. Everywhere James went, hate followed.

After James stopped working at the Rising Sun finding work was almost impossible.

James tried to paint portraits in Saint Charles Park, but found little employment. Even when he did get an offer for a sitting he received only a few pennies for his work no matter how brilliant the painting was.

James was able to continue getting some work at the brothels in Story Ville as a handy man or in security. With the money he made he basically was able to eat. He slept where ever he could.

James was fortunate in that some of the elderly gentlemen still remembered his mother, Sunflower. These men would hire James to help with chores.

At one of the brothels the madam gave James a trombone for a birthday gift. One of the gentlemen callers had left it and the Madam thought of James and his love of music. This trombone soon became a best friend for James. He was able to master this instrument very quickly.

James met a gambling man by the name of River Rick at one of the Houses in Story Ville. Rick's home was the Mississippi River and his bed was aboard the Natchez Queen. His game was draw poker.

Rick took a liking to James. He was impressed by James and his musicality. Through his friendship with River Rick and his talent with the trombone, James was able to get a job on the Natchez Queen. James became a member of a five piece band that performed for the guests.

James was a natural and took to this opportunity with a new zest for life. Life was great until River Rick was accused of cheating and took off during the night never to be seen again.

Unfortunately for James, because of his friendship with River Rick, he was asked to leave and lost his job on the Natchez Queen.

James was once again without a home and without a job. However, he still had his trombone and he still had his talent.

After his mother's funeral, John Wells disappeared into the bowels of New York City. He went into isolation and lived a life of misery in the slum that was known as Five Points for over ten years.

His bitterness and grief over losing not only his mother, but in his eyes his brother, was more than John could bear. He became a recluse, a beggar and a drunkard. His alcoholism fueled his temper and he would get in terrible bloody arguments with many Irish immigrants who were also living in desperate conditions of filth. He hated the Irish and the Irish hated him.

John Wells had very few friends. He felt he did not need anyone, with only one exception, Neko.

It was Neko who kept in touch with John during this time in his life. It was Neko who would bring him nourishment for his body. She would also bring him nourishment for his soul in that she was able to communicate with his mother in spirit. John would sit with her kitty in his lap and listen to Neko's words of comfort from his mother for hours at a time. Neko and her beloved pet kitty kept John from going insane.

John became a fixture of sort at various theatres that featured a new entertainment that was called "French Balls". He could be found begging in front of these palaces of pleasure.

French Balls were more or less strip tease clubs. Five Points had become well known for French Balls.

In the year of 1879 John Wells met a man at one of the theatres that was being investigated by law enforcement. He met a citizen who was of high esteem and had volunteered to testify as to what he had witnessed at one of the French Balls he attended as a detective under cover. This gentleman was also a man who dedicated his life to helping not only his fellow Irish countrymen but all citizens of New York City who were living in the most horrid conditions imaginable in the slums of Five Points.

For some reason, and he was not sure why, the man took a liking to John Wells. He became determined to somehow help the beggar. The man's name was "Lemon," John Lemon.

At first John Wells turned cold when Mr. Lemon approached him. Mr. Lemon was intrigued by the young Negro man who would sometimes draw portraits, or sing a song if asked. Most of the time he would just beg for money. Their first conversation did not go well at all. Mr. Lemon had a very thick Irish accent. When he extended his hand for a shake of introduction, John Wells looked the other way then spat at Mr. Lemon's shoe. Mr. Lemon did not give up that day. Something about this young and angry man was intriguing. He returned the next weekend to find John once again sitting in front of the theatre. Charcoal in hand busily drawing a portrait of a rather scruffy looking older man.

As almost a secret Angel took possession of his voice, Mr. Lemon asked if John would draw a portrait of himself. He was once again astounded by the young man's talent. John Wells was not impressed, he just wanted a few coins to go to the tavern where he would drink himself asleep. Then the pain would go away. Mr. Lemon asked the young angry man where it was he learned to draw. "I did what you asked, I want my coins", John Wells answered with a sneer. Mr.

Lemon complied with the request and thanked John Wells. I won't give up on you he thought to himself.

Mr. John Lemon returned many times and slowly a friendship somehow developed.

The one joy in John Well's life during this desperate time was his love for working with clay. Brick and Mortar.

It was John Lemon who was to set in motion life changing events for John Wells. He began to care for the young man who seemed to have nothing left in life. As this unlikely friendship developed John Wells asked John Lemon about his family in Ireland. Mr. Lemon told him about the hardships his family had to endure. About his grandparents and how they had brought him to America. Mr. Lemon was by no means born of wealth. His wealth came to him because of his good heart. He was a man of law and order being a detective, but he was also a man of great compassion. Slowly, ever so slowly John Wells and John Lemon became very close. Because of this friendship, John Wells turned from hating the Irish to understanding their passion's and loving them as family.

John Lemon knew of a woman in the Harlem area who needed some work done on her apartment building. She needed a brick wall repaired. John Wells was given the address along with a referral from John Lemon.

The elderly lady who answered the door did not recognize the very thin man who stood before her. The years of famine, drugs, alcohol, isolation and misery made John appear much older than his actual age of twenty nine. When she did realize the man who stood before her was John, she thanked the Heavens above. This elderly lady was Angel. Everyone now called her by her birth name which was 'Alice.' Angel Trumpet Alice, Sunflower's faith full American Indian friend. John's long lost weekend had finally ended. It had been over ten years.

Alice had been keeping in touch with Edward Clark. When she told Edward that John "long lost John" had returned, it came at a very difficult time in Edward's life. His wife Caroline had died six years past. Losing first Sunflower, then Caroline, had proven too much for Edward and he found little joy in life. John coming back into his life at this time proved to be a blessing for both men.

True to Edward's prophecy he told Sunflower many years past, Isaac Singer had made him a very wealthy man. Edward Clark was now part owner and President of the Singer Sewing Machine Company.

Edward Clark and Isaac Singer had one dream in common. They wanted to build a luxurious apartment building in the west side across from the newly developed Central Park. It was a bit out of the way, but the two men were convinced that this building would become world famous and an excellent address for the wealthy of New York City to live. The name that was given this apartment building was "The Dakota."

Edward approached John and asked if he would like to help build the Dakota? Building this would provide a wonderful way for John to heal and to reconnect with people.

After the Dakota was finished in 1884, John continued to help as a handy man for the residence. John also started drawing once again. He would set up his easel across from the Dakota and as he did many years in the past, drawing portraits in ink and also in charcoal.

John was able to make a meager living and soon was able to rent a small flat for himself. The only thing John had never had a desire to do again was to sing. Only when he begged would he put his voice to song. Now he wanted to sing once again for the simple joy of it.

It was at the Dakota, in 1886, that John found his singing voice again. He was working in the garden and singing "Dixie" when a beautiful woman approached him. He had seen her from time to time as she worked as a house maid.

"You sing beautifully sir," the young lady said with her eyes focused on John face with such intensity that at first he was taken back. "Hello, my name is Katherine. However everyone calls me Kitty." John held out a shaky hand and took hers. He surprised himself when instead of shaking her hand he kissed it.

Kitty had a natural beauty that was given her from her African American heritage. She was seventeen when she met John. The seventeen years difference in age made no difference. John was now thirty seven years old.

Mr. and Mrs. John Wells were married on October 28th, 1886. The couple had arranged for the ceremony to take place in Battery Park. This was also the date that the Statue of Liberty was dedicated and revealed to the people of the United State of America.

John and Kitty Wells moved into a small flat in Harlem. It was the same apartment building in which Angel Alice lived in.

In 1887 Kitty gave birth to a son. John was extremely anxious about the birth and was no help at all. Thankfully, Alice was at Kitty's side, and the birth went very well. The baby boy was named for his father. John Victor Wells the second, was followed by another son, James Paul Wells in 1890. In 1892 John and Kitty welcomed a daughter into their lives. She was named Sarah Ann. Angel Alice was Godmother to all the children.

In 1898 Kitty gave birth to twins. A daughter whom they named Molly Alicia. A son whom they named Desmond Eric. Angel Alice, who was now eighty years of age, was once again in attendance at the birth. So was John, who by this time was quite an efficient birthing expert.

Angel Alice squealed in delight when she saw the two babies. Her mind went back to the birth of John and James, forty eight years past, in which she was in attendance.

When John and Kitty believed that their family was complete, God once again blessed them with another child. At the age of forty one, Kitty announced she was expecting at a Christmas holiday party. The year was now 1909. John was now fifty nine years old.

It was now the year of 1904 and life for James was finally going to change for the better. It was in this year that he met a young man who had a fire for music that could not be put out. This young man was known as Jellyroll. His last name was Morton.

Jellyroll had a natural talent for music and he could play just about any instrument with an amazing ability. He would play the piano with fingers that flew across the keyboards. Jellyroll was not satisfied with just playing the standards; he created his own music almost at will. He was a musical prodigy and only sixteen years of age when James met him.

James was now fifty four years old. At this time in his life he had perfected his skills as a musician. He would appear with local bands in and around the French Quarter in New Orleans. He would also play in bands on some of the riverboats.

Jellyroll and James hit it off immediately. Jellyroll loved to hear about life in New York City and constantly talked about making his name known in New York City.

The two troubadours, James now 57 and Jellyroll now age 19 made plans to head north and the bright lights.

For three years James and Jellyroll played at saloons, brothels, gambling halls, hotels, private parties anywhere they could make a few dollars. They lived on the road side for most the time. They also lived on the kindness of people they would find along the way. They had many adventures.

Jellyroll enraptured his audiences where ever he appeared. He was a natural and people where drawn to him.

It was in Springfield, Illinois that James and Jellyroll parted company. Jellyroll had been given an opportunity he could not resist in Chicago. James continued his way to New York City to try to find his brother Johnny. Whom he had not seen for an over forty years. He was not even sure if his brother were still alive, nor was he sure if Johnny would even want to see him. He prayed that time had healed and Johnny had forgiven him for his mother's death.

"We will meet again my friend" Jellyroll told James. "Then I can meet your brother and together we'll make music once again as shining stars on Broadway".

On January 20th, 1909 James stood at the river's edge on a cold day with gray clouds that guarded the magnificence that is, and was, the New York City Skyline.

James was now fifty nine years of age.

The search for his brother would prove to be very difficult for James. It had been almost forty years since James had last been in New York City. It seemed as though everyone he had known were either dead or had disappeared.

The first place James thought he might be able to find Johnny was at the Leonard Street brothel. He could not find the house and learned that it had been destroyed in a fire many years past. No one remembered the brothel even existed. Even if they could remember, they refused to acknowledge it. Julia Brown had simply disappeared into history.

James tried to find his mother's dear friend Angel Alice. He returned to the tiny flat the four of them had lived at. He asked the elderly residents if they remembered an American Indian woman who lived there many years past. No luck.

His next plan was to find Edward Clark. He learned of his passing in the year of 1882. James knew that his mothers and Edwards relationship was kept secret from most of the family members. This would prove to be a dead end he reasoned with himself.

It seemed to James, as if his mother and brother never existed. New York City grew bigger and lonelier every day for James.

James was quite resourceful when it came to living on a dime. He had lived in hotels, flop houses, brothels, the YMCA and on the kindness of strangers and friends all his life. If needed he could survive homeless living in parks and roadsides. Trying to live anywhere in Manhattan was not always possible for James. He found acceptable living arrangements in Harlem. He would room with other musicians and make a modest living playing his trusty trombone.

His search for his brother took all his "extra' money which there was precious little of. However, as long as he had something in his belly and a song to sing, then he figured he was a blessed man.

Finally after almost a year of searching for his brother, James decided to visit Edward Clark's family. He knew that the Clark family was one of the most celebrated high society families in the city. This would prove to make it very difficult if not impossible for James to arrange a meeting with one of the members of the Clark family. However, a small voice in his head told him not to give up and keep trying.

James found out that most of the Clark family members were now living north of New York City in the city of "Cooperstown".

Cooperstown was over 200 miles north of New York City. James would have to hitch rides on rail cars, or do what he did best and that was walk. He was very self-sufficient and knew he could survive.

With his trombone in hand, a stick over his shoulder, and some garments rolled into a ball, while singing Dixie, off he went to Cooperstown. For most the journey, James lived on the land and slept off to the side of the roadway.

The journey started on January 21st and took him nine days to arrive in Cooperstown on January 29th. An average of 22 miles a day. Quite an accomplishment for a man of 60.

He learned the Clark family was involved in the construction of a new luxurious hotel in Cooperstown. He asked many questions of the workers who were involved in the building of it. Through his questions he was able to learn where it was that the Clark family now resided.

When he finally found the mansion where the Clark family lived, James realized that it would be impossible for him to just walk up to the front door and ring the doorbell! For one thing, a twenty foot high iron fence encircled and protected the residence. Inside the fence roamed some very protective guard dogs. Even if he could get to the front door, what would he say?

For three days James stood outside the gate, in very difficult and freezing conditions, wondering to himself "What am I doing here?"

Sometimes it seems destiny steps in and gives a helping hand. As James was about to leave after another day of really not having a plan and not knowing what to say or do anyway, the front gate swung open and a man of about thirty years of age walked out with a dog on a leash.

The resemblance was uncanny. James would not normally approach a white man without extreme caution tempered with humility. This time, he simply blurted out "Excuse me sir, is your father Edward Clark?" The man stopped to face the Negro man who asked him this question. "Why, no sir, my father is Alfred Clark. However my grandfather was indeed Edward Clark. Did you know my grandfather? My name is Stephan Clark."

James was then able to carefully explain his relationship to Edward Clark to Stephan, his grandson. He was very respectful and very careful realizing that he must not reveal his mother's occupation.

After James told of his special relationship with Granddad Edward he told Stephen of his search for his brother Johnny. "I was hoping that perhaps someone in your family might remember my brother."

James was happy that Stephen was being very respectful of his inquiry. Stephen thought hard but simply could not come up with anything to help James with his search. Then just as James was about to leave, Stephen asked James what he did for a living? "Well", answered James "Johnny and I were entertainers and we also were part time artists. We both drew portraits in Central Park". Johnny was also a mason and liked to work with brick and mortar". "I think I may just be able to help you sir" smiled Stephan.

"My grandfather and Mr. Isaac Singer were involved in the construction of a building in Central Park West. My grandfather Edward, I believe, was in charge and the foreman of this building site. I remember hearing from my father that granddad told him that good masons were hard to find back then. The building is called the Dakota and it is located on 72nd Street and Central Park West. Perhaps my grandfather hired your brother."

"When was the Dakota constructed?" James inquired. "I believe it was finished in the year of 1884" answered Stephen. "That was twenty five years ago", sighed James. "Yes", answered Stephen "it would be highly unlikely anyone kept records of the workmen." With that said James started to walk away after thanking Stephen for his time.

"Wait a minute" Stephen said "I do remember getting my portrait painted a few years ago by an artist who set up his easel right across the street from the Dakota. He was a Negro artist! Perhaps he was your brother!"

James felt like his heart skipped a beat and was about to leap from his chest. Impulsively he gave Stephen a hug. "Perhaps with a little help from our Lord you can find your brother! Would you like to see the portrait? It is hanging in our hallway" Stephen asked James. "I would very much like to see it sir" answered James. This was the first real lead he had gotten about Johnny since his return to New York City in over a year.

Stephen opened the large Iron Gate and together they walked up the long manicured walk way to the large and very impressive front door. Along the way James noticed that the bushes were shaped in the form of bears, giraffes and other zoo animals.

The entry way to the house was spectacular. James realized how influent the Clark family had become. James began to feel quite uncomfortable and insignificant. Stephen seemed to sense that in James and made an extra effort to make his guest more comfortable. "This way my friend", Stephen motioned to James as the two men walked on the opulent white marbled flooring.

The spiral staircase was surrounded by family portraits. James stopped to admire a beautiful painting of his childhood friend and father figure, Edward Clark. He recognized the signature of the artist, his own.

Memories of his mother flashed before him. His eyes misted up when he thought to himself that not a single picture of her had survived. His thoughts were interrupted by Stephen's voice "Here it is James. Here is the picture I had commissioned when I was about sixteen. That would make the year 1898. Does this look like your brother's work?" James could no longer stop his flow of tears. "Yes", replied a choked up James "this is my brother's work." Then James looked for the item he knew he would find. His brothers initials on the lower side of the portrait. "These are my brother's initials, "J.W.L. Wells. We both signed our names the same." He motioned for Stephan to look at his grandfather's portrait. "Look," James said with more than a touch of pride in his voice "same initials." Stephen was almost as excited as James at this point and asked "James you told me your last name is Wells. Why then did you and your brother sign J.W.L.? Why the L?" "It was a game we played. We signed the same so that it was hard to tell whose work was mine and which was Johnny's. We signed the "L" to honor our hero, President Lincoln," James replied with a smile.

James stayed for over an hour talking to Stephen about his Grandfather. Carefully avoiding anything that the Clark family would find offensive.

"Your mother was a good woman" Stephen stated "I would have liked to have met her. I can see the love you have for her in your eyes as you speak of her. My grandfather was a good man too. I can sense that she was a good friend to him. Find the Dakota and with God's help you will find your brother."

Stephen next asked James if he were hungry? James was empty inside and the food was most appreciated. James left with a belly full of grub and pocket full of hope. Wishing his new friend Stephen Clark "Happy Christmas".

It took James five days to get back to New York City. It had been a particularly bitter winter. It was a very difficult journey home for James. However the thought of finding Johnny warmed his heart, body and soul. Stephan Clark had given James enough money to hire a horse driven coach for his return.

James had planned his big day for February 9th. 1909. Forty years had passed since the death of their mother, Sunflower.

James reasoned that his best chance to find Johnny would be to go to the park, where long ago they set up their easels to paint portraits. If Johnny is indeed still drawing portraits then this would be a way to spend this day in which to honor their mammy. Drawing portraits was always a way for James and John to reflect and relax.

In the distance James could see a beautiful gothic building that had not been there the last time he was in this area of Central Park. The Dakota stood proudly beckoning him forward.

He could also see a man sitting in front of an easel busily drawing a portrait of a lady sitting on a bicycle. James was still a healthy and vibrant man, and he whistled at the young woman who was wearing those cute "Betty Bloomer's" which were the fashion hit of the day.

When James got closer to the artist he could hear that he was singing a tune. The song he was singing was "Daisy Bell"

"Daisy, Daisy, give me your answer do"

"I'm just crazy all for the love of you"

"It won't be a stylish marriage"

"I can't afford a carriage"

"But you'll look sweet upon the seat"

"Of a bicycle built for two."

James felt the presence of this mother and his grandmother Daisy at that moment and knew he had found his brother, Johnny.

He slowly walked up to Johnny, there he was, the mirror image of himself. James took a deep breath and walked towards him. Johnny looked up from his easel and started to cry at his shadow, who was his brother. The two men held each other tightly. Both never wanting to let go again.

As if an invisible hand guided her, a very small woman draped in a shawl and wearing a large hat appeared next to James and John. John wiped the tears from his eyes and re-introduced James to a friend from his past. "James, do you remember our mother's friend and spiritual advisor, Neko?"

Her eye's had not changed in forty years. He recognized Neko right away. "Yes, of course, I remember you dear Neko. Your words and prayers were of great comfort at our mother's service. Its way over due in coming, but thank you," James said to the little woman now into her seventies.

Then John proceeded to tell James how Neko would comfort him during his ten year seclusion. "Neko and her pet kitty were my only friends. I asked Neko if I could paint her. She has not let me do this yet, but perhaps that now you are here she will let us both paint her portrait." "Your brother John, has been very kind to me", Neko said then bowed to John. "I'm afraid my image would not be so pretty to paint." James lifted her hat to see that the years had been cruel and that the little Japanese woman had indeed lived a life of great hardships. She bore several scars. People can be so cruel, James thought to himself. He was glad to know that John had been kind to her and that together they had helped each other survive.

"Neko never forgot this date of February 9th and our mothers passing. We passed this day together many times in this park across from this building that we both love so much, the Dakota. She told me that she has had many conversations with our mother in Spirit. Neko always assured me that our mother loves us both very much and that you will return. I never doubted her," John told his brother.

"Neko also saved my life" John informed James. "She warned me a few years ago of a man she had known who had been watching me. She told me to be aware of the man with the cold eyes and cruel twisted smile. I knew the man instantly when he approached me from behind my back. I turned to see his face and I knew what to do next. Right before I turned to run I saw that he had a large knife. Neko saved my life!"

James put his arms around Neko. She was so tiny and frail, at four foot tall she was more like a little girl than a woman. "Thank you for saving my brother's life," James whispered into Neko's ear. He was surprised at what she told him next, "You can thank me, but the entity you should really thank is Judy." "Judy," asked James, "who is Judy?" "She is a small white kitty who is always at your mother's side. Your mother has told me that you will remember her if you try.

It was Judy who told me through her thoughts, that John should be aware of this man" Neko replied. "I do remember the white kitty we named Judy! It was Judy who was at our side during the draft riots when we really thought we might not make it through that long and terrible night. I do remember Judy, she had a black patch of fur that was shaped like a heart" exclaimed James.

James then saw that she had a small birth defect that was on the left side of her eye. A birthmark shaped like a heart.

"God Bless you James" Neko said "Your mother loves you and wants you to know that is was not your fault."

James and John held each other again. "I love you brother", James said in between tears "please forgive me." "I have, many years ago. I love you James". The brothers held each other with happiness beyond measure. When they turned to tell Neko thank you for her comforting presence, she was gone. Neither John nor James ever saw Neko again.

John had one more item to show James. John took James over to his easel and produced a small urn. In it were the ashes of their mother.

John told James that every February 9th; he would take the urn with him to the park to be near him. It was his way of honoring their mother as she did not have a grave site.

John thought that one day he would release his mother's ashes to be with nature in Central Park. "My hopes and prayers were that you too would be with me when I did this" John said. "When you did not appear I thought Neko would be the one to accompany me. Neko never gave up. She always told me to wait. James will come. She never gave up. She was right. Today is that day".

James and John walked together across 72nd and Central Park West Avenue to a clearing.

"James, my dear brother, this is the spot for our mother to return. She loved Edward Clark very much, as did he her. She would have loved the Dakota."

"Edward Clark and the Dakota turned my life from one of being destitute to one that included the love of my life, Kitty, and our five, soon to be six children" John said with great pride.

James smiled and told John that he agreed. Their mother's ashes should remain at this place".

James then told Johnny about meeting Stephen Clark. How Edward's grandson was responsible for his finding him. "It's a miracle Johnny, my finding you. Our mother and Edward are smiling at us right now. This is a happy day".

Together James and John opened the urn and let the wind take their mother "Sunflower's spirit to be forever in Central Park across the street from the Dakota.

The children were overjoyed to meet Uncle Jimmy. Kitty was very happy for her husband whom she knew missed his brother every day of their life together.

Uncle Jimmy was given a special honor. Kitty was expecting in the spring. She informed James that he would be the one to name the new baby. She asked him not to tell her or John his choice of a name until the baby's birth.

A baby girl was born in the month of June. James kissed her tiny head and then announced to her parents her name. "Her name is Alvina Sue," James proudly told them. Kitty loved the name choice. She knew why James had chosen Alvina but why Sue?

Both brothers were caught off guard by Kitty's question. John gave James one of those looks, "Yes, Brother, do tell why the middle name of Sue?" James cleared his voice and said "Sue was a country girl and a honkey tonk Angel I will never forget. Some may have thought Angel not appropriate, but not I. I loved Shoes'y Sue." With that Alvina Sue smiled and cooed (probably gas) as for John, he whispered into his brother's ear "Well done."

James and John continued to draw portraits in the park. They soon once again had a large clientele. As they drew portraits they would also sing.

James could hardly wait to share the music of Jellyroll with his brother. Jellyroll arrived in New York City in 1911. John agreed that this music was a gift from Heaven.

Jellyroll went on to become a man of legend and his new music was called "Jazz". James was nervous as he introduced Johnny to his young friend whom he called "Jazzman".

"It's an honor to meet you sir" Jellyroll said as he held out his hand to shake John's. "I feel as though I already know you. James told me about many adventures the two of you shared." Kitty gave John "one of those looks." John just smiled.

Times were good. Then war was once again on the horizon.

My Tutorials

"Anne Pressly"

This next message is dedicated to Anne Pressly.

I met Anne only once, and I will never forget her. Anne Pressly was a news anchorwoman for channel 7 in Littlerock, Arkansas.

On Monday the 20th of October 2008, Anne was beaten and stabbed in her home by an unknown intruder. Anne Pressly died on October 25th, 2008. She was only 26 years old. In honor of Anne I would like to share my memory of her.

In 2008 I decided to fly to Arkansas from my California home to celebrate my granddaughter Trinity's 5th birthday.

Her birthday is August 23rd. To have met Anne on this day makes meeting her even more special.

For Trinity's 5th birthday we decided to invite her friends for a birthday party at the Chuckie Cheese Pizza parlor near Littlerock.

Trinity loves Barbie Doll! As do many little girls including myself. I still have my first Barbie which was given to me by my grandma Dora at the age of six in 1958.

So for this special day the birthday party's theme was "Barbie". We had Barbie balloons, Barbie napkins, plates, gift wrap and of course a Barbie cake.

As we all gathered to sing Happy Birthday to Trinity and get down to the important task of opening the gifts, we were surprised to look over our shoulders to see some commotion going on at the back of Chuckies pizza parlor. From the parking lot I saw a channel

7 news van parked. It seems that the news team were to interview patrons of this Chuckie Cheese for the evening news program.

We continued our celebration with happy birthday sung with great enthusiasm. Then Trinity blew out the candles on the cake with Barbie's smiling face in the center. All five were blown out and the gifts were presented to the delight of our special party girl. Then something magical happened. A beautiful, real life walking talking smiling Barbie walked up to our little angel Trinity. Her real life name is Anne Pressly. I had to rub my eyes in disbelief. Anne is so beautiful with Honey blonde hair just below her shoulders. Her eyes sparkled and danced with joy.

Anne was the chosen reporter for this evening who was interviewing patrons at this Chuckie Cheese about a toy recall that had recently been announced concerning a led scare in toys that are imported from China.

Anne excused herself for interrupting our party and then politely asked if she could ask us a few questions for her news report that evening on channel 7 TV. We told her we would be happy to be interviewed.

Thankfully we had recorded this interview in which we would be able to share with Trinity in the years to come.

We were very proud of "Daddy Matt," who stepped up to the microphone and answered Anne's questions with sincere honesty.

At the end of the interview Anne wished Trinity a happy birthday and finished the report by holding up a Barbie Doll and explaining how frightful this situation was for parents who give these toys to their children. The interview ended with a fade out of a smiling Trinity holding her new Barbie Doll with the Barbie cake in the background. Anne thanked us and gave Trinity a birthday hug.

Anne's passing in such a tragic way can and does really shake your faith. Why did this happen? I believe, with all my heart and soul, that Anne's life will have a profound effect on many souls. Her death will change lives. Her sacrifice, somehow will have a positive effect on someone. This is the only way I can even hope to understand something as terrible as her murder. That I met her on August 23rd is perfect.

XOXOXOXOX

"I don't want to be misunderstood"

On page 49 in Eric Burdon's novel, DON'T LET ME BE MISUNDERSTOOD, Eric writes of a rather disturbing encounter he witnessed that involved John Lennon and his father, Alfred Lennon. This encounter happened at a popular pub in swinging London in the sixties.

Eric explains how he and John were having a drink at a London pub when John's father walked in followed by two reporters. John became very nasty to his long lost father whom he had not had any sort of relationship with for years.

There have been many written accounts of this uncomfortable event in John Lennon's life. Basically, from what I can understand, John told his father to "f" off (or words to that effect).

Eric explains that after some very nasty moments John made a show of putting down his glass and walked out. Eric writes "like a brother, I followed."

I include this passage in Chapter eight "Family" because it reflects the tragic effects that can happens to families though separation.

Eric's book is amazing. I highly recommend reading it.

XOXOXOXOX

"The Banger sisters"

A few years ago, while in meditation, I felt John was trying to get something across to me concerning "Family" but I just was not sure what it was. It was while viewing the movie "The Banger Sisters," that I received a profound message from Spirit.

The Banger Sisters—2002

Goldie Hawn and Susan Sarandon were the leading ladies in this very funny movie. In the "Banger Sisters" Goldie and Susan were now middle aged and reliving memories from their youth together. The Banger Sisters were groupies from the sixties era.

It was nearing the end of the movie when I was to receive my message from John Lennon:

In one scene, Goldie and Susan were going through some moments of doubt and pain; the girls needed some time to work out some issues.

The scene opens with Goldie and Susan sitting under a freeway bill board sign. The sign reads "Got Milk." The way the sign is lettered reminds the viewer of John Lennon and Yoko Ono signs that were posted all over New York City during the seventy's that read "War is Over," and "Happy Christmas."

What happened next blew me away! There was music that accompanied the sisters as they sat under the "Got Milk" sign. The song was "Don't let me be Misunderstood."

This is one of Eric Burdon and the Animals classic hits.

It made so much sense to me! Got milk = Mother's milk (the billboard) which made me think of John and Yoko and the billboard signs all over NYC. Susan and Goldie—two siblings-who represented James and John Wells. "Don't let me be Misunderstood" which is what I hope when someone is reading this novel and the messages I've received.

I went home and searched the movie to learn who had sang the song, "Don't let me be Misunderstood", in the Banger Sisters movie. It was covered by Trevor Rabin. He was a former member of the band known As "Yes." Perfect!

Another event in the life of John Lennon that is well documented is how John met Yoko.

Yoko has been involved with the art scene all her life. She had a showing of her work at the Indica Gallery, St. James (there's that St. James again!). As far as I can understand, John was curious about her work and decided to view it for himself.

He spotted one work of art which involved him climbing a ladder to the top where it led up to a very small note which was attached to the ceiling. There was only one small word on this note and the word was "Yes". The rest is history. John liked the art work and he fell in love with the artist.

I believe that I had interpreted the message from the movie "The Banger Sister's" correctly. Once again Sunflower's story began to fall into place.

XOXOXOXOX

"Alvina and Alvenia"

My mother's first name is Alvina. As I was writing the chapters about James and his love, I knew at once that her name was Alvina. I really had no messages to confirm this assumption and quite honestly just felt like I wanted to honor my mother's memory.

It was after I had written about Alvina that I discovered once again an amazing 'coincidence' within the pages of Eric Burdon's novel "Don't let me be Misunderstood". On page 283 of his novel Eric describes how he believes he may have found the original House of the Rising Sun in New Orleans.

It was at this location Eric discovered an old portrait of, as he describes it, "a smooth-skinned brown beauty". Eric gives a description of this woman in this picture as having wide eyes, a long nose that was long and thin, yet African. Her hair was piled high on her head.

Eric then realized that the woman who he was gazing at in the portrait resembled a woman he knew many years ago. This woman's name was Alvenia Bridges. Alvenia, was a very beautiful and well known girl friend of his.

Was this a painting of Alvina? Who later in life changed her name to "Alvenia." The painting was indeed of a beautiful light skinned girl of African ancestry. Was this the same woman who was employed by the Rising Sun and Madam Marianne?

XOXOXOXOX

"Rick"

The one thing I have learned as I try to understand the messages I receive from my loved ones, my Guides, and of course John Lennon, is that on the other side of reality we seem to have an incredible desire to touch the hearts of those we loved in the past lifetime just left. A desire so intense that it continues many years after the loved one's passing. Even to the extent that this love encompasses not only the present life but past lives too.

The messages are as varied as the sands of time and space. From all I've read, and all I've experienced myself, it seems like the most desired message to try to convey to those left behind and in mourning is that "I'm OK." I'm alive now behind the looking glass". Always the message is LOVE—even if it seems to the loved one who receives it as ridiculous, or sad, it is meant to convey some form of love.

Which brings me to a message I received in November of 2007 from a man I never met in this lifetime.

This message was from a man I know only as "Rick"

On Tuesday the 6th of November, 2007 my father was scheduled for abdominal surgery. Dad was now 75 and in great health overall. So we approached this operation with positive energy and great hope. However, I do not think any of us would deny that as the moment approaches, it is damm scary to go under the dreaded Knife.

As we waited for surgery time, dad and his wife Lori, my husband Randy and I spent some quality time with each other. We talked of many private moments, reflections and memories. One of the people we spoke about was a friend of dad and Lori's. His name is Rick.

Dad told us about Rick. How Rick worked as a bartender at a local casino where he and Lori liked to go. Dad explained that Rick was a very nice guy, who smiles a lot and is always friendly. Dad, Lori and Rick developed one of those special friendships we think of when we think of a great bartender. They would visit Rick about once or twice a month and always had a great time chatting with him, while dad and Lori played video poker at Rick's station.

Dad told me that just a month ago he and Lori had went to the casino and approached Rick's bar expecting to see him busy with his normal chores. This time was different. Rick was sitting at the side of the bar with his head down. Dad said he hardly recognized Rick. Even though it had not been that long of time since they had visited with him. Rick had in this time, lost a tremendous amount of weight and looked quite a bit older than his age of 53.

When Rick spotted dad and Lori he waved a hello to his friends. It was then that Rick told them about his illness. He had cancer and it had spread to his abdominal area. There was not much anyone could do. Rick was in horrible pain and could not eat.

Dad and Lori were in a state of shock. Not only was their friend terribly sick but dad was facing the same type of exploratory surgery himself. Dad had been trying his best to keep a positive attitude but this was blow.

As the day of dad's surgery approached dad and Lori decided to return to Rick's bar to ask how he was. They saw that Rick was not attending bar. Carl was. Carl greeted Dad and Lori with their usual beer and cocktail in hand. Dad took a healthy swallow of beer and asked Carl about Rick. Carl told him that Rick was now in a hospice. Not much more was needed to be said. Needless to say, dad and Lori did not stay long. Both dad and Lori knew that Rick would never return to the bar. Dad's surgery was in two days.

The hour of Dad's surgery had arrived. Once again, Dad, Lori, Randy and myself are waiting for the doctor so we can get this "over with!" I prayed a silent prayer for Dad and for Rick too. I kissed dad and told him I will see him soon. November 6th is also the day of my mother's birth and the date of my Grandma Dora, dad's mother's passing. I knew each of these incredible loving women would be at dad's side in the operating room.

The doctor warned us this surgery could take as little as two hours or as long as six hours.

Dad's surgery took a little over two hours. He was out and in recovery at noon hour. One hour later he was wheeled into the ICU unit. We were able to peak in on him at this time. He was sleeping soundly. All his vitals were good.

An hour later dad woke up. We kissed him and told him it was over. He smiled and went back to sleep. In another hour he was talking to us. I was amazed! He was very alert and from what I could tell not in much pain. Now we wanted to hear from the doctor. We knew by then, that the tumor was not malignant, but it was still scary.

After a couple of long hours the doctor finally came into the room. He told us the surgery went great! He had cut off a foot of intestine and had gotten the tumor out. No cancer anywhere he could see or tell of. We all celebrated! Now we just gotta heal. Then get on with life!

After dad's surgery, the next day dad was even better. He was starting to sit up. Doctor says he is one day ahead in his recovery!

Dad made the comment that he was ready to go home! After our visit Wednesday I told dad that Randy and I were going to celebrate tonight and go to the casino to try to get a Royal Flush on the poker machines.

Dad and Lori were happy to hear we were gonna have some fun. As we were about to leave dad asked us a favor. "Anything dad, what do you want?" I answered. "I would like you to visit the casino where Rick worked and ask how he is doing. I've been thinking about him a lot" dad told me. I noticed dad's expression and my heart ached. "Of course we will," answered Randy.

As I have just stated, our loved ones on the other side will come through with messages that are not always given us by the way of roses, birds in song, or the way we would expect. Rick's message will not make much sense to those of you reading this unless I give you a little poker lesson.

A Royal Flush, in poker, is very difficult to get. The odds of getting this poker hand are approximately one in every two hundred and fifty thousand hands! The royal flush consists of the cards ten, Jack, Queen, King and Ace of one suit. If you are at a poker machine and get one then you are going to receive a handsome reward. For $1.25 cent bet the reward is one thousand dollars! So obviously it does not happen very often!

That Wednesday night we celebrated dad's successful day with a night of fun that included playing video poker and trying to get that illusive Royal Flush.

After gambling at two or three casino's we decided to make our way to the casino Rick worked at. We made our way to the bar we knew Rick had tended for years. We each put in our twenty dollars and started to play poker. A nice looking man of about fifty years of age approached us.

Randy looked up from the video machine and asked the man if he knew Rick? The man looked sadly back at us and said yes he did. Randy told him that we were John and Lori's kids (Dad and Lori were very well known and loved at this casino) and that they were asking about Rick. I later learned that the man that night bartending was Rick's friend Carl. He then said, in a matter of fact way "Rick died". Neither of us knew what to say. Randy put in another wager into his poker machine. That's when it happened! A Royal Flush in Hearts!

The timing was perfect. To doubt that Rick had just sent us a wonderful gift would be such a dishonor to his memory. Both Randy and I were without words. It was breathtaking!

The next day we told dad and Lori about Rick. We also told them about our Royal Flush in Hearts. Dad got it right away. Dad is tuff as nails, but this got to him and he understood. We all knew that Rick's suffering was over and he was now in paradise.

We found out that Rick died the same day as dad's surgery on The 6th of November. As I stated, this date is also my mother's birthday and the date of my paternal grandmother's death.

The name of the bar that Rick bartended at is called "The River

Bar". The river that runs next to this bar is not the Mississippi but is the mighty Colorado.

I am very thankful to Rick for this message I was able to pass along to my father. We can all use a little booster shot of faith every now and then and your message was much appreciated as was the thousand dollar jackpot! God bless you River Rick and thank you!

XOXOXOXOX

"Julia Stanley"

About a month ago (today's date is June of 2012) Rev. Arlene wrote to me out of the blue and asked me if I knew what the number one song was on the day I was born. I told her I did not, but that I would look it up and let her know. I did and found that the number one song was a song by "Johnnie Ray," called "Cry." She did not need to tell me why she asked, I knew. John asked her to ask me.

Johnny Ray had a group of singers who backed him up on the recording. The official name of the group on the record is "Johnnie Ray and the Four Lads". Pretty amazing.

Before I fell asleep I once again thanked our Creator for all my blessings. At the end of the prayer I thanked my friend and guide John Lennon also. Just as I was about to fall asleep I heard a little voice in my head ask me. "Do you know the last name of my mother Julia?" I had to admit to the voice "No I do not". I had to get out of bed, turn on the light, find my copy of Imagine and search- for Julia's last name. Again I heard the little voice in my head giggle "you're gonna be surprised! Her last name is Stanley. Julia Stanley.

This is also the maiden name of my sister Vicky's love of her life Robin. I wrote to Vicky, Robin and Dorothy (Robin's mother) the next day to tell her of my discovery.

I promised Vicky, on my honor, I did not know this until last night. Oh I'm sure I read it before, but if I were to be asked this question yesterday on Jeopardy I would not have been able to answer with the correct last name. What am I to take from this? I believe it all has to do with motherhood. I also believe it has to do with Huey (Dorothy's late husband) wanting me to tell the love of his life that he is watching over her and loves her.

Just as I had done the night before I asked John to send me another message (I was on a roll!) I wrote Vicky the next morning. I had suspected that Vicky was Neko in her past lifetime. Now I was sure.

Dear Vicky, Robin and Dorothy:

Last night, I asked John while in meditation, to tell me more about Stanley. This is what I learned:

When John Wells lost his mother, thru death, and his brother, because he blamed him for his mother's death, he went into hiding. He left everything and everyone behind and lived in the slums of Five Points, in NYC.

During this time he became a drunkard, a drug addict, a homeless and hopeless human being. The only person who he kept close to him was Neko. It was Neko who would come to visit him during this time. It was Neko who was able to connect with his mother and talk to her in Spirit. Neko also brought with her a special pet cat that John was able to love. Neko helped John get through this ten year seclusion.

As I have told you, and is well known, John Lennon's way of bringing forth a message from the other side with the use of white feathers. Your white feather is Robin. Yes, there are white feathered Robins. They are rare and very special. As is your love for Robin. John, his mother Julia Stanley, and Huey Stanley all were responsible in helping bring together this love bond.

My dear little sister I believe in one of your many past lifetimes you were known as "Neko". John loves you very much.

I Love you

XOXOXOXOX

"John Lemon"

As I was working on Chapter 8, a strong feeling of de ja vue once again hit me. I just could not shake the feeling. A small voice in my head said these words. "My name is Lennon". "O.k." I said to the small voice, "I know that but why are you reminding me?" I then noticed my copy of the book "City of Ero's", on my book shelf. I felt something within its pages held my answer.

I looked in the glossary to see if there was perhaps a John Lennon who lived in New York City back in the late 1800's. Well, there was not a John Lennon but there was indeed a John Lemon.

Chapter 11 of "City of Ero's" by Timothy J. Gilfoyle is entitled, "Concert Halls and French Balls".

I have heard of the term French Balls but I really did not know what French Balls were until I read this chapter.

After the Civil War, French Balls in New York City reached their zenith. After reading this chapter I realized that French Balls were basically mass orgies! Or, at least that is what the police, conservatives, purity crusaders, and many other concerned citizens thought of them. It truly was a battle over sexuality in the city of New York that continued into the new century.

In this chapter I learned of John Lemon. I'm not sure if he was a policeman, a lawyer or a newspaper reporter. Whoever he was, he was important enough to testify in court sometime in 1894. Where he shared his eyewitness report that during his experience at Madison Square Garden, he witnessed prostitutes in various states of nudity, also sexual activities that included lap dances!

I could not find any more information about John Lemon other then what I read in City of Ero's. I do feel that because John Lemon was fighting corruption he met John Wells who was in a desperate situation when the two men met. I do believe it was John Lemon who set the wheels in motion to help John Wells out of his "Lost Weekend.

It is interesting to me that John Lennon and John Wells each had their "lost weekend." John Lennon's lasted a little over a year. John Wells, over ten years.

Almost a century separated the 'two Johns" however I do believe that the John Wells weekend would better John Lennon's as far as promiscuity and debauchery!

Were the 1870's more sexually permissive then the disco - cocaine 1970's? They just might have been if you happened to attend a French Ball back then!

Update: today is December 14, 2011. Last night I watched Dick Cavett's show that was telecast on May 11th, 1972. His special guest stars for this night were Shirley Maclaine and John and Yoko Lennon. May 11th 1972 was also Eric Burdon's thirty first birthday. John was also thirty one when this was taped.

This was the first time I had viewed this show in its entirety. I was thrilled to see Shirley Maclaine and I thoroughly enjoyed her thoughts on the politics of the time. I also enjoyed hearing her interesting views on spirituality. She is an amazing woman.

What really blew me away was when Mr. Cavett opened the show by letting his audiences know who his special guest stars were for the night.

"Tonight, we have a very special show. Our guest stars for tonight are"—Dick giggles and next grabs the cue cards so that he can show the audience. He laughs and says I guess we do not have John Lennon but a fellow by the name of "John Lemmon!" Mr. Cavett held up the cue card in order for the audience to read it, someone had mistakenly written "Lemmon."

Just to put a nice bow on my message I was reminded that May 11th, 1868 was a day in Sunflowers life that was perfect. Today I received a three cent nickel from my sister Vicky. It is a three cent nickel that is dated 1868. She sent me this coin having no reason other than she just felt moved to do so.

XOXOXOXOX

"My name is Lennon"

Nine years ago we met Allen. He is a proud African American with a kind heart.

When Allen came to apply for a job at the bike shop he really did not have a resume. We hired him because we liked his easy going personality. He has worked at our shop for over nine years.

Allen and I have a common love we share and that is music and the people who make this magic happen.

Like my friend Robert, Allen has a remarkable knowledge when it comes to music.

One day a little girl came into our shop with her mother. Allen looked up from his bicycle repair and smiled at her. He came out to greet her with a big hug and a kiss on the cheek.

When I finally got the chance to say hello to the little girl, who was now standing next to Allen, I found out that she was his God Daughter. I asked her what her name is and she said "My name is Lennon." I had to rub my ear. "What did you say your name is sweetie," I asked. "Lennon," she replied. I looked at Allen and asked him how does she spell it?" 'L.E.N.N.O.N' of course!

He next introduced me to Lennon's mother. I just had to ask her "is your daughter named after John Lennon?" "Yes" her mother answered. "John Lennon is my hero."

"Allen, I've known you now for over two years. Why didn't you tell me about your God Daughter," I asked after Lennon and her mother had left. "Well, now you know," Allen smiled followed by a wink. An easy going Rastafarian wink.

XOXOXOXOX

"Beautiful Boys"

This spiritual message from John Lennon started on a beautiful spring day in April of 2004. I had taken the day off work to do some of the spring cleaning I had been putting off. I was busily scrubbing the kitchen floor with little else on my mind other than getting the floor clean. My mood was happy. I turned on the radio, pulled back the window shades and got to work. Then it hit me. The room darkened and sadness enveloped me, for no reason! I looked over to Buddy, our orange tabby kitty, who sat across from me from where I was working. Gazing at me with his sad amber eyes.

I was crippled with an overwhelming desire to cry. Then my mind went numb with a memory I had long forgotten about. This memory was deep in my subconscious. I traveled back into time and the year of 1977.

This memory was brought back to clear recollection and I could not shake it. All my life I have tried to make up for having made the terrible decision to put to euthanize three kittens. Why would this memory come to me out of the blue?

I could not shake the memory, the sadness and the shame of what I had done. I actually shouted to whoever is doing this to me to stop it! I felt like I was literally losing my sanity.

I got up from my scrubbing duties sobbing. I went to my bedroom to try to stop thinking about this awful memory. My sweet Buddy cat followed me. I sat on my bed petting Buddy when I spotted a book I had purchased a few months earlier at a used book store in San Francisco. The name of the book is "Lennon", by Ray Coleman.

I had not, until this time, read the book. I mindlessly thumbed through the pages. I have never since had an experience such as this. Buddy my orange tabby kitty nuzzled up close to me. "I love Kitty's", I told him. His purring machine was in full force. I looked at John's face on the cover of the book and asked "Why John, why would you want me to remember?"

I started to settle down and again picked up the book. On page nineteen (the age of John Well's when he lost his mother) was a picture of John's aunt Mimi holding a kitty. Under this picture the caption read "Aunt Mimi, whom John grew to love and respect. This picture taken in March of 1971, shows her with a cat John brought home as a stray". I smiled realizing this picture was taken the year of my son Franks birth. I also have an Aunt Mimi. Her name is Mary Wells.

I love the picture. Then I turned to the front of the book to the inside cover. The book was used when I purchased it so I have no idea who this person is. In hand written form is a message which reads—

HAPPY BIRTHDAY SPECIAL NIECE

LOVE AND MISS YOU

'AUNT KITTY'

29 APRIL 1986

Our beloved Kitty "Buddy' died two weeks after this message on April 26th, 2004. Three days later on April 29th, we received his ashes. We brought Buddy back to his home.

XOXOXOXOX

"Kitty Wells"

It had been eight months since I received my "Aunt Kitty & Beautiful Boy's message when I decided to once again visit Reverend Arlene. The date was December 8th, 2004.

I was hoping that perhaps John would come through with a message about his passing as this date was the twenty fourth anniversary.

I was to receive a much different message from the always unpredictable John Lennon.

Rev. Arlene: "Sherry, are you a fan of Kitty Wells? John keeps mentioning her name to me".

Sherry: "Kitty Wells? Who is Kitty Wells?"

Rev. Arlene: "Interesting. You do not know of Kitty Wells? Anyway, he is quite adamant and keeps repeating her name."

Then suddenly my mind went numb when I remembered my sad day back in April when I was reminded of the kittens and what I had done. My heart was lightened when I realized that perhaps the reason John mentioned Kitty Wells was her name. Rev. Arlene knew nothing of this message indeed no one did. Only John.

I truly believe, in his loving way he was telling me, "The kitties are well." I still believe this but time and more messages brought forth more meaning and depth to the Kitty Wells message. I also know that Buddy is well also.

After my reading with Arlene I went home and searched the internet for the country western singer "Kitty Wells." I learned that she was born in 1919. Sunflower was born in 1819. One hundred years.

Kitty Wells had her biggest country western hit with a song called "God did not create Honky Tonk Angels". Pretty appropriate description for Sunflower! Also this hit was in the year of 1952. The year I was born.

Finally through many messages, I knew I was right and that Sarah Anne's (Sunflower's) last name was indeed Wells. Her mother, Daisy, loved to sing with all her heart and soul into the side of the wells on the plantation she lived many years past.

Kitty (Katherine) Wells was the love of John Well's life and the mother of his six children.

XOXOXOXOX

"Alice"

There have been times in my life, as I'm sure there have been for you also, that I get the blues and miss those people and furry family I can no longer communicate with. It does help to remember those happy times you had together.

Sometimes it helps me to write my thoughts and hopefully, be able to share my thoughts with others.

I have received precious few messages from my mother since her passing.

A few years ago I posted a tribute to my mother entitled 'Beautiful Dixie Daisy." At the end of the tribute I finished with "I miss you mom. Please say hello to grandma, Grandpa, and all my friends and family behind the looking Glass." I then asked if it was all possible if she could give me another message of love.

I wrote this tribute years before I had begun this novel. It was years before I had any idea that Sunflower was anything other than a pretty flower.

It was a few months after this that we lost our pet cat "Buddy". At this time I was receiving many cat messages. I began to wonder if perhaps Buddy was the name of one of John's kitties. At any rate I asked this question to others who receive messages from John Lennon. Did John have a kitty by the name of Buddy?

I got the answer from an online friend of mine. In her letter she told me that John, in a dream, told her to tell me about his pet kitty "Alice."

John did indeed have a kitty by the name of Alice. He loved Alice very much. John lost Alice when she fell to her death from the balcony of his upstairs apartment at the Dakota.

This was a dual message. John is letting me know about Alice his precious kitty, and he also wants to express his love for his mother's dearest friend, and the Godmother to his children, "Angel Alice."

She was also one of the many friends who were responsible for bringing him back to reality and out of his long lost weekend, in his lifetime as John Wells.

Alice has one more meaning and it is very special and is from my mother.

One of mom's favorite bedtime stories was" Alice in Wonderland". I can, as I type this, hear her sweet voice and feel her loving presence, as she read to me about Alice, sending me to the wonderland of dreams.

Mom is indeed with Alice and the smiling Cheshire cat, behind the looking glass of reality.

XOXOXOXOX

"Doug"

On January 20th, 2009 our family lost a dear member. His name is Doug. My brother in law. He lost his battle with cancer and stepped the other side when he was only forty four years of age. Doug was husband to my sister in law Bobbi. A father to three beautiful children, Dale, Shane and Shannon.

Doug's fight began when he discovered a lump on the side of his throat. He was having difficulty swallowing and thought he had a bad infection. Time went by. Many Doctor visits. Finally he was diagnosed with stage four throat cancer.

Doug did not have an easy exit. He fought a valiant fight.

On Thanksgiving Day of 2008 our family went to the hospital to share it with Doug. I had not seen him for a few months. By this time Doug's voice box had been removed. He was living on a stomach feeding tube and he also had permanent tracheotomy tube. With all these challenges, when our family walked into his room, he greeted us with a smile from ear to ear.

He could not talk to us but he could write down responses on his erasable clip board. His courage made it impossible to feel anything other than pride. His children lovingly held his hand and gave him kisses and hugs. I am unable to find the words to express how much Doug embodied human spirit for life at this particular moment. Courage beyond courage, and love beyond the word.

I had brought one gift for Doug on this Thanksgiving Day. It was Rollingstone Magazines special issue of the 100 greatest singers' of all time. This featured John Lennon on the front cover.

Doug and I did not have a real close relationship. We would meet at birthdays and holiday's then catch up on each other's lives. We never spoke to each other more than just a few minutes. We had our families, friends, pets etc. in common but not much more. However, one Christmas, many years ago, we discovered another common interest. John Lennon. We both agreed that John was our favorite musician, song writer, poet, humanitarian and house husband. So we had John in common.

That was the reason I brought this magazine to Doug that Thanksgiving Day in 2008.

The last gift I received from Doug is a framed picture of the Beatles. I have it now in my living room and think of Doug often when I look at it.

Words cannot express how sad it was too loose Doug. He loved his children and his wife, all of his family and friends with all his heart.

Here is how I learned that our family had lost Doug.

Randy and I were on a cruise in the Caribbean with our kids. When we left for this cruise Doug was home and although things were far from great, we felt at least he was not in the hospital and at home with his family.

On our return flight home we had a layover at JFK airport. It had been a week of no contact with our family while we were at sea. When we landed at JFK we noticed that we had a new message from Bobbi, Doug's wife, on our cell phone. This could not be good. Randy asked that I listen to the message.

I took the cell and walked over to the window. In the distance I could see the magnificence of the New York City skyline. Behind the skyscrapers were big gray clouds standing guard. "Hello John," I said before I clicked on the voicemail message, imagining at the same time I could see the Dakota.

Bobbi's message told us that Doug had passed. He passed away on January 20th. It was now January 23rd. Bobbi said she had not called until now because she did not want to upset our vacation.

I stood there at the window and knew John was once again with me for comfort. Not only me, our entire family.

I told Randy. To say we did not expect to hear that Doug had passed is not entirely honest. We all knew his battle was drawing near its end; it's just hope burns eternal.

When I boarded our jet for home, I was in a state of shock. We were flying Jet Blue. This airline features personal in flight television and music. I just wanted to hear some music as I sat down. Before I clicked on the music station I asked John and Doug to send me a message in the form of music. I put on my headphones and clicked it on. The song that was on was—"She Talks to Angels"—by the Black Crows. I knew at that instant that Doug is in Paradise. My mind went back into time when I met the little black kitty 'Crow' at the used book store in Duluth. I shuttered remembering how close we came to losing dad.

Time heals, but you never forget. We miss you, Doug.

James stood and gazed at the New York City Skyline on January 20th, 1909. I stood and gazed at the New York City skyline on January 20th, 2009. Exactly one hundred years.

God bless Doug, Bobbi, Dale, Shane and Shannon.

XOXOXOXOX

"Cooperstown"

As I was researching the history of Edward Clark's family, I discovered that Edward Clark's descendants moved from NYC to Cooperstown, New York in the latter part of the 19th century.

That indeed his grandson, Stephen, was responsible for the beginnings of the Baseball Hall of Fame in Cooperstown. Interesting also is that the Baseball Hall of Fame was opened on June 12th. Our daughter Crystals birthday is June 12th, of 1975. Another confirmation for me.

When I read that the Clarks had relocated in Cooperstown I realized that another interesting coincidence had occurred.

About ten years ago I met a man who told me that he was the

owner of John Lennon's birth certificate. When this man told me this, I could tell he was shocked that he had revealed this to me. He told me he had paid a huge amount of money for it in auction. He asked me to keep it to myself which I have and I will. This man is in the entertainment business and I believe he told me the truth. I will say that he was not born in Britain.

A few months after I learned of this birth certificate I received a special gift through the mail from this celebrity. I saw that his return address was from a city whose name seemed 'familiar' to me. At this time period, I must add that I was not aware of Sunflower's existence yet.

The name of the city this celebrity lived in is not exactly Cooperstown but very close. That's about all I can reveal.

I believe that what James discovered in Cooperstown, New York, was the beginning of a new life (birth) for the brothers who were separated for so long.

XOXOXOXOX

"J.W.L. Wells"

When I wrote this last passage about how James discovered two portraits, one of Edward Clark, the other his grandson Stephen Clark while James was at the Clark mansion, I was led to believe that John and James would sign their names with their initials J.W.L. on the finish artwork. Adding the "L" for Lincoln.

I thought I had gotten it right, however I also felt like something was missing. It took a little over six months to receive my message and re-write the pages.

Today is the 10th of August, 2012. It is also the birthday of my sister Vicky's life partner Robin. As I have revealed in an earlier chapter her last name is the same as John Lennon's mother Julia Stanley.

Today is also a day in which I have received perhaps one of the most amazing gifts from Spirit I've ever been given. Here is my latest!

About three weeks ago a young man came into our bicycle store to purchase a few parts. While he was there he happened to mention to me that his mother owns a newly opened antique-second hand store. I knew of the store and told the young man to wish his parents good luck from me. Then the young man informs me (for no reason I can think of at all) that his mother had just recently purchased a first edition Charles Dickens novel from a storage shed she had bid and won. Of course my interest went up several notches.

Today I decided that I must go to the store and see this book for myself. I must add that the little voice in my head was relentless! Go Now! So I went to the store in hopes to see this book by Charles Dickens.

I met Candy the owner of the store who was very gracious. I asked her about the book and she informed me that yes she did indeed have a first edition but that she had just sold it yesterday to the Gold and Silver Pawn shop in Las Vegas. The same pawn shop on History Channel's television show called "Pawn Stars".

Her husband, Donald, overheard our discussion and announced that just a few days' ago purchased a box of antique books at an estate sale. "Would you like to see them? The box is still in my car. I'll go get them" he informed me with great excitement. I could not say no, he was so excited. Donald returned with cardboard box of books. There were eight books inside the box. All the books were dated from the 1850's to the 1880's.

I told Donald thank you for showing them to me but that I'm really not an antique book collector. I just have an interest in Charles Dickens. He simply would not give up! He was so insistent that I purchase the books. I could not refuse him.

I picked four books which interested me. I had only brought twenty dollars and felt foolish but asked anyway—"Would you take twenty for these four?" I asked sheepishly. "Please take them all", he told me that he really wants me to have them. So I was now the proud owner of eight novels. The newest being published in 1880!

When I got back to the bike shop and looked at one of the novels

I could not believe my eyes. The name of the novel is—On Both Sides of the Sea. By M.W. Dodd. It is in very good condition.

The inscription is what blew me away! On the first page inside cover this is what someone had signed so many years ago.

To: J.W.L. Wells.—Please dear reader I am not clever enough to make this up! I knew immediately what I had left out! J.W.L. (Wells) of course! I left out their last name!

I next looked to see the published date of this book

I gasped when I read

New York—-M.W. Dodd, 506 Broadway 1868

1868 is the year; I believe Sunflower had quite a few encounters with Charles Dickens while he was on his second vacation & book promotion in America. On May 11th of 1868 I had written of Sunflowers perfect day at the art exhibit with her son's and the love of her lifetime, Edward Clark.

The signature above JWL Wells is ACS LENN??? I cannot make out the last few letters but I do not think it is Lennon but it is close. The Lenn is, to my eye, identical to how John signed his last name.

On the right and left upper corner of the first and second pages of this book is written this curious note—Hi 8—I have recently learned that this may simply be the placement number of this book when it was shelved at the library.

For me however, it is a way of John or James Wells telling their mother hello. If she were to have a favorite number then I would say it was the number 8. She was born in the 8th month. In my mind I am hearing a voice and this voice is telling me "if I were an octopus I would have eight arms to hold you. I love you Mammy".

So, did this little book belong to my son John or James Wells? Did it somehow make its way to find me some one hundred and forty four years later? I treasure this little gift from both my sons who signed their names J.W.L. Wells.

XOXOXOXOX

"Number 8 and Number 9"

9th month (September) in 2008—we received an incredible gift
from spirit in a most unusual way. We were at our annual bicycle
convention in Las Vegas where we were given an honor from one of
our bicycle company's.

We were told that we were in the top 25 Dealer's list. We were
given a beautiful engraved crystal with our shops name. We were also
given a Silver belt buckle. I looked at the back of the buckle to see a
number on it. I asked the owner of the company what was our official
number? When he told me #9 I jumped and shouted in joy! "We're
number Nine!" I could have not been more proud or happy!

XOXOXOXOX

"Betty Boop and the Walrus"

This next message was given me from my Grandma Dora and my
mother Alvina Dixie Daisy.

As always, I do feel that John Lennon had his part in this message
also. In my mind I see him sitting in a director's chair. He is wearing
a white fedora hat, blues brothers type sunglasses, a white double
breasted suit, shiny white Patten leather shoes, and he is smoking a
ciggie in one of those long holders.

Grandma and Moms message began in a dream I had in 2006.
One of those dreams we've all had in which it feels so real that when
you awake you know it was different from all other dreams. I'll never
forget it.

The Dream: begins with me standing at a podium on stage. I
am standing in front of an arena size audience. I seem to understand
that the audience is composed of everyone I've ever met, if only for a
moment, during my life as Sherry. The audience is absolutely silent.

Suddenly, a spotlight appears and shines down on a person who
is seated in the front row. She stands up and I realize who she is—my
grandma Dora.

I try to say something but nothing comes out of my mouth. I want to tell grandma how much I miss her and how happy I am to see her. I cannot find my voice! However I can tell by grandma's look that she understands and knows how much I love her. She is so beautiful.

Then a microphone appears out of know where next to her. She takes the microphone in hand and informs me "I just love Betty".

She smiles again. Then she shows me a nickel. "Let's put a nickel in the juke box and see what comes on." Like the Microphone, an old fashion juke box suddenly appears to her right. It is beautiful and seems to be made of gold! Grandma next takes the nickel and flips it high into the air.

The next thing I hear is perhaps the most beautiful music I have ever heard in my life! The song that came on the juke box was "When you wish upon a star."

I now see that there is another person sitting next to Grandma in the front row. It is Mom. I wake up.

When Grandma told me that she just love's Betty, I believed she was referring to her eldest daughter whose name is Betty.

I went on the internet to read about the song "When you Wish Upon a Star". I read that it won the Academy Award for best song in 1940. The year of John Lennon's birth. I also read that the character who sang it in Pinocchio was Jiminy Cricket. Not a Beatle but close!

The next day at work, I saw a small book lying on the guest table. It was a children's book that had been left. The book was "Pinocchio".

I was very amazed and very grateful for this special gift from Grandma Dora, Mom and Dear John.

However, I had a feeling that there was more than one Betty. I was right, there was another Betty and her last name is Boop!!

Now, I must flash forward into time. It had been over three years since I had this dream. I was at the library when I happened to see a book with the title of "The Afterlife Experiments" by Dr. Gary Schwartz.

It is not unusual at all for me to either purchase or check out books such as this. I find them fascinating. This book was no exception. I highly enjoyed it.

In this book we are introduced to Christopher Robinson, who is a psychic detective. He lives in Scotland. After reading about Chris I knew I had to try to contact him. Besides being a psychic detective, Chris has another specialty, and that is dreams. I wanted to share not only my dreams but my connections with John with Mr. Robinson.

I found his web site www.dreamdetective.com Chris and I shared a few emails back and forth. I was not sure where all of this was taking me until I received an email from Chris asking me if John Lennon had anything to say about August 8th?

I wrote Chris back and told him I could not think of any connection with John about the date of August 8th, but that I would write him if something turned up.

The next morning, the 9th of August was a Sunday. I woke up and turned on my favorite Sunday morning TV. Show "Sunday Morning" on CBS. The show featured two segments.

The first featured the date of August 8th. The host of the show told of how on August 8th, 1968 the iconic photograph of the Beatles walking across Abbey Road Studio's was taken. Ah! Ha! That's it I thought. That is what happened on August 8th! I'm glad I tuned in, I would have not known.

The next segment, featured on the Sunday Morning telecast, was about August 9th. On August 9th, 1929 America was introduced to a new American Icon. Her name is Betty Boop.

The Sunday morning show featured a cartoon in which Betty Boop is singing to a rather strange and wonderful creature.

In this famous cartoon Betty is being sung a song called "Minnie the Moocher"—by Cab Calloway. Cab Calloway's character in this cartoon is a Walrus! A rather strange looking ghost Walrus!

I learned that Cab Calloway was an incredible dancer, singer, band leader, song writer and that he also had quite the flair for fashion too! I found videos of Cab Calloway in which he wears a double breasted all white suit with shiny white shoes. Very familiar! Then I remembered how John Lennon looked the day he wed Yoko in Gibraltar near Spain! Same suit. In fact the little step he does reminds me of Cab Calloway.

Chris Robinson the dream detective helped me discover not only Betty Boop but also Cab Calloway by asking me to ask John about the meaning of August 8th/9th. The Dream detective found "Betty" for me!

I wrote back to Chris Robinson and thanked him for the helping me decipher my dream. I finished my letter with the Lyric I thought was from the Lennon/McCartney song "I am the Walrus." "Koo-ko-ka-choo"—to you Chris. Not realizing this lyric was from the Simon and Garfunkel song "Mrs. Robinson."

I was amused that I could make this mistake! How many times have I listened to "I am the Walrus", who knows! Maybe a million!

I believe this Mrs. Robinson mistake might be a reference to another life John may have lived. In her novel "The Lennon-Bronte Connection", Jewelle Lewis writes about her belief that another of John Lennon's incarnations just may have been Branwell Bronte. That Mr. Bronte was in love with a married woman by the name of Mrs. Robinson! Amazing! Jewelle's first novel "Just Imagine", published in 1995, is about the life she shared with another of John Lennon's incarnations in sixteenth century England. His name was John Baron; her name was Katherine St. James. I highly recommend both novels.

As I have stated in an earlier message my sister Vicky's mother in law's last name is Stanley, her maiden name is Robinson. Just another connection.

Cab Calloway recorded a song called "Saint James Infirmary". Eric Burdon, who many believe is the Eggman from the song, "I am the Walrus" recorded a version of—St. James Infirmary—also.

Just to put a cherry on top of the cake—St. James is the name of the street in New Orleans where I was told may be the site of the original House of the Rising Sun. I do not believe this true, instead I have a strong belief that this is the address of the brothel Sunflower lived and worked at. The same that was operated by Madam Rose. Nope not a coincidence. Koo-Koo-Ka -choo Mrs. Robinson! Goo-Goo-g-Goob—Eggman! Boop-Boop-Be-do—Betty Boop!

Sometimes ya just gotta love it! We just love Betty!

Just a little reminder—August 8th and August 9th. The number 8 for Sunflower the number 9 for her son John.

XOXOXOXOX

"Daisy Bell"

In 2007 I received a wonderful message from John Lennon that was given to me right before Mother's Day.

One of my favorite movies is "2001 Space Odyssey.

Stanley Cubic's Epic movie was made in 1968. I find it hard to believe that this movie masterpiece was made of forty three years ago! The film, in my opinion, is way ahead of its time.

Now onto my message from John.

Once again my message came from Arlene via a reading.

On this day Rev. Arlene, once again, revealed many personal observations and advise for me. Some of it felt relevant, some not so. It was delightful to see her once again and as always nice to feel connected with our Creator and our unseen friends.

One little moment during this reading, of which I have on recorded tape, Arlene asked me if I know of a song called "Daisy Adieu?" I told her I did not know of such a song and asked her why? "Oh, she says, I just keep hearing a song that has something to do with Daisy. John is humming a song and I just cannot quite connect". That was all that was said on this subject and we continued talking about something else. Then the session ended.

After I left Rev. Arlene's office, I went to the front desk to talk to Bill (not real name) the owner of the Spirit of the Moon. After we had talked a few minutes Arlene came out and joined us. She asked Bill if he knew of a song called "Daisy Adieu?" Bill is an accomplished musician himself and he could not remember such a song either. "I just can't get this tune out of my head", she then said in a whispered voice "John, he's being relentless!" Arlene continued humming at that point.

Then I realized that the tune was not Daisy Adieu but Daisy Bell or as the song is better known by "A Bicycle built for two".

Arlene, Bill and myself began singing the song together. Reverend Arlene was thrilled when we sang the lyrics as she did not remember the song was about a bicycle.

The next day I could not get the tune out of my head! All day long I hummed and sang "Bicycle Built for Two", while I worked at the bicycle shop. Allen heard me humming it and asked if I had recently watched his all-time favorite movie lately? I asked what movie was this. He informed me "2001 A Space Odyssey". He then told me that "Daisy Bell" was used in this movie's musical score. I told Allen that no, I had not viewed the movie for some time and that I did not realize this song had been featured in it. "Yes, it was", Allen answered "remember when Hal 9000 was switched off by Dave? Daisy Bell was the first song the computer Hal 9000 learned from his programmer". "Oh, Yeah, your right", I replied. I knew then instantly that John was behind all of this and I said this to Allen. He just smiled.

So I went home and researched John Lennon and 2001 a Space Odyssey and immediately received lots of data on this subject.

It seems John Lennon was fascinated with this movie. There were rumors that John watched 2001 countless times. It could be said that it is his favorite all time movie. John Lennon did make a statement that all church services should show this movie before Sunday service began.

Well how about that I thought! I had no idea that John had loved this movie. Now I do. I do feel that the message of Daisy Bell has many meaning's for me and for John.

First—it is a hello to me from my mother Daisy in this life and my former life.

Second—it is a clever reference to my current life's profession—bicycles!

Third—I feel it is a statement on reincarnation. For those of you who have viewed 2001 Space Odyssey- Do you remember the last scene of Dave the astronaut floating within his mother's womb? I have always thought this scene represented that Dave was returning home to earth in a reborn body

On a personal note: I was thrilled I received this message just a couple of days before Mother's Day. Perfect.

Fourth—I have always felt that John Lennon really loved riding bicycles and was fascinated with them too!

Finally I know that this is the song that John was singing when James finally found him as he painted a portrait of a girl, sitting on a bicycle, wearing those cute "Betty Bloomer's" across from the street from the mighty Dakota.

Daisy Bell was composed by Henry Dacre in 1892.

First heard in the Bowery, New York City.

James finally found his brother Johnny in Central Park at West 72nd Street. February 9th, 1909. So many nines! Oh yeah—Hal 9,000 model.—I repeat so many nines!

XOXOXOXOX

"How our kitty Judy saved our lives"

As I have reveled in previous chapters, I have received many spiritual messages where the wonderful magnificent feline is the messenger.

Judy was our white kitty who passed away on October 26th,

2010. This was also Randy and my 36th wedding anniversary. Judy was all white with several black islands (patches) of fur. One of these islands was in the shape of a heart.

It was in 1995 that Randy and I were seriously thinking of relocating to northern California when we read that a bicycle shop was for sale in Fort Bragg. At the time Judy was only about two months old so we could not leave without her. So she went with us to Fort Bragg which was about a twelve hour drive from our home.

We did not make the move, but we did have a delightful visit with my Uncle Fred and Aunt Mary Wells. They resided in Mendocino, California. At the time Grandma Dora was visiting them so we had a lovely visit with Grandma too. I'm forever grateful that because of the shop for sale we made the drive. I'll never forget this visit.

On our drive home we decided to stop for lunch in Willits, California. We stopped at one of those little family diners that clung to the main highway in the older part of the City. It was October so it was quite cool. We parked our car in front of the diner so that we could see it while we had our lunch. We made sure Judy was comfortably sleeping in the back seat. We locked the door and left her.

The diner was delightful as was the home cooked food. We made the comment to each other, how friendly everyone was at this establishment. Good food, good people as the saying goes.

What happened next is forever ingrained in my memory. Our car was parked parallel to a very busy highway. We approached the car and looked into the window to make sure Judy was not going to jump out. Randy put the key into the front passenger door and I stood behind him. He carefully opened the door and reached down for Judy. As he did this I realized then that someone was standing behind me. I turned to face a very evil looking man. His eyes were piercing. He saw that I was looking at him and he motioned for me to look down. He had a very large hunting knife he was pulling out from its sheath. I froze. I did not know what to do. He was obviously going to stab either Randy or myself.

Randy in the meantime was having issues getting Judy. By this time I had moved up behind Randy so close that he could not close the door. "Move", he told me "I can't reach Judy and she'll get out! I've got to close the door dammit." I stepped back to face the man. At the same time Randy reached Judy and stood up with her in his arms. I saw the man's face change from evil to good. I turned to see that Randy still had his back to me, but now he was holding Judy and she was now facing me and the man.

I was so frightened by then I did not know what to do, if I screamed he might stab me! Finally Randy turned to face me and hand me Judy so that I could get into the car. I took Judy in trembling hands. "What's wrong with you?" Randy asked me in frustration. "Judy could have gotten out!" I could not believe Randy would say this to me with a man and a really big knife standing behind me! Then I knew why, the man had simply disappeared, silently gliding away as if he were a ghost.

I was snapped back into reality when I heard Randy exclaim "Shut the damm door." I shut the door and as we drove away I began blabbering like a crazy woman. "Did you see him? Did you see that man? He had a knife and he was going to stab either you or me. I think he wanted to rob us!"

Randy never did see the man. We drove back to the diner but we could not find him. We did see that there were some shady looking characters but not the man with the cold cruel eyes and evil snicker.

After reflecting on this later, I believe that the man was going to try to rob us. I believe that he thought Randy was bent over reaching for his own weapon in the car. So the man hesitated. When he saw Judy, his plan changed. In my heart I believe that the little black and white kitten softened his heart and he changed his plan. I believe this.

XOXOXOXOX

Chapter 9

MAMMY

THE YEAR WAS NOW 1914, and this time the war was in Europe. America had not yet joined the fight as far as sending troops into battle yet, but everyone knew it would soon come to pass.

Both James and John were deeply patriotic men. As the fever of war began to grow, so did patriotism.

At the age of 64, James and John Wells had "Started over," and began to appear on stage at various cabarets and theatres in Harlem. Then as their two man show grew in popularity, they began performing in Midtown and off Broadway.

James and John were billed as the J&J Brothers. They would appear on stage in black face, tux with tails, white gloves and white Patten leather shoes.

In 1917, America officially declared war on Germany and began to send troops into harm's way.

Also in that year, a new and very moving song from George M. Cohan could be heard throughout the city. The song was called "Over There." James and John now opened their act with this brilliant song. By now, John and James had perfected their voices and blended them in perfect harmony.

James Paul Wells, John and Kitty's second born son, had enlisted into the army in the year of 1917 at the age of twenty seven. His brother Desmond Eric also joined the army to fight for his country when war was declared. He was nineteen.

Desmond Eric adored his older brother James Paul and wanted to make him proud. Desmond would tell his family that he was going to fight for America and become a sky pilot.

Desmond never realized his dream and was not able to become a pilot. However, he was proud to have been able to serve alongside one of the most decorated Units in World War One. This "colored" unit was known as the "Harlem Hell Fighters' who were a part of the Army's 369th division.

Desmond Eric Wells died in battle at the age of twenty years.

Everyone in the Well's family, along with all of his many friends, were saddened by the loss of Desmond. He was an especially out going and happy person. Just being near Desmond could make a gray day blue and cheery.

Desmond's twin sister, Molly Joe, had great difficulties coping with the loss of her twin brother, however, because of the loving family she was a part of, she was able to go on. Her older sister, Sarah Anne, became her best friend and the two were never to leave each other's side for the rest of their lives.

James Paul Wells, because of his talent with the clarinet, was able to perform with the regimental Jazz band leader Lt. James Resse Europe.

James Paul did see action in the war. The atrocity's he saw were imprinted in his memory forever. He was never the same.

His talent for music saved him from living a life of misery. He became a fixture of sorts at the clubs in Harlem, especially at a club on Lenox street that later became known as the Savoy Club. It was in this atmosphere James Paul tried to start a new life.

Unfortunately, along with a love of music, came a love for a demon who would sing a song in his ear that was more tempting then any woman he had ever met. This woman's name was Heroin

In 1918, the war was over. James and John continued to sing patriotic songs and perform a show dedicated to the country they loved and the country that their son and nephew gave his life. Always opening their show once again with "Dixieland".

At every performance the J&J brothers would have the M.C. announce that their show was dedicated it to all the brave African Americans who served and gave all for America. After performing Dixieland, James and John would sing a very moving rendition of "Over There." Performed first at a slow tempo then a change to the upbeat tempo for which song is known for.

At the end of the song James and John inserted Desmond Eric's name into the lyrics.

On August 23rd, 1920, James and John celebrated their 70th.

Their big day began with a walk with two of their grandchildren in Central Park. James and John had no idea that a big surprise birthday party was planned for them.

When James and John approached West 72nd and Central Park West, across from the Dakota in the exact area they would go to remember their mother, they were greeted by just about everyone they had ever known. Their loved ones were waiting, hiding behind trees and bushes for James and John to arrive. What a celebration! There was singing, dancing, clowns, balloons, and a cake that was large enough it seemed to feed the entire city!

Many of John and James friends were in the music business so the air was filled with the sound of voices in song, violins, horns, guitars, accordions, harmonica's, drums, and even a stand up piano! James blew his trombone for all he was worth.

Just as the celebration was getting under way a bio winged flying machine flew overhead. On the side of the air plane printed in huge letters was "Louie's Flying Circus." The air plane circled above

several times then dipped its wings at the celebrants in Central
Park. James, John, Kitty, and everyone at the party realized it was
Desmond Eric's way of wishing his father and Uncle Jimmy a happy
birthday. As the "Sky Pilot", flew into the morning clouds, John and
James saluted the plane.

The grandchildren had saved all their penny's and nickels to buy
their papa John and Uncle Jimmy a very large kite for their birthday
present. After most of the guests had returned home, James and John,
along with all the grandchildren and Kitty, tried to fly the kite.

At one point John slipped and fell into a puddle of mud. James
dipped his hands into the mud and chased his brother like he did
when they were young boys. The grandkids laughed and laughed.

The kite never did fly but everyone sure had a grand time in
trying to get it up in the air.

When everyone left, John and Kitty stayed behind to celebrate
in private. Under the stars, the two "Youngsters at heart", made love
in Central park.

James and John's show was by now a very polished and well
received show that was a part of the vaudeville tours around midtown and off Broadway. The J&J brothers would appear on stage
in the black faced minstrel tradition. Wearing the finest of tuxedo's
with tails, Patten leather shoes that were shined to the "nines."
Their ensemble was finished off with a top hat and gloves. Their
performance would usually include five songs.

On the occasion of their 72nd birthday, J&J invited many family
members and friends to the August 23rd performance. J&J had a
special dedication at the end of their performance for that nights
show. On this night, they began their show with their usual Set
list.

J&J would open the variety show with the singing of the National
Anthem. James and John had a rather unusual version that was
"jazzed' up a bit. It was very well received.

The second song they sang was "Dixieland" or "I wish I was in

Dixie." sang traditionally slow. A harmonica man would accompany them.

The third song, J&J asked James Paul to accompany them. James Paul (John's second born son) was now a very skilled clarinet player. When he was able he would sit in with his dad and Uncle Jimmy. This was one of those times. The song was "Over There" of which J&J dedicated to all our valiant soldiers who include our son and nephew James Paul and Desmond Eric. Then J&J saluted James Paul who bowed and saluted them in return.

The fourth song was dedicated to Grandma Daisy. The song was "Daisy Bell" or as it had become better known as "Bicycle built for two." During this song J&J would sit on a tandem bicycle while a few pretty women wearing "Betty Bloomers" danced behind them. The pretty girls would tease and tickle J&J as they sang the song. James was able to show off his trombone skills and get off the bicycle and chase the girls while blowing his horn. The audience loved it.

The fifth and final song was a collaboration of two popular songs. J&J combined "Swanne River" with "My Mammy."

The closing lyrics from these two songs as interpreted by James and John were:

Mammy how I love you

How we love you

Our dear ole Mammy

We'd walk the world to be, among the folks in

D.I.X.I.E. ven now we miss you.

Then just as James and John were to sing the final lyrics, they blew a kiss to the Heavens above and sang——

We'd walk a million miles for one of her smiles from our Mammy.

Usually this would end the show with a bow from J&J to the

audience. This night, the show ended with the bow then a turn toward center stage where a huge picture now stood.

A single spot light now shown on a life sized painted portrait of their mother Sunflower.

James and John had painted this portrait from memory of how they remembered their mother the morning she attended Abraham Lincoln's speech at Coopers Union. Dressed in her long black satin dress with blue and white trim. A small hat tilted to the side with a single white feather on top. Long black gloves that held her mother Daisy's black trimmed fan with the beautiful blue butterfly's on it.

It was a picture of beauty and grace from her two sons who missed and thought about her every day in every way.

James and John sang "happy Birthday" to their beloved Mammy.

Sunflower thanked her sons the next day when James, John, and Kitty along with their nine year old grandson, Johnny Eric the third, went to visit the new Sea Aquarium.

This aquarium had a huge tank in which, just like the painting that John and James had viewed many years past, featured many octopus, sea urchins, star fish along with many varieties of sea weed that floated along with the motion of the water.

Johnny Jr. took his granddaddy's hand and exclaimed with great excitement, "Grand-daddy look! It looks like an octopus garden in the sea". James and John smiled when the memory of the painting at the art gallery instantly came back to both of them. "Yes, it is indeed an octopus garden you are right Johnny Jr.", grand-dad John said, then added "and look, the octopus has eight arms to hold you".

Then John felt a light touch on his shoulder. He felt two little pokes. He turned to see a young light skinned Negro girl who was holding a single flower. The flower she held was a large and very beautiful sunflower. The center of the sunflower pod was in the shape of a heart. The flower girl asked John if he would like to purchase a flower for his sweetheart. With tears in his eye's John bought every sunflower she had in her cart.

She had nine.

John and James together planted the sunflower seeds in their apartment garden and also in the garden at the Dakota. As they did this, a light sweet wind kissed her beloved sons on their cheeks. A mother's love is never far.

The seed's in turn, every spring, come back to life

My Tutorials

"Starting over"

This is really more of a personal observation then a message from spirit. I believe we do repeat events from our prior lives over and over again as we progress in our journey of eternal life.

John Lennon's last album was called "Starting Over." As we all know he really was about to start over with new music.

John Wells was also starting over at the age of sixty four with a renewed interest in performing his music.

XOXOXOXOX

"J&J Towing.

I have no proof of this just memory. I promise you however I am not clever enough to make this up!

A day or two after I began writing chapter nine, I was given a nice confirmation. As I pulled into our bicycle shop parking lot, across the street I saw that a very large truck was parked. I had to blink twice and rub my eyes! The name on the side of the truck printed in huge letters was "J&J towing." Update: Oct. 15th, 2012.

I have seen this truck (J&J) Towing many times since I first posted this. It appears when I need a lift in spirit. It is uncanny how many times this has happened.

XOXOXOXOX

"Molly and Desmond Wells"

"Ob La Di Ob La Da", was penned by Paul McCartney and was influenced by Reggae music.

John Lennon had no part of it. In fact he did not like the song at all. Calling it Paul's granny song. John did not even want to be a part of its recording. He finally gave in and played piano when it was recorded.

The song was included in the Beatles "White" album in 1968.

In 1976 "Ob La Di Ob La Da", appeared as a single.

The "B" side was "Julia." A memorial song from John to his mother Julia.

After reading all of these facts about this song, I realized this little granny song, has a lot to say and it's all said in one lyric—

"LA LA LA LA LA", "LIFE GOES ON"

Paul's granny song is beautiful.

XOXOXOXOX

"Molly"

I received confirmation from spirit that Molly was indeed the name of John and Kitty's twin daughter through a most amazing set of circumstances.

I attended a writer's club meeting where I was introduced to a lovely lady by the name of Molly. Molly is a sweet lady in her late seventy's. I immediately liked her and got a kick out of her feisty personality.

I did not want to let anyone at the meeting know who I thought my Spirit Guide was. I read a portion of Chapter one, Life Begins in New Orleans, to this group of writer's. Leaving out any reference to John Lennon. Boy was I nervous! I was shaking like a leaf.

After I was through my fifteen minute read I told the group that whom I believe my guide is, was killed by gunfire in his last former lifetime. I also informed this esteem group that he was "somewhat' famous in his last incarnation. I left it at that.

Well, I guess thinking back that for Molly to realize his identity was not really all that much of a long shot; however, of all the people in the writer's group, she would have been my last choice to figure out who he was.

Right after this Ob La Di Ob La Da came on the radio (in perfect timing once again!) It just felt right that Desmond and Molly were the names of John and Kitty's twins.

XOXOXOXOX

"A message from George Harrison"

George wrote and recorded a song called "Savoy Truffle" which appeared on the Beatles White Album in 1968. Most agree it is a song George wrote about heroin abuse and cravings for chocolate.

George Harrison has only come through a few times during my readings with Reverend Arlene. Once he appeared in her mind's eye looking like the "Zig Zag" man on the paper used by many to construct marijuana joints and ciggies.

It was during this reading that Arlene asked me why he would appear to her like this. I told her I had no idea. I went home and searched the Internet with simply "George Harrison and Zig-Zag". I quickly received my answer.

George Harrison appeared in a movie called "Shanghai-Surprise." This movie was made in 1986-. In this movie he makes an appearance as an entertainer in a club. He appears for only a few seconds and unless you know, he is hard to Recognize. The name of the club is "The Zig Zag Club." The movie is not about heroin but is about Opium.

Because of this message I was able to put together the sad Zig Zag pieces of the life and times of James Paul Wells Jr.

XOXOXOXOX

"Our friend, Louie"

This next message is dedicated to our friend Louie.

Louie was one of our outside salesmen from one of our major bicycle suppliers. He became not only a valued business partner; more important he also became a friend.

Louie was a handsome proud American of Hispanic ancestry. He reminded me of Ricardo Montalban. He had a head full of white hair of which he was very proud of. He also had a winning smile and a way about him that endeared him to his many bicycle shops he serviced. Even when we had to give him a hard time about a product, he always handled tough situations with professionalism and a smile. Everyone loved Louie.

The last time we saw Louie was right before Christmas of 2007. We all noticed that Louie had lost some weight. Louie assured us that he was fine, just feeling a bit "under the weather." As was Louie's custom, he walked into our shop door with a Christmas gift for us. Every year he would bring in a very big tin of cookies. Not just any cookies, these were gourmet chocolate cookies shaped in the form of hearts, squares, and triangles.

I was embarrassed this year in that I did not have a gift for Louie. So before he left I told him that I would make it up at our next bicycle convention in Las Vegas and take him out to a special show. As he drove off, I blew him a kiss and wished him "Happy Christmas Louie."

This was the last time I was to see Louie. He passed away ten days later on December 30th.

Louie's funeral was held at Saint Joseph's Catholic Church in his home city. The cathedral was filled to standing room only. Louie had many friends and a very large loving family.

Before going to the service I reached into the cookie tin Louie had brought us for Christmas and took out a heart shaped cookie to take with me to Louie's funeral.

On January 11th, 2008 just two weeks after Louie stepped to the other side, we decided to drive to Las Vegas to visit with friends of ours who live in Henderson which is only a few minutes from Las Vegas.

Our dear friends, Ron and Karen, graciously invited us to stay with them in their beautiful home. We were visiting with them when Karen asked if we would like a cookie. She then brought out the exact cookie tin Louie would bring us every Christmas! I had never before seen this particular tin of cookies except every year when Louie would bring them.

I realized at that moment that Louie had just left us a beautiful message. I did indeed connect with my friend Louie just a few miles from the city of Las Vegas.

XOXOXOXOX

"Flying a kite"

It was shortly after I received Louie's wonderful cookies message that I went to visit Rev. Arlene once again.

It was during this reading that I received a wonderful message from John for Yoko.

Rev. Arlene: "John is showing me a kite. He is telling me of a kite flying adventure. He and a woman tried to fly a kite one day but they were not successful in getting it to fly. They gave up. However he sure had fun trying to get it to fly. He tells me that it was even more fun after they gave up."

At this Point Arlene got embarrassed and say's "That's enough John, I get the picture. I get it!" We both giggled.

I was curious who the lady might be so I chose the obvious choice of Yoko Ono. I wrote to her address on the internet and asked her if John and she ever flew a kite?

My letter to Yoko

During a prayer and reading session I believe John wanted to tell someone he loves very much that one of his happiest moments was of flying, or trying to fly, a kite. It seems this kite did not fly very well, but it sure was fun trying to attempt it.

Like I said, I am not sure who this message is for, but I wanted to ask you, so I am asking.

Love and hugs

Sunflower

I received a reply from Yoko soon after I sent this message on February 1, 2008

Yoko Ono writes:

"Yes," We tried to fly a kite, and it did not work. That was in a park in London near Richmond.

Yoko

XOXOXOXOX

"My mother, my Mammy"

October 27th, 2004 I went to visit Reverend Arlene for what was my third time to have a reading. It had been over six months since my last reading with her, so I figured she would not remember me. From the way she received me when I entered the room, I was right.

As always, she started my reading with a prayer of thanks to our Creator.

As of this date, Rev. Arlene was aware that I had a Guide by the name of John who communicated with me. She knew he would send me messages in the form of synchronicities and coincidences. I had been very careful not to mention anything about the Beatles or John's last name Lennon to her. I made sure I did not have any clues in the form of clothing pins or anything. It was important that our connection was pure.

I was hoping to have a connection with my mother more than any other person at this reading. I told Rev. Arlene of this desire.

These next few lines of communication are exactly what was

said and happened during this reading. I have it on tape dated 10/27/04.

Arlene: "What else can we do for you?"

Sherry: "Well as always I would like to know if my Guide John has anything to say to me. Hello John, come on in." (My cheeky attempt at humor).

Arlene: "John is turning a large ring around on his finger. He keeps pointing to this ring as a point of reference for you. It is a very top heavy ring with a red gemstone. Did John have a ring like this?"

(Note) This reading occurred in 2004. This was the first of two times that John made reference to a "Ring". The second time was during a reading in 2007, which I referred to in Chapter six. I am 100% sure that John is referring to the red gemstone ring that was featured in the Beatles movie "Help". I am also sure that John brings up this ring to help me remember the ring that Edward Clark gave to his Sunflower.

During this reading I made no mention that John's friend Ringo was known for wearing rings. As I stated, it was extremely important to me, at this time, that Arlene did not know who my Guide John was in his former past lifetime.

Sherry: "Well, I do not know. John probably had many rings. I think he liked jewelry but I'm really not sure".

Arlene: "Oh, now he is showing me his hands. Did John work with cars or did he work with a dark substance which would be on his hands?"

Once again, I did not realize at the time the importance of the dark substance on his hands. It is a reference to John Wells's love of masonry. The dark substance was clay.

Sherry: "John was an artist".

Arlene "O.K. good. Now I know I have the right person. He is showing me his dark hands. His hands are covered with this dark sticky stuff. However his finger nails are very clean. Did John like Eddie Cantor?"

Sherry: "I don't really know. John was an entertainer himself, and I suppose he might have liked Eddie Cantor. I really do not know".

Arlene: "Well, John is showing me Eddie Cantor who wore white gloves and black face make-up and moved his hands like this… (She then moves her hands like the entertainers did when they would perform in black face make up).

Sherry: "Oh my gosh! Yes, of course Eddie Cantor! Mammy! I can't believe it! This is really funny and very embarrassing too! Reverend Arlene no one knows of this! How could you know this?"

Arlene: "What dear one?"

Sherry: In the morning when I get ready for work, I pull back my hair and apply foundation. I put this dark make-up on thinking it makes me look tan. Anyway as I do this I sing a little tune. No one hears me as I perform this ritual as I am by myself. Well at least that's what I thought until now. Apparently John and my mother—my Mammy—are watching! This is embarrassing!"

Arlene: "Ha! Ha! Ha! What do you sing?"

Sherry: "As I apply this very dark foundation I sing this— "Mammy, how I love you! How I love you, my dear ole Mammy! I want the world to see, how I love thee—my dear Ole mammy D.I.X.I E", I love you.—- I don't really know the words to this song, but these are the words I sing. My mother's name is Dixie".

Arlene: "Ha ha ha very funny. Wonderful"

So this was the start of many "Mammy" messages. Others followed. However on this day I did indeed receive a message from John and from my beloved mother Alvina Dixie Daisy.

XOXOXOXOX

"A gift from Doug and Bobbi"

As I wrote in a previous chapter our family lost a dear member on January 20th, 2009. His name is Doug and he is my brother in law. Doug and I shared a mutual love for John Lennon.

Only a little over a month had passed since his death when his wife, Bobbi, was at our local Target shopping for some items when she spotted a book display. The featured novel was Phillip Norman's newest novel entitled "John Lennon".

Bobbi said a little voice in her head told her to buy the book for me. She reasoned with herself that I probably already own it, as she knows of my collection. However, she thought to herself it did not matter if I did. She wanted to purchase me a copy from her regardless.

She bought the book and gave it to me a few days later. When she handed it to me I felt a rush of emotion and blinked hard to keep the tears back. I was really touched that she would think of me and purchase this book. Bobbi is a hard working single mother doing the best she can. I know how hard it is to make ends meet with three young children and an assortment of furry family who depend on her. She works very hard at a very physically demanding job. She is a meter maid.

I cannot begin to understand her loss. I will not pretend to understand what she went though as her husband died in her arms. There simply are no words adequate. So for her to think of me and buy me this book, only weeks after she lost husband, is an honor.

"I had to buy you this book", she told me. "I think it is from Doug too. I hope you do not already have a copy". I swallowed hard and told her "I do not have this book and yes it is from Doug too. I'm also very sure there is a message for me somewhere within the pages. Thank you". I hugged her.

Then I watched her walk back to her truck to continue her day's work schedule of reading water meters. As she drove off she rolled down the window smiled and flashed the peace sign my way. "I love you", I said to Bobbi. Then I told Doug the same and I also told him thank you for giving me this special book.

It did not take me long to find the message I was hoping for.

Since receiving my "Mammy", message from John in 2004 I've always felt there was going to be more to it. I had no real proof that John Lennon was somehow attracted to the music or memory of Al Jolson or Eddie Cantor. All I had was the reading in which he refers to entertainer's black face make-up. However this was to change when I read John Lennon by Philip Norman. I once again highly recommend this novel to anyone who is interested in reading about the life and times of John Lennon.

The first Chapter of John Lennon is entitled "War Baby". It is a chapter about John Lennon's family history. In this chapter I learned that his grandfather, who shared the same name as his famous grandson, was a part of a very popular form of entertainment in America which soon caught hold in the British Isles at the turn of the century. It seems American Minstrel troupes were the hit of the day. These white entertainers would paint their faces black, wear oversized pantaloons and sing sentimental songs about life in the southern region of America. Singing songs about the Swanne River. John's grand dad was part of this music scene of the late 1800's.

When I read this I realized that John was telling me that his biological grandfather had indeed performed as a black faced minstrel, I was amazed! I had absolutely no idea of this before receiving this book to read.

Then I read on to learn more about his father "Alf" who was also known as "Alfred (Fred) Lennon". On page five of Lennon by Phillip Norman I read that Alfred could sing all the popular songs from the World War 1 hit parade. That he also loved doing impressions of Charlie Chaplin. When I read this paragraph I laughed because I've always thought John Lennon looked a bit like Charlie Chaplin also known as the beloved "Little Tramp". I then remembered how at a reading years ago Reverend Arlene thought that John was impersonating Mr. Chaplin when he appeared in her vision that day.

The next paragraph Mr. Norman wrote about how Alfred loved to sit on his grandfather's knee at Christmas time. Apparently Alfred must have had problems with his legs as he wore "Tiny Tim "leg irons.

Tiny Tim, as mentioned in Mr. Norman's novel, was also a confirmation. Charles Dickens was a huge influence on both John and James Wells. That influence continued into both men's future incarnations.

I believe this next excerpt from Phillip Normans book is perhaps one of the most loving and confirming messages I've ever received.

Alfred "Fred Lennon" loved to entertain his fellow sailors when at sea. He loved to sing the songs and do impressions of Al Jolson. He would paint his face with black shoe polish and sing Mammy and Dixie. The anthems that were very popular in the twenties. Again my mind went back to Reverend Arlene asking me if my special friend on the other side of reality was Al Jolson or Eddie Cantor, or if perhaps my Guide was a huge fan of these entertainers? This was before she knew my Angel was John Winston Ono Lennon.

After reading this paragraph I realized that this message was from three generations of the Lennon's. I was in tears when I read the very last sentence—these songs were—- Anthems to "Mammy" and "Dixie".

My thanks and love again to Doug and Bobbi for helping me discover this incredible message of love and tribute to John's biological father and grandfather.

XOXOXOXOX

"Goodbye"

Mr. Elias Howe- 1819-1867

Elias Howe died October 3rd, 1867. He served in the Union Army from 1862 to 1865. He was an honorable man who was also a passionate abolitionist. He died a wealthy man, but he never did receive the recognition some believe he should have for his invention of the sewing machine.

In 1965, The Beatles, made their second movie called "Help." The movie is a zany comedy about the Beatles being chased by an Eastern religious group of thugs. It is a fun movie with a fantastic musical score by Lennon & McCartney

At the very end of the movie, just before the credits begin to roll, there appears a large Singer Sewing Machine on screen. Under this sewing machine appear these words:

"This movie is respectfully dedicated to Elias Howe. Who in 1846 invented the sewing machine?"

The movie "Help" has absolutely nothing to do with sewing machines! However "Help," does make quite a statement, in its own way about religion.

Isaac Singer 1811- 18751

Isaac Singer died in Torquay, England on November 23rd, 1875.

He never returned to America after he was suspected of being a bigamist. The man who was an admitted womanizer is forever credited by most for inventing the sewing machine. This incredible machine that liberated millions of women from the drudgery of hand sewing.

Isaac Singer, when asked about this, was reported to have said "because of the sewing machine now women have more time for their "irritating," never ending gossip and chit chat."

Singer Sewing machines are now one of the most recognizable trade names in American history.

Edward Clark 1811- 1882

I have thought a lot about Edward Clark. Do I know him in this lifetime? I have to admit I'm not quite ready to say yes or no.

This next excerpt is from another book I own called simply 'The American People'—page 309—

Despite their marketing success with clothing and shoe manufacturers, sewing machine makers dreamed of selling their wares to the many thousands of women who were sewing by hand for their families. But the purchase price was too high for most family budgets. In 1856, Singer's partner, Edward Clark, came up with the idea of allowing buyers to pay for their machines in installments. The plan succeeded brilliantly. The very next year, sales of Singer machines almost tripled. Clark, then hit upon another marketing concept-the trade-in. The Singer Company offered $50. For "old sewing machines of any kind" that could be used to finance a new machine. Sales took another leap forward. Profits produced by these innovative schemes allowed improvements in the production of sewing machines that halved prices by 1859. Technological and marketing innovations combined to put machines into the hand of ordinary Americans.

I had until I read this, thought of Edward Clark as primarily very successful attorney who's most predacious client was Isaac Singer. I now think of Edward Clark as a very successful business man and entrepreneur.

I have also read that Edward Clark was indeed a very devoted fine art collector. He made several journeys to Europe where he purchased many valuable paintings. His journeys were after Sunflower and his beloved wife had both passed away. That he would re-unite with John Wells in the year of 1880 actually fits into the fabric of his lifetime.

Edward Clark died a very wealthy man and lived his final days in Coopers town, New York.

I learned about Edward Clark's interest in art collecting after I had written about Sunflower's perfect day at the art Gallery with Mr. Clark and her sons. I believe that day was a perfect day in his life also.

I'd like to think it was.

Madame Marianne LeSoleil 1840- (?)

When the House of the Rising Sun closed its doors for business permanently in 1874, Madame Marianne LeSoleil was only thirty four years of age. Money had become her sole ambition in life. Because of this, she had very few friends and no family. Alvina was her only companion, however as time went by even this friendship ended in heartbreak.

Madam Marianne was a very bitter woman. Bitter because of her love for money and little else. Bitter because her family had moved and wanted nothing to do with her. Bitter because she was unable to trust or love anyone.

No one is sure what became of her after 1874. Some say she committed suicide. Others say that she lived a lonely life of isolation and despair. Whatever her demise, she disappeared into history and very little is known.

Alvina 1870- (?)

Without Madam Marianne to guide her, Alvenia had no desire to continue as a working girl.

Fortune smiled on her when she met a gentleman from Natchez, Mississippi. Like James, whom Alvina never forgot, he loved the new music called Jazz. He was her Jazzman. His name was George. Alvina (she no longer wished to be called Alvenia) and George married and moved to Natchez. Their home was near the bridge that spanned the mighty Mississippi River where together they would hold each other under the moonlight. On many nights they would listen while the wind would carry music from Natchez and its many music halls.

Then after the music made by man stopped, Alvina and her jazzman would listen to the music of the river, the wind and the many animals who called this special paradise home.

Alvina and Jazzman George lived a full life and were blessed with many children and grandchildren.

James Paul Wells Jr. 1890-1940

James Paul Wells Jr., went on to become a respected and successful musician.

It was during the roaring twenties era that he began to play the saxophone along with his clarinet with success.

Living in Harlem, it was only a matter of time before he was introduced to some of the most brilliant band leaders of this era. One being the brilliant band master Cab Calloway.

James Paul did play as a stand in for Mr. Calloway's band, the Missourians, at the Savoy Club. His musicality was show cased in two of Mr. Calloway's most memorable songs, "Saint James Infirmary" and "Minnie the Moocher."

James Paul lost his battle with a demon who was never far from his side, heroin. He died a lonely and forgotten man in the year of 1940.

James and John Wells 1850-1922

James Wells died in the month of September in the year of 1922. John Wells died a month later in October. Both men were seventy two years of age.

John Wells was survived by his wife Kitty Wells, and their four surviving children. John and Kitty had nine grandchildren.

James and John were met on the other side of the looking glass mirror of life by their Mammy and their grand-mother Daisy.

Along with the people John and James had known in their lifetimes, was a man whom they did not remember, but realized instantly who he was as he approached them in Heaven.

During their lifetimes, James and John had asked their Mammy who their father was. To which she would reply "Jesus". Both James and John thought she was a bit irreverent, but then again they knew her sense of humor. So James and John figured she did not know the answer to their question and just let it be. Besides, like their Mammy always told them, "We are all one and the same anyway."

The man, who approached John and James Wells as they entered Heavens entry way, was a tall and very handsome black man. He had long hair worn in the custom of his African ancestry. His eyes were full of love and compassion. He had a smile that complemented his natural beauty to perfection. If God were to create a man who would embody "Everyman" this man would be the model.

As the man approached James and John he was singing a song that had sweet tones of the Caribbean. The song he was singing was about "ONE LOVE." He introduced himself "Hello, I'm your father, my name is August. Many will soon know me all over the world as Bob."

Sunflower and Daisy smiled and together with James and John walked hand in hand as thousands of white feathers led the way towards the light that shines in all of us FOREVER.

"Nine Miles to Heaven"

Over five years ago in 2007, I received a fantastic message from Mr. Bob Marley. I was at the laundry matt (once again) when a young man asked me if I knew how Bob Marley died. This was a wonderful "coincidence" as I had just asked my friend Allen the same question the day before. I knew when this happened that someday I would be involved in some kind of message that would connect John Lennon, Bob Marley and I.

It took a little time but the connection happened and I am much honored to have been a part of this message of love between Bob Marley and John Lennon.

On June 15th, of 2009 we boarded a jeep for a journey to Bob Marley's village of birth in Jamaica. This village is called '9-mile-. I smiled to myself when I learned the name of Bob Marley's birth city and gave John a secret thumbs up in appreciation of the number 9 once again. Which of course we all know is a special number indeed.

Our guide's name was George. He was a man of about 40 whose appearance gave no clue as to what he did for a living. I was expecting to see a Rastafarian warrior dressed in the Jamaican colors, long dreads, while all the time smoking a large joint. Nope, George wore khaki shorts and colored shirt along with a very official looking badge. His hair was neatly cropped and his manner was most professional. He introduced us to our driver who smiled from the front seat of our little safari jeep. In his thick accent George welcomed us. "We shall go to see Bob today. I hope you enjoy our drive to the beautiful village of 9-mile through the jungle". We were in for a treat.

There were a total of nine of us (how appropriate and true!). We were joined by a couple from Puerto Rico and their two children. A son who was about 19 and their daughter who was 17. Along with this family was a man from India. This man from India was very "straight laced" and quite honestly not really sure why he had signed up for this tour! Then there was Randy and I. Along with our Guide George and our driver the number equaled nine. So the nine of us started our journey for Nine Mile.

Our little jeep was equipped with an ancient stereo set with crackling speakers that reminded me of days of old at drive in theatres. George turned on his microphone and started his narrative. Telling us about the flora and fauna we would see. Along with the history about the country side as we drove along the bumpy road. In between his narrative George would filter in the music of Bob Marley.

The couple from Puerto Rico began singing along with the music. Their two teen-aged children sang along too. I was quite impressed as my safari companions knew all the words to these songs. Songs I was not familiar with. I could tell that my new friends were very devoted fans of Bob Marley. My friend from India (Charles) did not know any of Bob's music. Telling me that the only reason he signed up for this tour was that it looked interesting. Something different.

At first the drive was filled with music and sunshine. Then the jungle road got very narrow, hot, scary and bumpy. All the while the music of Bob Marley boomed in the background of our driver's rather interesting sound system.

After about an hour's drive we stopped at a small shop. George told us to stretch our legs and informing us that we could purchase some refreshments if we wanted.

First a word about this road side store. Well, it's not exactly like our local Stop and Go back home. The first thing I noticed as I stepped out of the jeep was a very skinny dog! She looked at me with sad eyes and I had to turn away. Not that I thought she was abused or anything like that, it's just I am not used to seeing dogs this skinny. "This is my dog Mom", a little voice came from my side. I looked to see a beautiful young girl of about nine. Her skin was the color of honey. She had long braided hair and dark black eyes with eyelashes no makeup could hope to duplicate. She wore a simple dress of white cotton. She was barefoot. I bent down and petted her dog who looked up at me and smiled. The girl then touched my hand.

The store was in reality an old house with no doors between the rooms and ancient walls with old posters pinned to them. There was some shelving with small canned goods. I mindlessly wondered the store looking for something to purchase. All the while, the little girl and her dog followed me in silence. She never asked me a thing. She simply followed me.

I found my way to the counter and asked to purchase a diet coke. Silly me "No Mam, we have no diet cola", the clerk informed me and then opened an old cooler to retrieve a brand of cola I was not familiar with. Thinking to myself—go ahead take a walk on the wild side "I'll take it", I told the clerk who smiled at me with a smile that was toothless!

The little girl continued to follow me. She looked at the cola in my hand and I could tell she was puzzled why I was not going to drink it. I opened the can and took a swallow. I was shocked to taste how sweet it was. I really thought it was horrid tasting so I guess I made a face, although I was trying not to offend, I just could not help myself. The little girl giggled when I made this face. I smiled and offered her a drink. She giggled and said "No thank you Mom". I guess she was familiar with this cola!

"All aboard" George informed our little group. I climbed into the back of the jeep. I turned around to see the little girl and her skinny dog standing outside the store. Her beauty was breathtaking.

As we drove off I waved good-bye to her. She held up her hand and flashed me the peace sign. I did the same back to her. Nothing more needed to be said. In my mind when I think of Jamaica I will remember her as "Jamaica's daughter".

We drove on for another hour. At this point the teenage girl in our little group of explorer's got car sick, so we had to pull off the road. Well, a few miles further, I need to stop also. I'm afraid the combination of the winding road, sweet drink, and hot weather got the best of me also. Needless to say we asked George to pull over several more times.

I found a little patch of grass, let go and felt better. George approached me and asked if I were all right? I sheepishly got to my feet and said "yes". "Good thing you not sit on the poison Ivy", he informed me as I climbed back into the jeep. "Oh Great I thought; now he tells me!"

I was beginning to feel like my new friend from India Charles, "What am I doing here?" I thought to myself in silence. The music continued to crackle as we bumped along.

I will say that by the time we arrived in 9-Mile I was more than ready to get out of that jeep! Everyone else was in a jubilant mood. We walked into the little gift store then continued up a very steep pathway which lead to the small house that was in fact Bob Marley's boyhood home.

Our new Rasta Guide, "Joe" did indeed look the part! Now I'm not going to say that there was any ganja being smoked, as I do encourage anyone who is open minded to take this tour, but I did see quite a few people smoking. The aroma of skunk was in the air.

The first building we walked into was in fact Bob Marley's home he grew up in. It was a very small house with only a few rooms. Joe guided us to a small room with a single bed, some pictures and a desk. That's about all there was to this room. Joe informed us that we were in Bob Marley's room. It was very small and very humble, and very special.

The next building contained the tomb of not only Bob Marley but also his mother. We were able to take a picture of his mother's tomb but were told no pictures of Bob Marley's tomb were allowed.

Bob Marley's tomb is beautiful white marble. A huge tapestry of Bob is hanging on it. Many other treasured photos' are on the walls that surround his tomb.

Somewhere on the tour candles were given as a way to honor Bob Marley once you entered the Mausoleum that held his tomb. I had not taken a candle so when I entered I asked Joe for one. "I'm sorry, I do not have one to give you, mum", he informed me. I told him no problem as I did not need one anyway. Bob will know my thoughts and I will remember this moment forever. I then pointed to my head. Joe smiled.

As I walked around the tomb I noticed that there were little tokens left by many visitors that were laid along the side's that formed a shelf on the tomb. Little treasures that included pictures, crosses, flowers, peace signs, and yes I saw a couple of rolled cigarettes (?) and other small trinkets left for Bob Marley from those who love and honor his memory.

I then realized I wanted to leave something. I reached into my purse and took out the first thing in my hand. I have carried this item with me to many places. It was given to me from my friend Lily from Australia. "Lily" who talks to Angels. This gift was, like Dr. Rio's gift of small pieces of brick, from John Lennon's boyhood home in Liverpool "Mendips".

My gift from Lily was a keychain she had purchased at a small store next to John's boyhood home. This key chain had a picture of John singing while seated at a piano. Next to him was a sign which had one word printed on it. The word was "peace'. I loved this key ring.

I knew it was the perfect gift to give to Bob Marley from John Lennon and his boyhood home to Bob and his boyhood home. "Mendips to Nine Mile". However it was hard for me to give up this little treasure.

I held the key ring in my hand for a few minutes. I knew I was being asked to leave it. I kissed John's image. I felt much moved. I started to cry as I put the key ring down amongst the other gifts. I was not crying because I was going to leave the key ring, I was crying for John and Bob.

I then heard a voice behind me ask "What is dat you are giving to Bob?" It was then that I saw Joe had tears in his eyes too. I told him about my key ring and its meaning. I asked him if these items were thrown away after a while. Joe informed me that nothing is ever thrown away that was left for Bob. That after a while the items are donated to the family or museums. They are considered sacred. He then told me that some items are left at Nine-Mile. Then he took my hand and told me that a few very special items are taken and put on top of Bob Marley's tomb. Never to be removed.

He hugged me again and told me that he is one of the entrusted Guardians of the tomb and he can decide which items deserve this honor. I'll never forget what he told me next "I Love John Lennon very much. Bob and John are soldiers and brothers one and the same. I shall put your item from John and you in its rightful place. It shall go on top of Bob's tomb. It shall remain there forever. I promise you this".

We both agreed this was appropriate. I gave Joe a farewell hug and I next told him "We are ONE". "Yes, we are", Joe told me. I walked out the door of the Moslem, and I thought I heard "tink" as the keychain met its final resting place.

The journey back to Ocho Rio's aboard the jeep was in silence. It seemed each of us was in deep thought about our visit to Nine-Mile. I asked Charles, my reluctant friend from India; if he is now glad he went on this tour? "I'm very thankful that I was guided to this sacred journey", he informed me. "As am I'.

Update May 2012: A few nights ago, I asked a question, while in prayer, if Bob Marley was contented with what I have written about him. The reason I asked is because I must admit I still, as of this date, know very little about him. I would classify myself as a casual fan of his music, life and times. I also know very little about his religious Rastafarian beliefs.

I received my answer to my question to Bob in less than a day.

I walked to our post office to mail my sister Kathy a birthday card. The walk is only about a block. On the way I noticed a small children's plastic toy laying all alone on the parking lot pavement. I gave it little thought and continued my journey. When I got to the post office a little voice in my head told me to pick up the toy.

"It is yours to keep." I picked up the toy and realized who it from immediately. It is a very small plastic "Lion". It was from Bob Marley. The "Lion of Zion." Very Spiritual and perfect.

AUTHORS NOTE: The young lady who is featured on the cover of this novel, is a model for Thinkstock imagery. When it came time to pick out a cover for my novel I was directed to Thinkstock.com. I found her with such ease that I know I was guided. This young lady could be the twin sister to the little girl I met in Jamaica at the convenience store. She is also, in my minds mirror, how I imagine Sarah Anne Wells appeared at the age of 11 +.

Thank you Mr. Bob Marley for this wonderful gift!

"We Are One"

"I've seen Angels from Heaven,
Flying saucers in the sun,
And must make my Easter Sunday
In the name of the rising sun".
—*Jimi Hendrix*

And so I come to the final chapter of this my continuing life in this reality.

Today is the Saturday before Easter Sunday. Tomorrow millions of people will dress in their finest and attend a church of their choosing to worship in their own way. Little children will squeal in delight as they hunt for eggs left by an elusive bunny. Strange isn't it? Yet perfect too! For we all started as an egg! Therefore we are all Eggmen and Eggwomen!

I have often wondered why John Lennon could be so sarcastic when it came to religion. Would a God of Love and Compassion forgive him for his biting tongue?

A few years ago, on my drive to work on a sunny Sunday morning while listening to Breakfast with the Beatles, John's song "God", came on the air. The lyrics in John's song are beautiful yet puzzling.

"God is a concept. In which we measure our pain".—

In this song John expresses his non beliefs which include not believing in Jesus, Elvis, Beatles, Zimmerman, Yoga——At the conclusion of the song he expresses his true belief—Yoko and me—that is his reality.

The song came to a conclusion as I parked my truck in front of our local deli. I've heard this song many times. I've always thought it quite profound. I like the song but I also don't like the song! Then I wondered. Would God like the song?

My answer came quickly once I entered the Deli and ordered

my lunch. At the register was a tip jar. In this tip jar was a dollar bill. Someone had printed a message on this dollar. The message read "God Loves John". How perfect!

John's prayer for humanity is his masterpiece "Imagine". Some may think it an anti-religion song. Not I. I believe it is a very Spiritual song.

Martin Gerschwitz is our dear friend whom we met many years ago when he was the keyboard and violinist for Eric Burdon's band, "The New Animals." Martin, Randy and I have traveled many roads together all over the USA. Some memories are hard to remember as we drank way too much and partied way to hard. Other memories are etched in my mind and seem like just yesterday.

One memory is when we walked to Ground Zero, in New York City on February 9th, of 2002. Afterwards we walked to Saint Peters church just blocks away. In front of this church were grave stones that were still covered with the hallowed ashes from 9/11.

In 2008, Martin invited us to one of his one man recitals at a very popular Christian Church near our city. At this recital Martin played not only Spiritual songs on his Hammond B-10 organ, but also some classic rock songs along with his own beautiful originals.

At the end of his show, Martin once again dedicated his final song to Randy and myself. I knew what was coming. "Imagine". I was somewhat "apprehensive" about this. How would the congregation feel about this song? I should have known better. The congregation applauded in appreciation not only for Martin and his incredible rendition but also for John's prayer.

This brings me to this question. "Does John love Jesus?" Once again I am reminded of the session with Reverend Arlene I had many years ago in which I asked John "who is Jesus?" His answer "you mean the man with the beard from Nazarene?" "Of course John", I replied in disbelief at his indignity. "Well", John replied "he sure can hold an audience". Rev. Arlene and I laughed and laughed. Then John went on to answer my question. His answer was "Love". I really like that.

I would like to share a message from Spirit that came to me on New Year's Eve 1998-1999.

Randy and I had traveled to Telluride, Colorado to ring in the New Year with Eric Burdon and The New Animals at the Sheridan Opera house. After a fantastic show we were able to go back stage to share our thoughts and love with the band.

I admit I had more than my share of festive refreshments and was feeling more than a little brave.

I had a conversation with Eric in which I said something to him that to this day amazes me that I was so bold. I told Eric that he is one of my hero's. That he will live forever through his voice. Humanity will be listening to you sing "House of the Rising Sun", forever. I then told him that John Lennon loves you very much. I could not believe my ears that I had said this to him. To my surprise he kissed my cheek and gave me a big hug.

We then formed a conga line and proceeded to dance down the narrow stairs of the venerable Opera house that led us to the dance floor. We rang in the New Year of 1999 singing Auld Lang Syne. Then the D.J. turned up the volume to Paul McCartney's beautiful love song to his wife Linda "Oh Darlin". We formed a circle and sang along with Paul and the other boy's in the band.

After this we went outside to finish the night's festivities and return to our hotels. We discovered that Eric's car was stuck in the snow. The band, along with the help of a few fans, shoveled the snow from under the tires. Eric (being the star) and I (because I was wearing much too short of a mini skirt) stood at the side watching. Then Eric said something to me I will never forget. With the full moon shining its beams on the snow behind him, I saw a sly smile form on Eric's face as he said to me "John Lennon and I were born on the same day." I could not believe he said this. "Ha! Ha! Ha! Your wrong Eric, you and John do not have the same birthday. You're too funny." Then he informed me "I'm right. You'll find out. If I'm wrong then I owe you a toe sucking" (I've learned over the years that artists and musicians have a certain, shall we say, interesting way of expressing themselves!). Well to this day I've never had a pedicure.

Now back to the question that has puzzled me for many years. Why would John Lennon want to connect with me? Back to the autograph on the back of my beloved John Lennon jacket on which Eric Burdon first whispered "Hello Johnny," then signed:

"John: I remember the 'ONE'

My question—who is the ONE?—

My answer and the reason for John Lennon being in my life and connecting with not only myself but many others—He simply wants every one of us to know this simple yet wonderful message—

We are the ONE. Every one of us. Every living entity, including our Mother Earth and the Universe. Anything that has a spark of life within. That Illusive little spark of energy that no scientist can explain. Put those sparks together and that little spark is God of which we are all a divine part of.

"WE ARE ONE" and we will go on forever. It's just the way it is. The really great news is that in Heaven——

"All We Have and need is Love". I have found my truths!

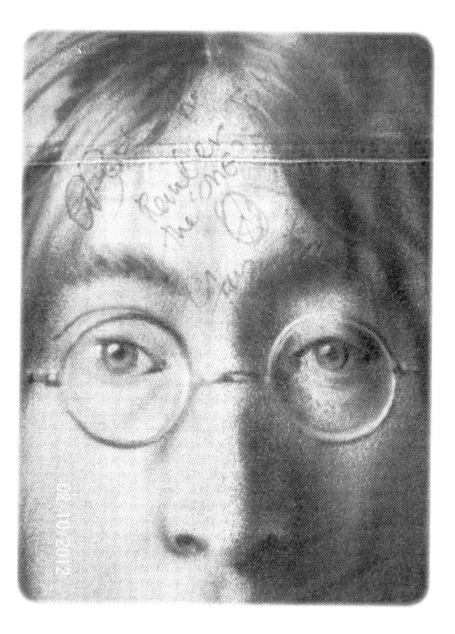

Epilogue
My final thoughts (I promise!)

I have not had a reading with Reverend Arlene in two years. The last one being December 8th, 2010. I do keep in touch with her through emails, and try to attend a church service when she is the guest minister. I'm very proud of her accomplishments. She is very devoted to the American Indian traditions and their Spiritual beliefs. Last year I attended my first drum ceremony and found it fascinating and very enlightening. She will forever remain my friend who helped me find my answers. www.arleneandtheancients

I do not attend as many rock n roll concerts as I did a few years ago. However I do continue to follow the amazing life and times of Eric Burdon. He is about to present to the world a new collection of music entitled "Till Your River Runs Dry". He has a fan site called "I'm gonna change the world". I just love the man's spirit. He continues to search for his own truths be it thru his music, artwork, and his biographical novels. He is forever young in not only my eyes, but in the eyes of fans all over the world who adore this man of peace. Fight on Sky Pilot. Peace and happiness always Eggman. www. ericburdon.com

I turned sixty last year; I guess it's another milestone. My husband and I still own and operate our family bike shop and yes we are still "Watching the Wheels."

Today is June 1ˢᵗ, 2013. My granddaughter Olivia's fourteenth birthday. This will be my final message. Our city is having a 'Dog Day's' of summer fund raiser and pet adoption day today. Yesterday I went to the shelter to donate. Going to the shelter is not something I can do easily. I so admire the wonderful people who work at the shelter. These amazing people are truly the ones who love animals the most.

As I stood waiting to talk to the Shelter director I tried to keep my eyes diverted from the cages. I finally could not avoid looking and turned to face the many kittens. Beautiful babies in need of a home. I swallowed hard. As I stood there trying not to be effected, a young woman and a staff member walked to a cage where a beautiful furry baby with sad blue eyes came up to the edge and softly meowed. I heard the staff member tell the young woman that this kitty is sick. She will need a few days before she can be considered for adoption. My heart ached. I then saw the staff member give her a card with a number to call. The lady left. The kitten went to the corner of her cage and made muffins. I felt so sad. I next noticed a man with his son come into the shelter. His son looked to be about 11 plus years of age. I could tell by how excited the young man was that something wonderful was going to happen. A new family member and best friend was about to be taken home. I next noticed something on the man's tee shirt that made me smile and know that my friend John was with me. The tee shirt had two words on it.--- "THE GOONIES." ---- After reading this my mind went back into time and I could see John Lennon, at the age of 11 plus, sitting in front of his telly watching Peter Sellers his favorite Goonie. John's humor and timing once again, spot on.

I knew then that everything will be ok. Everything is as it should be. Small voice in my head told me, the sick kitty will find a loving home soon.

I end this with this final thought----There are so many religions and so many beliefs. Why can't we all get along? I really have no problem at all with what hat you choose to wear, even if you don't wear any hat at all. As long as you basic belief is centered on love. As for me, I do believe in Jesus, I do believe in Buddha, I do believe in all the Saints and humanity which include some very special rock stars.

Thank you for reading I've got John. I hope you found something within these pages to inspire you to live a happy life that includes music, laughter, friends, and family (be it skin, fur, scales or feathers.) Most of all love. Yes, it is true ALL WE NEED IS LOVE SWEET LOVE.

As for me, I walk with Sunflower Sarah Anne Wells on a daily basis. She and I are one.

Acknowledgements and Recommended Reading

All You Need is Love
By Jewelle St. James

City of Eros
By Timothy J. Gilfoyle

Don't Let Me be Misunderstood
By Eric Burdon

John Lennon
By Cynthia Lennon

John Lennon: in their own write
A loving tribute from his friends and fans
By Judith Furedi

John Lennon
The Rolling Stone Interview
By Jann S. Wenner

Lennon
By Ray Coleman

Lennon-Bronte Connection
By Jewelle St. James

Loving John
By May Pang

The American People
Howe—Frederick—Davis—Winkler

Movies, Documentaries and pt. shows I would like
to acknowledge. Some are my favorites some just
helped me along the way of my Spiritual journey.

Abe Lincoln Vampire hunter 2012

A Hard Day's Night 1965

Banger Sisters 2002

Being There 1979

Casino Royale starring Peter Sellers 1967

Christmas Carole starring Patrick Stewart 1999

Close Encounters of the Third Kind 1977

Concert for Bangladesh 1971

Dick Cavett Show : The John and Yoko interviews 1971

Dr. Strangelove 1964

Forrest Gump 1994

Gangs of New York 2002

Help 1965

How I Won the War 1967

Magic Christian 1969

Jazz Singer Starring Al Jolson 1927

Jim Nabors Christmas in Hawaii 1981

Oh Brother, Where art Thou? 2000

Pink Panther 1963

Pinocchio 1940

Post Cards from the Edge 1990

Shanghai Surprise 1986

Snow Fall on New Year's Eve 1999

The Beatles Anthology 1995

The Birds 1963

The Goon Show British radio and television 1950

The Little Tramp 1921

The Lovely Bones 2001

Whale Dreamers 2006

2001 A Space Odyssey 1968

THANK YOU

I wish to first thank our Creator for this wonderful thing most of us take for granite and that thing is—Existence.

Thank you to my four wonderful sisters Kathy, Vicky, Robin and Bobbi. Your belief in me helped me to finish this novel.

Thank you Reverend Arlene. Without you I would have never connected the dots of my Spiritual journey.

Thank you Dorothy Robinson Stanley for taking your time to correct my many boo' boo's in this novel.

Thank you to all my family and friends be you made of skin, scales, feathers or fur. I love you!

Thank you to everyone I've ever met in this lifetime!

Thank you to all my unseen Guides on the other side of the Looking Glass for all your help in guiding me towards the right light.

Thank you Martin Gerschwitz for being so talented and for sharing this with us. Ain't life Grand?

Thank you Eric Burdon for making me feel so young each and every time you walk onto the stage. I would, however, like to ask you just ONE question. Why in the world would you trade your great-great uncles track medal for a pair of cowboy boots? LOL XOXOXOXOX

Thank you Creator for blessing me with my children Frank, Crystal, Matt and Heidi

Thank you Creator for blessing me with my grandchildren Kyle, Olivia, Trinity and Noah

Thank you #9

Thank you to my husband and best friend Randy White

Reverend Arlene Raedel and me 2009

A note from Reverend Arlene

I can only say that it was one of those memorable days when Sherry and
I met. She is so understated in her demeanor and when you touch into
her spirit it is such a joy as it is pure in its intent and honesty Now, I
have to share with you that Sherry did not come alone. She came with
a loving spirit who I came to acknowledge as John Lennon. There are so
many instances of proof of life. As these unveiled themselves, it was then
that I was able to 'see' the real John Lennon not the publicity John.
I was not a fan of John Lennon, but I came to really appreciate his stubborn
heart when it came to the possibility of world peace and the weight of his
words and music and the impact and richness of a heart left behind.

Reverend Arlene Raedel